PRACTICAL TEST DESIGN

D1605257

Printed by Amazon POD

BCS, THE CHARTERED INSTITUTE FOR IT

BCS, The Chartered Institute for IT, is committed to making IT good for society. We use the power of our network to bring about positive, tangible change. We champion the global IT profession and the interests of individuals, engaged in that profession, for the benefit of all.

Exchanging IT expertise and knowledge
The Institute fosters links between experts from industry, academia and business to promote new thinking, education and knowledge sharing.

Supporting practitioners
Through continuing professional development and a series of respected IT qualifications, the Institute seeks to promote professional practice tuned to the demands of business. It provides practical support and information services to its members and volunteer communities around the world.

Setting standards and frameworks
The Institute collaborates with government, industry and relevant bodies to establish good working practices, codes of conduct, skills frameworks and common standards. It also offers a range of consultancy services to employers to help them adopt best practice.

Become a member
Over 70,000 people including students, teachers, professionals and practitioners enjoy the benefits of BCS membership. These include access to an international community, invitations to a roster of local and national events, career development tools and a quarterly thought-leadership magazine. Visit www.bcs.org/membership to find out more.

Further Information
BCS, The Chartered Institute for IT,
First Floor, Block D,
North Star House, North Star Avenue,
Swindon, SN2 1FA, United Kingdom.
T +44 (0) 1793 417 424
F +44 (0) 1793 417 444
(Monday to Friday, 09:00 to 17:00 UK time)
www.bcs.org/contact
http://shop.bcs.org/

PRACTICAL TEST DESIGN
Selection of traditional and automated test design techniques

I. Forgács and A. Kovács

The
Chartered
Institute
for IT

Printed by Amazon POD

Published by BCS Learning and Development Ltd, a wholly owned subsidiary of BCS, The Chartered Institute for IT, First Floor, Block D, North Star House, North Star Avenue, Swindon, SN2 1FA, UK.
www.bcs.org

Paperback ISBN 978-1-780-1747-23
PDF ISBN 978-1-780-1747-30
ePUB ISBN 978-1-780-1747-47
Kindle ISBN 978-1-780-1747-54

British Cataloguing in Publication Data.
A CIP catalogue record for this book is available at the British Library.

Publisher's acknowledgements
Reviewers: Francisca Cano Ortiz, Sudeep Chatterjee, Stephen Hill
Publisher: Ian Borthwick
Commissioning editor: Rebecca Youé
Production manager: Florence Leroy
Project manager: Sunrise Setting Ltd
Copy-editor: Katharine Bartlett
Proofreader: Barbara Eastman
Indexer: Rachel Oakes
Cover design: Alex Wright
Cover image: iStock © Oleg Lopatkin
Typeset by Lapiz Digital Services, Chennai, India

CONTENTS

LIST OF FIGURES AND TABLES

AUTHORS

István Forgács PhD was originally a researcher at the Hungarian Academy of Sciences. He has had more than 25 scientific articles published in leading international journals and conference proceedings. He is the co-author of the book *Agile Testing Foundations: An ISTQB Foundation Level Agile Tester guide*. His research interests include test design, agile testing, model-based testing, debugging, code comprehension, and static and dynamic analysis. He invented and published a partly automated method the implementation of which efficiently solved the Y2K problem so that a single tester was able to review 300,000 lines of code per day. As a result, he left academic life in 1998 to be a founder of Y2KO, the startup company implementing this project.

He is also the founder and Chief Executive Officer of 4TestDev and is a former CEO of 4D Soft. As such he led several projects funded by the European Union and others financed by national grants, where he worked together with large companies such as CERN, the European Space Agency, the Food and Agriculture Organization and the Fraunhofer Institute. He is a member of the Agile Working Group of the International Software Testing Qualification Board (ISTQB) and of the Hungarian Testing Board.

Dr Forgács is the creator of the 4Test method and initiator of the related tool Harmony, which is a test design and scriptless test automation platform for continuous testing and DevOps. He gives successful test design and model-based hands-on training.

Attila Kovács is currently a professor at Eötvös Loránd University, Budapest, Faculty of Informatics. His research interests are in software engineering, software quality, number theory and cryptography. He is the author of numerous scientific publications. He received an MSc in computer science and mathematics and a PhD in informatics. His teaching activity covers a wide range of subjects, including several courses of mathematics and software engineering.

He spent three years at the University of Paderborn, Germany, and four months at the Radboud University, Nijmegen, the Netherlands. He received an award for outstanding research from the Hungarian Academy of Sciences (Young Scientist Prize) in 1999. He is a project leader of several research and development projects, and consults for companies on issues including software quality, software testing, safety and reliability. He is an ISTQB and International Requirements Engineering Board trainer, and a founding member of the Hungarian Testing Board. He was the Program Chair of the 2016 Hungarian Software Testing Forum, the largest industrial software testing conference in Central Europe.

FOREWORD

Are you a serious software tester? A software tester who wants to know not only how to select and design effective and efficient tests but who also wants to know why those tests work? A software tester who is ready to take a deep, intensive dive into the topic? A software tester who knows that you can only learn test design by practising test design, using realistic exercises? If so, this book is for you.

Forgács and Kovács deliver a masterful tour through the most important behavioural test design techniques. Each technique is explained thoroughly. Each technique is illustrated with examples, which is always necessary with complex topics. Further, they include code segments to illustrate exactly why these techniques work, showing specific defects the resulting tests will catch.

Because of their willingness to drill all the way from the technique through the tests to the specific defects in the code, this book will appeal beyond professional software testers. The field of testing, and who is interested in testing, has expanded quite a bit, thanks to the advance of concepts such as Agile and Lean methods, DevOps, continuous integration and continuous delivery, and continuous deployment. So, if you are a technical tester, a software development engineer in test, or a developer who cares about properly testing their code, this book is for you.

Just like writing good code, designing good tests requires hands-on practice to learn. This book provides an excellent, realistic example system to use as the basis for such exercises. Forgács and Kovács deliver a system that is universally understandable, that of a ticket vending machine. Better yet, their ticket vending machine successfully steers between the Scylla and Charybdis of such an exercise basis, avoiding being on the one hand so trivial as to be useless for learning or on the other hand being so complex as to distract from the techniques being taught. From my own experience writing books on test design and creating courses on test design, I know how hard it is to create a good basis for exercises, and how critical it is to do so.

So, if you have reached a point with your knowledge of software testing where you need to challenge yourself, to gain deeper understanding, to become ready to put sophisticated test design techniques into practice, then, I'll say it again, this book is for you. Invest the time to read the explanations of the techniques, carefully study the examples, and work through the exercises. Your return on that investment will be a significant step forward in your software testing skills and abilities.

Rex Black
President, RBCS Inc.
Past President, ASTQB
Past President, ISTQB

This is the testing book I've been waiting for. It's nice that the authors understand and include some testing theory, but what sets this book apart in my mind is that it is written by practitioners who also have real pragmatic testing experience and a deep understanding of important issues. Also of critical importance in these days of ubiquitous embedded systems and the internet of things (IoT), is that the authors recognise and explicitly state issues related to hardware that also have to be considered. For example, in their running example of the ticket vending machine, they mention various types of testing that would have to be included, related to the physical machine. I've found that most students, and even many practitioners, just assume that the only possible problems that need to be considered are ones related to the code itself.

Other nice features are the device the authors use at the beginning of each chapter, a brief summary of what is to come ('Why is this chapter worth reading?') as well as a brief wrap-up that comes at the end of the chapter ('Key takeaways'); and that each chapter has non-trivial examples and exercises.

Finally, it is really important that the authors have included issues related to testing systems developed using modern software development strategies such as Agile and DevOps.

This is a book that both students and practitioners can use to hone their software testing skills.

Elaine Weyuker
University Distinguished Professor
Member, US National Academy of Engineering, ACM Fellow, IEEE Fellow

ACKNOWLEDGEMENTS

We are grateful to all of those whom we have had the pleasure to work with during this book-writing project: colleagues, friends, specialists.

First and foremost, we thank our editor for her professionalism and strenuousness. Her feedback on our book was thoughtful, thorough and supportive.

Second, we acknowledge all of our reviewers. They did an excellent job: Péter Földházi, Zsolt Hargitai, Terézia Kaukál, Zoltán Micskei, Gábor Árpád Németh, Ceren Sahin and Kristóf Szabados. Grateful thanks go to the official reviewers as well. Any remaining errors and omissions are the authors' responsibility.

Great appreciation is given to the crew at the Hungarian Testing Board for their continuous support.

We are grateful to Bianka Békefi for implementing our key example, the ticket vending machine (TVM), and for reviewing the manuscript very carefully. Special thanks to József 'Joe' Csuti, for seeding tricky bugs into the TVM code, even if we could find them. We are also grateful for László Czippán who helped us with some coding. Many thanks to Dalma Bartuska who made exploratory testing for the TVM.

Attila sends special thanks to his department leader, Péter Burcsi, who granted him peace in the book-writing period.

Nobody has been more important to us in the pursuit of this project than the members of our families. We acknowledge them for the continuous and strong support they gave us.

István: this almost two-year journey would not have been possible without the support of my family. Thank you to Margó, my wife, for encouraging and inspiring me all the time to follow my dreams. I am especially grateful to my parents, who have supported and believed in me my whole life.

Attila: I would like to thank my family members for their patience and continuous support, especially my sons, Bendegúz and Barnabás, my love and my parents who always believed in me.

ABBREVIATIONS

AC	acceptance criteria
AETG	automatic efficient test generator
API	application programming interface
ASCII	American Standard Code for Information Interchange
BDD	behaviour-driven development
BPMN	business process modelling notation
BVA	boundary value analysis
CD	continuous deployment/delivery
CI	continuous integration
CPH	competent programmer hypothesis
CT	classification tree
DAG	directed acyclic graph
DFA	deterministic finite automaton
DP	defect prevention
EFSM	extended finite-state machine
EP	equivalence partitioning
ET	exploratory testing
F	false
FDD	feature-driven development
FSM	finite-state machine
GDPR	General Data Protection Regulation
GSM	global system for mobile communication
GUI	graphical user interface
GW	GraphWalker
HRF	high-risk function
IoT	internet of things
ISTQB	International Software Testing Qualification Board
JDK	Java Development Kit

KDT	keyword-driven testing
LAN	local area network
LOC	lines of code
LRF	low-risk function
MBT	model-based testing
OA	orthogonal array
OCL	Object Constraint Language
SBE	specification by example
SBTM	session-based test management
SDET	software development engineer in test
SDL	specification and description language
SDLC	software development life cycle
STT	state transition testing
SUT	system under test
T	true
TAC	test data adequacy criterion
TCP	test case prioritisation techniques
TCP/IP	Transmission Control Protocol/Internet Protocol
TDD	test-driven development
TFT	thin film transistor
TSC	test selection criterion
TTCN-3	Test and Test Control Notation Version 3
TVM	ticket vending machine
UI	user interface
UML	Unified Modelling Language
V&V	verification and validation

GLOSSARY

Many of the following definitions are based on the ISTQB Glossary, available at https://glossary.istqb.org.

Black-box testing: Functional or non-functional testing without referencing the internal structure of the component or system.

Boundary value analysis: A black-box test design technique in which **test cases** are designed based on boundary values of **equivalence partitions.**

Business rule-based testing: A black-box test design technique used to determine test scenarios and test cases for business logic.

Cause–effect graph: A graphical representation of inputs and/or stimuli (causes) with their associated outputs (effects), which can be used to design test cases.

Classification tree testing: An approach of **equivalence partitioning** that uses a descriptive tree-like notation. The equivalence partitions are hierarchically ordered.

Combinative testing: A black-box test design technique in which the number of tests can be described by a linear function of the maximal number of parameter values.

Combinatorial testing: A black-box test design technique in which test cases are designed to execute specific combinations of values of several parameters.

Competent programmer hypothesis: Programmers create programs that are close to being correct, i.e. the specification and the appropriate code are close to each other.

Decision table testing: A black-box test design technique in which test cases are designed to execute the combinations of inputs and/or stimuli (causes) shown in a table.

Defect prevention: A process that identifies, analyses and collects defect information in order to prevent implementing new defects in the code.

Diff-pair testing: A **combinative test** design technique that requires each value of any parameter to be tested with at least two different values for any other parameters.

Domain-based testing: A black-box test design technique that is used to identify efficient and effective test cases when more parameters can or should be tested together. It establishes, builds on and generalises **equivalence partitioning** and **boundary value analysis.**

Equivalence partitioning: A black-box test design technique in which **test cases** are designed to exercise disjoint partitions by using at least one representative input value of each partition. If a single input detects (or not) a failure then the system behaves the same way for all other inputs in the same partition.

Exploratory testing: An approach to testing whereby the testers dynamically design and execute tests based on their knowledge, exploration of the test item and the results of previous tests.

Model-based testing: Testing based on or involving models.

Mutation testing: A method of testing the tests, in which slightly modifying the original code creates several mutants. A reliable test data set should then differentiate the original code from the well-selected mutants.

On-the-fly testing: An approach to testing where **test cases** are created on the fly and executed immediately based on the running application.

Orthogonal array: A two-dimensional array constructed with special mathematical properties. Namely, there is an integer t so that for every selection of t columns of the table, all ordered t-tuples of the symbols, formed by taking the entries in each row restricted to these columns, appear the same number of times.

Risk analysis: The overall process of risk identification and risk assessment.

Scenario-based testing: A test design technique focusing on the interactions between an 'actor' and the system, with different roles and environments.

Session-based testing: A software test method that aims at combining accountability and **exploratory testing** in order to provide fast defect discovery, creative **on-the-fly test design**, management control and reporting metrics.

State transition testing: A black-box test design technique in which the behaviour of an application under test is analysed for different input events in a sequence. The technique models the specification via states and transitions, which are covered according to a test selection criterion. In this technique both the valid and invalid transitions are checked.

Test case: A set of preconditions, inputs, actions (where applicable), expected results and postconditions, developed based on test conditions.

Test data adequacy criteria: Rules for validating whether enough testing has been executed.

Test design: The activity of deriving and specifying **test cases** from test conditions.

Test path: An execution path showing the control flow when executing a test case.

Test script: A sequence of instructions for the execution of a test.

Test selection criterion: The criteria used to guide the creation of **test cases** or to select **test cases** in order to limit the size of a test.

Test suite: A set of **test cases** or test procedures to be executed in a specific test cycle.

Use case testing: A black-box test technique in which **test cases** are designed to execute scenarios of use cases.

User story: A high-level user or business requirement commonly used in Agile software development to capture a software feature from the end-user point of view. It typically consists of one sentence in the everyday or business language and acceptance criteria for validation.

White-box testing: Testing based on an analysis of the internal structure of the component or system.

Dear Reader,

Thank you for picking up our book. This book is about specification-based test design.

We promise that you will learn a lot, and that after having read it, you will be a much better tester than before. The book not only assists in the deeper understanding of software testing but also strongly supports preparation for various professional exams (for example, those of ISTQB).

Each chapter is self-explanatory, and we refer to the necessary parts of each for all needs. Each chapter includes at least two elaborated examples. There is (at least) one for demonstrating the described method, and another, which presents the method through a common example. At the end of each chapter, there are exercises to be solved. We strongly suggest doing these exercises. You can find their solutions in Appendix D.

The entire book contains useful information, although we separate the must-read and worth-reading parts out. The worth-reading parts are denoted by a book icon in the margin; however, you can solve all the exercises without reading these parts.

A hint/tip is denoted throughout by a magnifying glass icon in the margin.

An anecdote is denoted throughout by a speech bubble icon in the margin.

Happy reading,
I. Forgács and A. Kovács

PREFACE – TESTING IS COMPLEX

Would you think, dear reader, that testing is easier than developing code? Some people think 'Yes, of course', since programming is hard, and requires a lot of skill to be able to do it effectively. Testing, on the other hand, is just monkey typing and watching the results, right? Other people think 'No, by no means', testing is hard, and excellent testing is far more difficult than excellent engineering, since excellent software testing requires thinking out of the box, requires selecting and applying test design techniques in combination, and requires intuition for finding tricky bugs. Others think that it **depends** at least **on complexity**, which is probably the most common answer.

Probably all of you know a test automation engineer, a recognised superman or superwoman, who incorporates the knowledge of developers and testers. However, non-testers sometimes believe that testing requires only some logical thinking and that is all. Test job applicants might think that learning some basic test design methods, a bug tracking system, and a version control system is enough for a testing career. The sad truth is that it is not enough. Testing is not only designing and executing some test code. A tester is an architect, a designer and far more. Testing is an art, a craft, a discipline. However, there's still a long road to traverse before testing occupies a worthy place in the engineering universe.

When the former company of one of the authors of this book was looking for testers, lots of non-IT people applied for the available positions. Some were economists, lawyers and there was even a policeman. Most applicants believed that a tester's job is similar to a soccer referee's job – everybody knows how to do it. There were also positions for Java developers and in that case, all the applicants were Java developers.

The good news is that this book is for everyone who wants to know why testing is complex, and in many cases, why it is even more complex than coding. Here we try to demonstrate some aspects of this.

STARTING POINT

Our starting point is a specification containing requirements on how to optimally arrange several rectangular and square shapes in a minimal quadrant. With this, we demonstrate the advantages of conscious test design and describe the usefulness of implementation-independent testing. This example served as an exercise for tester applicants in a company. Everybody who was able to solve this problem, later became a good tester. The applicant's task was to figure out a single test case, that if the implementation of the specification was faulty, then there was a high probability that the test would detect the bug.

SPECIFICATION: SQUARE-FILLING

For this example, applicants were given three kinds of rectangular shapes with their length and height, A = 1x1, B = 2x1 and C = 2x2.

Rectangle B is not allowed to rotate into the rectangle 1x2. The input is a finite random list of these rectangular shapes containing at least one shape from each type.

Example

Input:

1x1 – 3 pieces,

2x1 – 4 pieces,

2x2 – 1 piece.

The task is to insert the objects into a square with the smallest possible size.

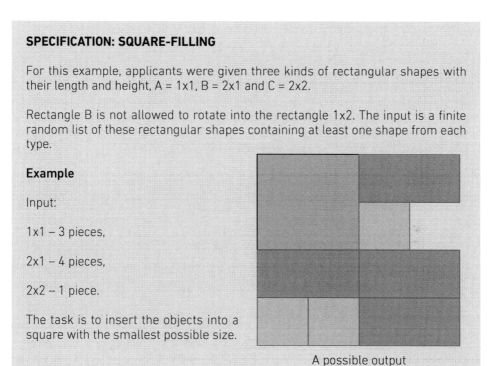

A possible output

Clearly, to create the appropriate test case, the tester should know something about the potential solution, which involves the following steps:

1. Summarise the area of the shapes.
2. Compute the square root R of the total area.
3. If R is an integer, then this can be the size of the minimum square.
4. If R is a non-integer, then let's select the closest integer S for which S > R. Then S can be the size of the minimum square.
5. Starting from the top left of the minimum square, let's place the 2x2 squares from left to right. When a row is full, we continue the placement of the shapes in the next row beneath the full one.
6. If there are no 2x2 shapes, then we place shapes 2x1 in the same way.
7. Finally, we place all the remaining 1x1 shapes into the empty parts of the minimum square.

8. If the shapes do not fit into the minimum square, then increase S by one, and

9. Place the unplaced shapes into the empty space in the way described in steps 5-7.

Then, the tester has to select an **order of the input shapes**. Even if the tester knows the above method, it is not easy to create the appropriate test. To create a test for which a faulty solution will most probably fail, the tester has to know something more. Really, the tester also has to know that squares with odd sizes are more difficult to fill in. The reason is that if the size is odd and we start filling the minimum square with 2x1 shapes as described in step 5, then some 2x2 shapes cannot fit. This knowledge is necessary for the tester but not necessary for the developer.

Consider the test case design. If the input forms are in the order in which the minimum squares are filled only by selecting the following form and inserting them into the first empty space, the test case is ineffective. An odd-sized minimum square is more challenging for testing than an even-sized one, as already mentioned.

EXAMPLE: 7X7 SQUARE

Input:

1x1 – 7 pieces,

2x1 – 7 pieces,

2x2 – 7 pieces.

Since the area is 7+14+28 = 49, the size of the minimum square is 7. The input can be: T = [1x1, 1x1, 1x1, 2x2, 2x1, 2x1, 2x2, 1x1, 2x2, 2x2, 2x2, 1x1, 2x1, 1x1, 1x1, 2x2, 2x1, 2x1, 2x2, 2x1, 2x1]. The output is the following. The numbers represent the order of insertion.

The author gave the above input to all of the interviewees after they had come up with their solutions. They immediately realised the problem with their solution when they were not able to insert the rectangular shapes into the 7x7 square. This test case always worked.

There are some other questions to consider:

    a. should the objects fill the minimum square entirely? or

    b. leave some empty places in the square? or

    c. should the total area of the objects just exceed a square?

Of course, the last option is the worst. Namely, a wrong solution may result in a possible arrangement, since we have lots of space to fill. The less extra space is available, the greater the chance that a faulty solution fails. Therefore, the first is the best selection for a reliable test.

There is another area where testers have difficulties. A developer always knows when they are finished. When the implemented code is working, and the unit tests have passed then the developer gives the code to testers for further testing. However, it is not obvious when the tester is finished: how many test cases need to be designed and executed? The answer is: **it depends**.

If the goal is to test the suitability of an applicant for a job in the company, then this one single test is enough. Through this we learn if the applicant is able to solve the problem and implement their solution. However, if the task is to test a larger system and faulty implementations may cause serious problems, then additional test cases need to be created. For example, we have to test the size of the minimum square. It means that we have to select a suitable *test selection criterion* to restrict the number of test cases.

Our simple square-filling example shows that testing can be as complex as coding. Software complexity grows to the limits of our ability to manage that complexity. Testing complex software systems is one of the biggest challenges in our engineering life. Developers ensure that the software meets the specifications, business owners ensure that software systems meet the business's operational needs, and testers provide them with information about the quality. To reach the main goal of the software development process, which is a high-quality output, one will have to plan, design and conduct reliable tests.

There are various types of test design techniques, each of which is suitable for identifying a certain type of defect. Therefore, the challenge lies in selecting the *right set of relevant test design techniques* for the particular application. By designing appropriate test cases, the complexity of the quality assurance costs and time can be reduced. However, in practice, the known techniques are applied together, which raises the complexity and difficulty of the test design. This book deals with the question of how to manage these issues.

There are wonderful books and papers on software test design (see the references at the end of this book). In this book, we not only describe and explain the different methods of test design but always show **why to use** and **how to use them** by applying a **realistic software specification**. Also, the book always shows alternative solutions and points out why something is inappropriate. Many examples in the book are based on an implemented version of a software specification, therefore 'real faults' can be detected.

The book explains and evaluates the most important and applicable methods generally and specifically, unfolding their fault-finding capabilities. The different test design techniques will be connected and applied together. We also present the theoretical background of the techniques and their relations to real-world solutions. The presented examples are complex but do not require any special domain knowledge. The book covers all the usable *test design techniques* and the ways to validate them; it contains new methods, ideas and test selection criteria.

THE STRUCTURE OF THE BOOK

This book consists of 15 chapters and four appendices. The main chapters contain the test design techniques following a common structure. We start with the description of the method and demonstrate it by applying simple examples. We then may show complex examples as well. Then we select an appropriate part of our key example, the ticket vending machine (TVM), to also demonstrate the technique. The next part is the method evaluation, describing the types of defects, applicability, advantages and shortcomings of the technique. For interested readers, we present a short section of theoretical background. We summarise the chapters with key takeaways, followed by some exercises.

The first chapter introduces and summarises the whole testing process, placing the test design into it. We also consider some basic methods, which are necessary for test design.

In Chapter 2, you'll find our basic example, the TVM, which is implemented in Java. We use this example throughout the book.

In every test design technique chapter, we select a reasonable part of the TVM for demonstration. In the last chapter, we test the whole application. As the implementation of TVM was too good (thanks to our developer Bianka), we asked our experienced Java architect to seed some tricky bugs into it.

In Chapter 3, we deal with risk management and test optimisation. You will learn how to optimise testing to minimise the total system development life cycle costs based on risk and complexity analysis and by applying an appropriate set of test design techniques.

In Chapter 4, we demonstrate the importance of defect prevention, a cheap and reliable method of avoiding defects, and show you how to perform it.

Following these chapters, which describe how to support and complete test design, we consider all the important traditional test design techniques.

Chapter 5 contains domain-based techniques. You will learn about equivalence partitioning, boundary value analysis and domain analysis from more different perspectives than in other books. We will show you an optimal test selection criterion, which will be used later in our examples.

In Chapter 6 we deal with state transition testing. You will learn about state transition diagrams and tables. We present interesting examples for demonstration and introduce new test selection criteria. We show how state transition testing, equivalence partitioning and boundary value analysis can be used together in the case of more complex specifications.

In Chapter 7 you will learn business rule-based test design techniques. Specifically, we deal with decision table testing and cause–effect graphs. Decision tables guarantee that every possible combination of condition value is considered.

Chapter 8 is about scenario-based testing. We start with use case testing, which is used widely in developing tests at the system or acceptance level. Then we follow with user story testing, and we introduce Gherkin syntax.

Chapter 9 is about combinative and combinatorial testing. Combinative testing requires only a linear number of test cases, yet these tests may detect bugs caused by different issues in parallel. Here we introduce a new method, diff-pair testing. Then, we describe the combinatorial methods and we show you the strengths and the weaknesses of them.

In Chapter 10 you will learn about exploratory and session-based testing. We apply them for testing the whole TVM containing natural and artificial bugs and we show you the results.

In the next chapters, we move from traditional test design to automated test case generation, that is model-based testing (MBT).

In Chapter 11 we provide an overview of MBT in general and show you why it is promising.

In Chapter 12, you will become acquainted with Gherkin-based MBT. We will show you how to prepare a model through iterations, and how to make models for complex cases when more test design techniques are used together.

Chapter 13 is perhaps the most practical chapter, where we introduce you step-by-step to the GraphWalker, a graphical MBT tool. We demonstrate random test execution as an extension to the test design techniques.

In Chapter 14 we test the whole TVM by applying multiple techniques and compare the results. You will learn how many natural and seeded defects are found by applying different techniques and test selection criteria.

The final part is Chapter 15 with conclusions and recommendations.

1 INTRODUCTION

WHY IS THIS CHAPTER WORTH READING?

This introductory chapter explains the importance of software testing, and covers what test design is, how we can put test design activities into the software development and testing life cycle, why tests should be designed, what factors affect test design and when test design should be done.

THE IMPORTANCE OF SOFTWARE TESTING

Software is a vital part of our everyday life. It helps in navigating to destinations, communicating with people, driving production, distributing energy resources, taking care of people's health, and so much more. We use software for entertainment, for scientific research, for driving companies forward. There is embedded software in cars, trucks, locomotives, aeroplanes, mobile phones, electronic equipment and so on. Controlling and ensuring the quality of these software systems is vital. We need to check, that is test, software because things can always go wrong – humans make mistakes all the time. Despite this, the human aspects of producing quality software are indisputable even if artificial intelligence comes to the fore.

ISTQB certifies software testers worldwide; there are books, articles, documents, webinars, and blogs supporting the knowledge transfer of testing. In this book, we mainly draw on the terms of the ISTQB Glossary (2018a).

Let's list a few goals that should be considered while testing software systems:

- ensuring the overall quality of the systems;
- customer satisfaction;
- reducing the risk of failures;
- cost-effective maintenance.

The most important goal of testing is to ensure good quality software by optimising the project costs in a way that all the parties involved gain confidence in the product – see

Chapter 3. To be able to do this, a tester has to harvest information on system behaviour. One of the main reasons for gathering information is the execution of test cases. The test case is an essential notion in software testing: simply, 'a **test case** is a set of preconditions, inputs, actions (where applicable), expected results and postconditions, developed on test conditions' (ISTQB, 2018a). At this point the main questions are:

- How do we design the tests?
- Which test cases are the most appropriate for a given situation?
- How can test intensity be determined?
- How many test cases do we need?
- How can we validate the tests?

In answering these questions the process of **test design** is essential.

WHAT IS TEST DESIGN EXACTLY?

Test design is one of the most important prerequisites of quality. We design tests to support:

1. defining and improving quality-related processes and procedures (quality assurance);
2. evaluating the quality of the product with regards to customer expectations and needs (quality control);
3. finding defects in the product (testing).

Fortunately, or unfortunately, it is a creative process on its own, but also one that requires technical expertise.

> More than the act of testing, the act of designing tests is one of the best bug preventers known. The thinking that must be done to create a useful test can discover and eliminate bugs before they are coded - indeed, test-design thinking can discover and eliminate bugs at every stage in the creation of software, from conception to specification, to design, coding and the rest.
>
> (Beizer, 1990)

Test design depends on many factors. Figure 1.1 summarises the relevant entities of the traditional testing life cycle including test design activities.

Preceding test design activities – test planning and test analysis

In this subsection we describe the main activities that precede and influence test design.

Figure 1.1 Test design in the test software development life cycle (SDLC)

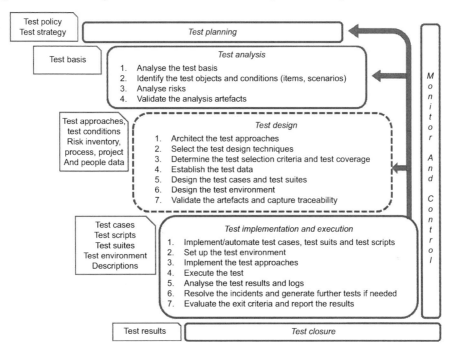

Test planning

The **test planning** process determines the scope, objective, approach, resources and schedule of the intended test activities. During test planning – amongst others – the test objectives, test items, features to be tested, the testing tasks, human and other resources, the degree of tester independence, the test environment, entry and exit criteria to be used, and any risks requiring contingency planning are identified.

> The ISO/IEC/IEEE 29119-3 *Standard for Software Testing – Test Documentation*, recommends the necessary documents for use in defined stages of software testing.

A **test policy document** represents the testing philosophy of the company, selecting the frames that testing parties should adhere to and follow. It should apply to both new projects and maintenance work. The **test strategy** is defined as a set of guiding principles that influences the test design and regulates how testing is carried out.

The **test approach** defines how (in which way) testing is carried out, that is how to implement a test strategy. It can be proactive, that is the test process is initiated as early as possible to find and fix the faults before the build (preferable, if possible), or reactive, which means that the test design process begins after the implementation is finished. The test approach can be of different (not necessarily disjoint) types such

3

as specification-based, structure-based, experience-based, model-based, risk-based, script-based, fault-based, failure-based, standard-compliant, test-first and so on, or a combination of them. For example, a risk-based approach is applied in almost all situations.

The proactive test-first approach starts with analysing the specifications, then applying risk analysis. Based on the result of this analysis one can select the appropriate techniques to design the test cases. The riskier code needs more techniques to be used in parallel. The test design can then be extended with structure-based testing, that is coverage analysis to create additional test cases for uncovered code.

Test monitoring and control
Test monitoring is an ongoing comparison of the actual and the planned progress. Test control involves the actions necessary to meet the objectives of the plan.

Although monitoring and control are activities that belong to the test manager, it is important to ensure that the appropriate data/metrics from the test design activities are collected, validated and communicated.

Test analysis
The test engineering activity in the fundamental test process begins mainly with **test analysis**. Test analysis is the process of looking at something that can be used to derive quality information for the software product. The test analysis process is based on appropriate project documents or knowledge, called the **test basis**, on which the tests are based.

The test analysis phase has three main steps before the review.

1. The first step is to **analyse the test basis thoroughly**. Possible test bases can take the form of business requirement documents, systems requirement documents, functional design specifications, technical specifications, user manuals, source codes and so on.

2. The second step is to **identify the test objects (features, scenarios) and conditions** by defining what should be tested.

   A **test condition** is a statement about the test object, which can be true or false. Test conditions can be stated for any part of a component (or system) that could be verified by some tests, for example a function, transaction, feature, quality attribute or structural element.

   A **feature** is an attribute of a component or system specified or implied by requirements documentation.

   A **test scenario** is a business requirement to be tested, which may have one or more tests associated with it.

   The advantages of using test scenarios are:

   a. They help to achieve more complete test coverage.

   b. They can be approved by various stakeholders.

   c. They help to determine the end-to-end functionality of the test object.

Projects that follow Agile methodology – like Scrum or Kanban – usually do not use test scenarios: they apply user stories, sometimes use cases. We note that both are test objects, and a user story – which is an informal, natural language description of some system features – contains information about the test conditions.

A test object may consist of different **test items**. A test item is a specific element to be tested.

EXAMPLE FOR TEST OBJECT AND TEST ITEM

To clarify the notion, a **test object** can be login functionality, while a **test item** can be a username or password field in the login form. A test condition for this scenario can be an assertion for usernames such as 'a username shall start with an alphabetical or numeric value'.

It is usually advisable to determine the test objects/conditions at different levels of detail. Initially, high-level objects/conditions have to be identified to define general targets for testing. Subsequently, in the design phase, the objects/conditions will be groomed towards specific targets. Applying this type of hierarchical approach can help to ensure that the coverage is sufficient for all high-level items.

3. The third step of the test analysis phase is **risk analysis**. For each elicited (mainly high level) test object the risk analysis process determines and records the following risk attributes:

   a. the impact of malfunctioning (how important the appropriate functioning of the test is);

   b. the likelihood of malfunctioning (how likely it is to fail).

   Later, during test execution, the risk inventory supports the organisation of the tests in a way that the high-risk items are addressed with more intensive testing – see Chapter 3.

   An effective risk analysis is a result of contributions from different stakeholders: managers, technical and business people, customer representatives and so on. Risk analysis is a continuous process.

   We note that risk analysis is always necessary, not only in risk-based testing. The reason is that we should optimise the costs and effort of the whole test development process. Risk analysis performed during the test analysis phase refines the risks identified during test planning.

4. The last step of this phase is spent validating the identified artefacts, test objects, main scenarios and test conditions, and the risk inventory by applying reviews.

Present activity – test design

After the test analysis, the **test design** comes into the picture. The test design depends on a few factors:

- The result of risk and complexity analysis – see Chapter 3. This is the starting point of the test design techniques to be selected.
- The way the software development process is organised (for instance, V-model vs Agile).
- The knowledge and experience of the people involved.
- The available (sometimes limited) resources.

Based on these and other factors, the test design can be performed in seven steps (see Figure 1.1):

1. First, the **test approaches** are worked out, which means that it should be planned how the product quality together with the cost optimisation goals can be achieved via the approaches defined earlier, taking into consideration the elicited test conditions, code complexity and risks. Here we consider consistencies with standards, processes, flows, measures, user experience and so on.

2. After planning the test approach, the **test design techniques** are selected that meet the testing objectives and the result of risk and complexity analysis. In general, it is advisable to select test design techniques understandable to other stakeholders. Real systems usually require using more than one test design technique together. Table 1.1 shows some test techniques related to different test design categories and test bases.

Table 1.1 Test bases, test design categories and test design techniques

Test basis	Test design category	Test design technique
Informal requirements	Specification-based	Equivalence partitioning
		Boundary value analysis
		Decision table
		Cause and effect graph
		Classification tree
		Ad hoc testing
Semiformal or formal requirements	Model-based, Model checking	State transition testing
		Syntax testing

(Continued)

Table 1.1 (Continued)

Test basis	Test design category	Test design technique
Structure (e.g. code)	Structure-based	Control-flow testing
		Data-flow testing
		Path testing
		Condition testing
		Mutation testing
Experience	Experience-based	Error guessing
		Exploratory testing
		Attack testing
		Checklists
Faults, failures	Fault-based, failure-based testing	Taxonomy-based testing

3. The next step is to determine the **test case selection criteria** (for simplicity we refer to this **as test selection criteria**).

First, let's consider the types of test cases. When a test case checks valid functionality then it is called a **positive test case** (or sometimes 'happy path'); when a test case checks invalid functionality, then it is called a **negative test case**. Both positive and negative testing are equally important for quality software. Negative testing helps to find more defects, but it is done once positive testing is completed.

Usually, we distinguish **high-level** (abstract) and **low-level** (concrete) test cases. An abstract test case provides guidelines for the test selection using tables, lists and graphs. A concrete test case realises the abstract one by describing the preconditions, test steps, expected results, postconditions and by assigning concrete input values to it. Sometimes, the level of detail is forced by an outside authority (DO 178-C in avionics, for example). A good test case satisfies at least the following:

- **Accurate:** has a clear purpose.
- **Effective:** able to verify correctness or able to uncover faults depending on the test target.
- **Economic:** no unnecessary steps, cheap to use.
- **Evolvable:** easy to maintain.
- **Exemplary:** has low redundancy.
- **Traceable:** capable of being traced to requirements.
- **Repeatable:** can be used to perform the test several times.
- **Reusable:** can be 'called' from other test cases, avoiding duplication and therefore the room for human error.

A TEST CASE AS AN 'EXAMPLE'

A test case can be seen as an example for the specification. Examples are very useful measures of understanding anything. They can also be used to understand software specification, user stories and so on. In most cases, a test case is a good example. For example, if we test a login feature with test data, we can see that it is also an example for demonstrating some part of the login process.

Good test cases are understandable examples for any stakeholders. The project owner can validate the specification or user story; the developers can implement better code because of a deeper understanding. The tester is supported by the examples and gets feedback from the examples/test cases. Moreover, and this is also important, if test design has been done, we do not omit the test.

In agile testing, the *Specification by Example* (Adzic, 2011) uses this approach, that is the Agile team creates good examples, which can be considered as test cases and also as part of a specification. By applying examples, the problems in the specifications/user stories can be detected very early on.

The test selection criteria determine when to stop designing more test cases, or how many test cases have to be designed for a given situation. The test selection criterion for the equivalence partition method, for example, may result in designing a different number of test cases for each equivalence class.

It is possible to define different ('weaker' or 'stronger') test selection criteria for a given condition and design technique.

EXAMPLE FOR WEAK AND STRONG TEST SELECTION CRITERIA

Assume that during test design a technique was selected for a test condition where the input domain was partitioned into 100 disjoint subdomains. A 'weak selection criterion' with respect to the criterion and technique means for example choosing at most one item of test data from each subdomain. A 'strong selection criterion' means for example choosing test data on each of the borders between the subdomains, test data 'close to' the borders and test data from anywhere else in each subdomain.

There is an important notion closely related to test selection criteria, namely, **the test data adequacy criteria**.

While test selection criteria are defined concerning the test design, that is independently of the implementation, test data adequacy criteria are defined concerning program execution. Both test selection and test data adequacy criteria, however, provide a way to define a notion of 'thoroughness' for test case sets. By applying these criteria, we can check whether our test set is **adequate** and no additional testing is needed. We can call both test selection and test data adequacy criteria with regards to thoroughness.

The adequacy criteria define 'what properties of a program must be exercised to constitute a thorough test' (Goodenough and Gerhart, 1975). Satisfying a stronger adequacy criterion implies greater thoroughness in testing. The test data adequacy criteria validate whether the designed test cases are efficient concerning the testers' expectations, and are applied after the test cases have been executed. Test data adequacy criteria focuses on validating the fulfilment of a specific code coverage and on the creation of additional test cases to detect specific types of defects.

THEORETICAL BACKGROUND

Let's formalise these notions. Consider a program P written to meet a set of requirements $R = \{R_1, R_2,...,R_m\}$. Suppose now that a set of test cases $T = \{T_1, T_2,...,T_k\}$ has been selected to test P to determine whether or not it meets all the requirements in R. The question arises naturally: is T good enough? Or in other words, is T adequate? Hence, adequacy is measured for a given test set designed to test P to determine whether or not P meets its requirements. This measurement is done against a given adequacy criterion C.

A test set is considered adequate concerning criterion C when it satisfies C. Let D_C be a finite set of sub-criteria items belonging to criterion C, called **coverage domain**. We say that T covers D_C if for each coverage item x in D_C there is at least one test case t from T that tests x.

The test set T is considered adequate concerning C if it covers all items in the coverage domain. Similarly, T is considered inadequate concerning C if it covers only j items of D_C where j < n and n is the number of the coverage items. The fraction j/n is a measure of the extent to which T is adequate concerning C. This ratio is also known as the coverage of D_C concerning T, P and R. The coverage domain may depend on the program P under test or on the requirements R or both.

The examples below demonstrate test selection and test data adequacy criteria and the difference between them.

EXAMPLE FOR TEST SELECTION CRITERIA

Regarding the test design-related aspects of test selection criteria, consider the following requirements:

R1. Input two integers, say x and y from the standard input device

R2. If x and y are both negative, then print x + y to the standard output device

R3. If x and y are both positive, then print their greatest common divisor to the standard output device

R4. If x and y have opposite signs (one of them is positive and the other is negative), then print their product to the standard output device

R5. If x × y is zero then print zero to the standard output device.

After analysing the requirement set, R = {R1, R2, R3, R4, R5} one can see that R is consistent, does not contain redundancy and is deterministic. Let's choose the test approach as a specification-based one. Suppose that the program P satisfies the requirement set R. Let's specify a test selection criterion (TSC) as follows:

TSC: a test set T for the program P is considered adequate if for each requirement r in R there is at least one test case t in T such that t tests the correctness of P with respect to r.

In our case the coverage domain is R itself. With the test set T1 = {([-2, -3]; -5), ([2, 3]; 1)} (i.e. for input x = -2 and y = -3 the expected output is -5, for input x = 2 and x = 3 the expected output is 1) then T1 covers R1, R2 and R3, but does not cover R4 and R5. Hence, T1 is inadequate with respect to TSC and the coverage of T1 is 3/5 = 60%. The test set T2 = {([-2, -3]; -5), ([4, 2]; 2), ([2, -4]; -8), ([2, 0]; 0)} is adequate with regards to TSC, having 100% coverage. The appropriate test design technique for this scenario is called equivalence partitioning (see Chapter 5).

EXAMPLE FOR TEST DATA ADEQUACY CRITERIA

```
1.   function coverage_demo
2.   begin
3.        int x, y;
4.        input(x, y);
5.        if x < 0 and y < 0 then
6.            output(x+y);
7.        else if x > 0 and y > 0 then
8.            while x ≠ y
9.                if x > y then
10.                   x = x-y
11.               else y = y-x;
12.           output(x);
13.       else if sgn(x) * sgn(y) = -1 then
14.           output(x * y);
15.       else output(0);
16. end
```

In the pseudocode above the function *coverage_demo* is implemented. Line 3 contains the declarations, line 4 the input from the standard input device (requirement R1). Lines 5–6 contain the code for the requirement R2, lines 7–12 the Euclidean algorithm for requirement R3, lines 13–14 the code for requirement R4, and finally, line 15 contains the code for requirement R5.

Consider the following **test data adequacy criterion (TAC):**

TAC: a test set T for the program P (coverage_demo) is considered adequate if each statement in P is traversed at least once.

The coverage domain now is the set of all possible statements in P. Let the test set be T2 = {([-2, -3]; -5), ([4, 2]; 2), ([2, -4]; -8), ([2, 0]; 0)} as before. In the first test case ([-2, -3]; -5) the path 1-2-3-4-5-6-16 is executed. In the second test case ([4, 2]; 2) the path 1-2-3-4-5-7-8-9-10-8-12-16 is executed. In the third test case ([2, -4]; -8) the path 1-2-3-4-5-7-13-14-16 is executed, and in the fourth test case ([2, 0]; 0) the path 1-2-3-4-5-7-13-15-16 is executed. Hence, this test set is inadequate with regards to TAC. The coverage of T2 is 14/15 = 93% (the statement in line 11 is not covered).

Adequacy and full coverage can be achieved by T3 = {([-2, -3]; -5), ([2, 3]; 1), ([2, -4]; -8), ([2, 0]; 0)}.

Observe the difference between test selection and test data adequacy criteria. During test design we considered R3 as a simple requirement in the previous example, which can be covered by a single test case. On the other hand, the implementation (see lines 7–12) is more complex and may require more test cases.

Table 1.2 shows some coverage domains with test selection/test data adequacy criteria. Definition is an assignment statement, such as x = 1. Use occurs when the variable is read from memory, such as z = x + 1. Definition–Use pairs exist for a definition and a use of the same variable so that there is a program path between them where no other definition for that variable occurs.

It is important to note that some authors define test selection coverage as simply the same as code coverage. However, although test selection coverage and code coverage are both useful to assess the quality of the application code,

Table 1.2 Coverage domains with adequacy criteria

Coverage domain	Adequacy criteria
Boundary values	Test selection: • One dimensional • Multidimensional
State transitions	Test selection: • Random • State coverage • Transition coverage • 0-switch coverage • 1-switch coverage • 2-switch coverage

(Continued)

Table 1.2 (Continued)

Coverage domain	Adequacy criteria
Data	Test selection: • Random • One or some data pairs • All data pairs • N-wise (extension of pairwise) • All combinations Test data adequacy: • All Definition–Use pairs, etc.
Control flow	Test data adequacy: • Statement coverage • Decision coverage • Branch coverage • Path coverage
Paths	Test data adequacy: • Depth level N
Decision points	Test data adequacy: • Decision coverage • Simple condition coverage • Condition/decision coverage • Modified condition/decision coverage • Multiple condition coverage

code coverage is a term to describe which application code is exercised when the application is running, while test selection coverage relates to the percentage of the designed test cases with regard to the requirements in the selection criterion.

Please keep in mind that neither test selection nor test data adequacy criteria tell us anything about the quality of the software, only about the **expected quality of the test cases**. When deriving the test cases, be aware that one test case may exercise more than one test condition, and thus, there is the opportunity to optimise test case selection by combining multiple test coverage items in a single test case. At the end of this chapter, you can find a simple but complete example which explains these notions.

There is another important notion related to test selection. In a multivariate domain, we can apply different fault models to predict the consequences of faults.

The **single fault assumption** relies on the statistic that failures are only rarely the product of two or more simultaneous faults. Here we assume that fault in a program occurs due to the value of just one variable. On the contrary, the **multiple fault assumption** means that more than one component leads to the cause of the problem. Here we assume that fault in the program occurs due to the values of more than one variable.

Single fault assumption also means that we test only one input domain with one test case, and if it fails, then we know the location of the fault. By applying multiple fault assumption we can design fewer test cases; however, in the case of a failure, we should make additional test cases for bug localisation. There is no rule for which method is better.

4. The next step is to **establish the test data**. Test data are used to execute the tests, and can be generated by testers or by any appropriate automation tool (produced systematically or by using randomisation models). Test data may be recorded for reuse (e.g. in automated regression testing) or may be thrown away after usage (e.g. in error guessing).

The time, cost and effectiveness of producing adequate test data are extremely important. Some data may be used for positive, others for negative testing. Typically, test data are created together with the test case they are intended to be used for. Test data can be generated manually, by copying from production or from legacy sources into the test environment, or by using automated test data generation tools. Test data creation takes many pre-steps or test environment configurations, which is very time-consuming. Note that concrete test cases may take a long time to create and may require a lot of maintenance.

5. Now we can **finalise the test case design**. A test case template contains a test case ID, a trace mapped to the respective test condition, test case name, test case description, precondition, postcondition, dependencies, test data, test steps, environment description, expected result, actual result, priority, status, expected average running time, comments and so on.

For some software, it may be difficult to compute the proper outcome of a test case. In these cases, test oracles (sources of information for determining whether a test has passed or failed) are useful. Test management tools are a great help to manage the test cases.

Where appropriate, the test cases should be recorded in the test case specification document. In this case, the traceability between the test basis, feature sets, test conditions, test coverage items and test cases should be explicitly described. It is advisable that the content of the test case specification document should be approved by the stakeholders.

A **test suite** (or test set) is a collection of test cases or test procedures that are used to test software in order to show that it fulfils the specified set of behaviours. It contains detailed instructions for each set of test cases and information on the system configuration. Test suites are executed in specific test cycles. In this book we use a simplified notation for a test case, for example TC = ([1, a, TRUE]; 99), where the test case TC has three input parameters 1, a, and TRUE, and expected value of 99. Sometimes, when the expected outcome is irrelevant with regard to a given example, we omit it from the test case. The notation TS = {([1, a, TRUE];

17), ([2, b, FALSE]; 35)} means that the test suite TS contains two test cases. Sometimes we simply list the steps to perform in a test case. Unfortunately, the specification sometimes contains issues that have to be corrected. For example, it may contain solutions or implementation details. This is completely wrong. The customer should not tell you how to implement the functionality they need. It is the developer's task to implement the user's needs in the best way. The test design is similar, as designed test cases have to test the implementation-independent specification, therefore cannot contain any implementation-dependent element.

Example for a test containing implementation details:

- Click on the LOGIN button
- Write 'smith' into the 'Login name' box
- Write 'aw12K@S' into the 'Password' box
- Click on 'OK'

There are many ways you could activate logging in and submitting a log-in request. Think mouse clicks, taps on screen, keyboard shortcuts, voice control and so on.

Here is the implementation-independent version:

Example for implementation-independent tests – CORRECT:

- Login as 'smith'
- Password is 'aw12K@S'
- Action: confirm

When the implementation is ready, and the tests are executed, coverage analysis reports the untested parts of the code.

Now it is high time to create additional test cases to cover the uncovered code. However, **it is not test design; it is test generation**.

6. The next step is to **design the test environment**. The test environment consists of items that support test execution: software, hardware and network configuration. The test environment design is based on entities like test data, network, storage, servers and middleware. The test environment management has organisational and procedural aspects: designing, building, provisioning and cleaning up test environments requires well-established organisation.

There is an emerging technology concentrating on unifying testing and operation, called TestOps. It can be seen as a 'process of using a combination of engineering artefacts, test artefacts, and field artefacts and applying the process of software analytics to improve the V&V [verification and validation] strategy' (Kurani, 2018). In other words, the testing and operation processes are integrated into a single entity aimed at producing the best software system as quickly and efficiently as possible. TestOps provides continuous feedback to the testing team to ensure that failed tests are identified and addressed as early as possible. TestOps allows organisations to deliver high-quality software quickly and cheaply.

We do not consider test environment design in this book. This is a different, but emerging, topic.

7. Finally, validate all the important artefacts produced during the test design including the control of the existence of the bi-directional traceability between the test basis, test conditions, test cases and procedures.

The following list summarises the important factors to be considered during test design:

- test approach;

- level of risks;

- test design technique;

- test selection criteria, and their coverage;

- fault assumption;

- type of test defensiveness;

- whether it is concrete or abstract.

> The output of the design process aggregates descriptions of prioritised test scenarios, test cases, appropriate test data and the controlled test environment.

Subsequent activities – test implementation and execution, test closure

During the **implementation and execution phase**, the designed test cases are implemented and executed. After implementing the test cases the **test scripts** are developed. A test script (or test procedure specification) is a document specifying a sequence of actions and data needed to carry out a test. A script typically has steps that describe how to use the application (which items to select from a menu, which buttons to press, and in which order) to perform an action on the test object. In some sense, **a test script is an extended test case with implementation details**.

When test automation is determined to be a useful option, this stage also contains implementing the automation scripts. Test execution automation is useful when the project is long term and repeated regression testing provides a positive cost–benefit.

The next step is to set up the test environment. In greenfield projects (which lack constraints imposed by prior work), extra time should be allowed for experiencing and learning. Even in a stable environment, organising communication channels and communicating security issues and software evolutions are challenging and require time.

In some cases (performance testing, security testing, maintenance testing, etc.), the testing environment should be a clone of the production environment. Moreover, it is not enough to set up the environment; a plan should be in place for an update and reset when needed. In large-scale projects, several environments are present and need careful management and maintenance. Well-designed configuration management of the environment and testware is also important.

Next, the finalisation of the approach comes via test case implementation. At this point, everything is prepared for starting the execution, manually and/or automatically, which can be checked with the entry criteria. Some documents may help to localise the items that will be tested (test item transmittal documents or release notes).

The existence of the **continuous integration environment** is important for test execution (depending on the SDLC, and the type of project and product). The execution process is iterative, and in many cases, it is the longest step of the fundamental test process. Here, scripted techniques are often mixed with other dynamic techniques such as exploratory testing. The outcome of a test can usually be:

- **Passed**, if its actual result matches its expected result.
- **Failed**, if its actual result does not match its expected result.
- **Blocked**, if the test case cannot run because the preconditions for its execution are not fulfilled.
- **Incomplete**, if the test case did not complete its execution for various reasons.
- **Inconclusive**, if it produces a result that is not clear and requires further investigation and so on.

Once an issue is detected, it should be investigated whether it was really a result of a software defect. Logging the results is critical. Test logs are like gold dust and should be analysed thoroughly. The levels of logging depend on the test approach, the life cycle, regulatory rules, the project's phase and so on. Logging information is especially useful in experience-based testing. In the case of failed tests, an incident management process begins. The analysis of the test results is extremely important since it serves as the basis of the feedback mechanisms. Testers have to gather all kinds of information during actual testing, which is then extracted and used to evaluate progress, data adequacy, coverage values, improvement possibilities and so on. For example, if the test design was not adequate, then some new tests **must be designed**. On the other hand, if code coverage was not appropriate, then new tests **must be generated**.

In extreme cases, the test management has to replan the test project to lower the quality risk. At this point there is important feedback for test design. In test evaluation and reporting, the test logs are checked against the clearly defined exit criteria (e.g. checking the test execution progress for high priority test cases, checking the status of all outstanding defects, etc.). Sometimes the exit criteria have to be modified with agreement from stakeholders. The result of the exit criteria evaluation is important information for all kinds of stakeholders; they want to know what happened during testing so that they can make the right decisions about the software project. A good test reporting tool is indispensable.

The **test closure** is a complete test report that gives a summary of the test project. It formally closes the project, collates all the test results, provides a detailed analysis, presents metrics to clients and assesses the risks with respect to the software as a whole.

WHY SHOULD TESTS BE DESIGNED?

We are not living in an ideal world. Nothing is perfect, including software. Developers make mistakes. The role of testers is to create tests, which reveal any mistakes made by the developers. The most secure way of doing this is to test the software for every possible input. However, this is impossible. Even for very simple code containing only two 32-bit integers, the number of test cases is 2^{64}. Assuming each test execution takes 1 microsecond, the total testing time would be 2^{58} seconds, which is more than 10^{36} years and is incomparably more than the time elapsed from the Big Bang till now.

Well, even if exhaustive testing is not possible, there may be a general method or algorithm that generates reliable tests for every code. A reliable test set T has the property that either for each $t \in T$, t passes if and only if the code is correct or there is at least one test t for which the software fails.

Unfortunately, it has been proved by Howden (1976) that there is no such method or algorithm. The consequence is that testing is not able to detect each bug. The only thing we can expect is to be able to design our test cases so that:

- we can find as many bugs as we can, and
- spend as little time with testing and bug fixing as possible.

Software testing is a team responsibility. High-quality and efficient test cases can only be achieved when everyone involved in test design is aware of this.

Another alternative could be to apply ad hoc methods to tests without designing any tests. Companies who apply this trial-and-error approach, suffer from a buggy code base and low-quality products. Ad hoc testing is similar to ad hoc coding – the result can be catastrophic. By applying test design, we are able to:

- create efficient and reliable test cases;
- stop creating new test cases when the available ones are enough;
- automate test cases when needed;
- document the design as part of the testing activity;
- make test design documents alternative specifications understandable by stakeholders;
- maintain the test cases in accordance to some modifications, that is delete obsolete and design new test cases;
- select test cases to be re-executed after modifications.

Of course, test design is necessary but not sufficient for some of the points above. It is important to note that applying test design does not bound thinking and creativity. On the contrary, it offers a strong ground for test case quality and for creative thinking.

Designing tests has some advantages:

- possibility of reproducing a test;
- increase of faults found;
- long-term maintenance of the system and test automation support;
- an objective approach to the testing process.

However, it is not always necessary to apply test design. It is only to be applied if it adds value. Sometimes it is unimportant to systematically test a component implementing a less important 'nice to have' feature. For important functions, however, more care is needed. The test quality for these components is provided by an adequate test design.

In many organisations, the test base is often converted directly into a test case. But the tester will still implicitly use test design techniques during the conversion. Basic knowledge of the test design techniques and their principles still has added value.

A standardised way of working makes the tests more independent, separating the design from the execution. Note that test selection criteria enable tests to be designed more efficiently.

Test design and test execution can be automated. Test suites can automatically be generated by software using model-based testing, model checking or symbolic execution. **Model-based testing** tools generate test cases from a model, such as an activity diagram, Petri net, finite-state machine (see Chapter 6), timed automaton, Gherkin code (see Chapter 12) and so on. **Model checking** is a technique for automatically verifying the correctness of a program or automaton. It ensures, for example, that all the paths of a simple program are exercised. However, it requires that both the model of the system and the specification are formulated in a precise mathematical language (e.g. B, Z or Larch). By **symbolic execution**, we are able to generate tests directly from the code that will expose the bug when the software is running. These methods do not make the test design superfluous. On the contrary, these techniques necessitate a good test model, which can only be created if appropriate test design techniques are applied.

WHEN DO WE DESIGN TESTS?

Nowadays it is widely accepted that test execution has to be done as early as possible. Especially, 'shift left' testing (where the testing processes move to the left on the project timeline) requires integration testing earlier. Test design has to be done as early as possible as well, but before coding in all cases. Specifications, use cases and user stories are appropriate source documents for implementing the code. In addition, designed test cases can significantly improve the documents the developer will start with. Good test cases are in fact examples that lead the developer during implementation.

Early test design is a very effective defect prevention method. Lots of bugs are design errors. Test design before coding involves the validation of the specification, removing most of the design problems.

Early test design eliminates the problem of involving testers too late and lowers the problem of increased testing effort. Moreover, in most cases, the overall testing effort can be reduced.

IMPORTANT TEST DESIGN-RELATED CONSIDERATIONS

Test design techniques are like lighting up the landing strip. They help you to find the right way in order to pick the right data. In safety-critical systems test design techniques are recommended by standards (e.g. DO 178C in aerospace systems, BS EN 50128 in the railway industry).

This section deals with the effect of test data selection and mutation testing on the test design. Test data is not random – it must be chosen **systematically**. Regarding test data selection we will use two important hypotheses in this book. These are explained in the following two subsections.

Competent programmer hypothesis

The first hypothesis is the **competent programmer hypothesis (CPH)**, which was identified by DeMillo et al. (1978), who observed that 'Programmers have one great advantage that is almost never exploited: they create programs that are close to being correct.' Developers do not implement software randomly. They start from a specification, and the software will be very similar to their expectations, hence, close to the specification.

CPH makes test design possible. If the implemented code could be anything then we should test the application to differentiate it from an infinite number of alternatives. This would need an infinite number of test cases. Fortunately, based on CPH we only have to test the application to separate it from the alternative specifications that are very close to the one being implemented.

To demonstrate CPH, let's consider our **example for test selection criteria** in the 'Present activity – test design' section above, where the requirements are the following:

R1. Input two integers, say x and y from the standard input device

R2. If x and y are both negative, then print x + y to the standard output device

R3. If x and y are both positive, then print their greatest common divisor to the standard output device

R4. If x and y have opposite signs (one of them is positive and the other is negative), then print their product to the standard output device

R5. If x × y is zero then print zero to the standard output device.

The test set T2 = { ([-2, -3]; -5), ([4, 2]; 2), ([2, -4]; -8), ([2, 0]; 0) } is adequate. However, an alternative specification can be the following:

R1. Input two integers, say x and y from the standard input device

R2. If x and y are both negative, then print x + y to the standard output device

> **R3. If x and y are both positive and less than 100,000,** then print their greatest common divisor to the standard output device, otherwise *print the smaller value to the standard output device*
>
> R4. If x and y have opposite signs (one of them is positive and the other is negative), then print their product to the standard output device
>
> R5. If x·y is zero then print zero to the standard output device.

Assume that the developer implemented this specification. In this case, T2 would not be adequate as all test cases would pass, yet the code is wrong. What's more, any positive pair of test input below 100,000 would not be reliable. Assuming that the implementation can be anything we easily modify the specification again so that selecting any number of positive test input pairs would not be reliable.

Fortunately, because of the competent programmer hypothesis, it is unrealistic to implement the modified R3, since this requirement is far from the original, and the probability that a developer swaps them is minimal.

Coupling effect

The second hypothesis we will use in this book is the **coupling effect**, which states that a test data set that detects all simple faults in a program will also detect more complex faults. Here a simple fault means a fault that can be fixed by making a single change to a source statement. On the other hand, a complex fault is a fault that cannot be fixed by making a single change to a source statement. To reveal these complex faults, we suggest applying the Delta Debugging methodology, which automates debugging by systematically narrowing down the places where failures can occur (Zeller, 1999).

Test design defensiveness

The last notion that influences the test data selection and test design is its type of defensiveness. A **defensive test design** considers all possible input for designing the tests. Defensive testing designs test cases both for normal and abnormal preconditions. For instance, an invoked system should always test that the input file exists or not, is empty or not, contains the right data in the right order or not and so on.

Contract-based test design assumes that the preconditions stated in some 'contract' always hold and guarantee the fulfilments of some postconditions. In the previous example, we do not have to test the appropriateness of the input each time the system is called. Based on the contract, we assume that everything is OK with the input (i.e. preconditions are fulfilled), however, if security is an issue, then the defensive testing (and design) remains the only possibility.

Black and white-box mutation testing

Another important aspect of test design is **mutation testing**. In mutation testing, we are not directly concerned with testing the program. Rather we introduce faults into the code to see the reliability of our test design. Therefore, mutation testing is actually not testing, but 'testing the tests'. The method is to slightly modify the original code, creating a mutant of it. We can make several mutants and a reliable test data set has to 'kill' all of them. A test kills a mutant if the original code and the mutant behave differently. For example, if the code is $y = x^2$ and the mutant is $y = 2x$, then a test case $x = 2$ will not kill the mutant while $x = 3$ will.

The main problem with mutation testing is with cases of equivalent mutants. They are the false positives, that is equivalent mutants keep the program's semantics unchanged, thus, cannot be detected by any test. Unfortunately, the decision whether two pieces of code are equivalent or not is an undecidable problem in general.

Mutation testing was introduced in the late 1970s by DeMillo et al. (1978) and Hamlet (1977). An excellent survey containing 250+ references on this topic is published by Jia and Harman (2011).

Mutation testing is applicable when the code is ready. The question is how to test our test cases when we have no code and thus white-box methods are out of the question.

Fortunately, a black-box solution can be introduced as well. Let's assume that we have two specifications that are slightly different. The question is whether we can have a unique test set, which would test both specifications reliably. The answer is obviously no. To see why, let the task be implementing Specification A. Let Specification B be another specification, which is not equivalent to Specification A. Assume, on the contrary, that we have a unique perfect test set for both. Assume that the developer accidentally implemented Specification B bug free. In this case, no test will fail, though the code is not equivalent with Specification A, hence, some behaviour of A is not tested, which is a contradiction.

We can therefore slightly modify our specification and check whether there are any test cases that would be different for the test sets in the two versions. If there are, then the different test case(s) separate(s) the modified specification from the original one. Hence, we can create alternative specifications to prove that every test case we designed is necessary and there are no missing test cases. On the other hand, if an alternative specification consists of the same test cases, then some test is missing. Unfortunately, this process is very costly, and thus not always appropriate in practice.

SUMMARY

In this chapter we gave a general overview of software testing. We discussed its importance and the role of test design in the full testing life cycle. Among other notions, we explained test selection and test adequacy criteria, test coverage, test cases, a test suite and some related concepts, including the competent programmer hypothesis, coupling effect, test design defensiveness and black-box mutation testing.

2 EXAMPLE SPECIFICATION: TICKET VENDING MACHINE

This chapter presents the specification of a ticket vending machine (TVM) software. In the book we demonstrate various test design methods based on this specification, among others. In Chapter 4 it is separated into user stories by one of the author's small Agile team. We call it **final version**. This refined specification is the basis of the model-based test design. The final version has been implemented. The ticket vending machine example is easy to understand but non-trivial to test.

The ticket vending machine is a vending machine that produces tickets. The typical transaction consists of a user using the display interface to select the type and quantity of tickets. After successful payment, the ticket or tickets are printed and dispensed to the user.

- **Ticket types**. There are three types of tickets:

  a. standard ticket valid for 75 minutes on any metro, tram or bus line;

  b. short distance ticket valid within five stations on a single line of any metro, tram or bus;

  c. 24-hour ticket for unlimited metro, bus, and train travel for 24 hours from validation.

  The price of the tickets can be modified, currently (a) is EUR 2.10, (b) is EUR 1.40 and (c) is EUR 7.60.

- **Initial screen.** Coins to be accepted: 5c, 10c, 20c, 50c, €1, €2. Banknotes to be accepted: €5, €10, €20 and €50. Initially, the three types of tickets are shown with the quantity to be bought, which is at the beginning set to 0. A 'Reset' button is also found on the screen by which the number of tickets can be reset to 0. Buttons '+' and '-'are beside the ticket types to increase and decrease the number of tickets to be purchased.

- **Selecting tickets.** The customer can buy tickets of one type only. If all the amounts of the tickets are zero, then any of them can be increased. After that, the ticket type with the non-zero number can be increased or decreased by clicking on '+' or '-'. The maximum number of tickets to be chosen is 10. '+' and '-' are unavailable when the number of tickets is 10 or 0, respectively. If the selected amount of tickets is greater than 0, then the buying process can start.

- **Buying process.** Payment is possible by inserting coins or banknotes. The ticket machine always shows the remaining amount necessary for the transaction. For the remaining amount to be paid, the machine only accepts those banknotes for which the selection of the smaller banknote does not reach the required amount. €5 is always accepted. For example, if the necessary amount is EUR 21, then the machine accepts €50 since EUR 20 will not exceed EUR 21. If the user inserts €10 and then €2, then even €20 is not accepted since the remaining amount is EUR 9; EUR 10 would exceed the necessary amount. The remaining amount and currently acceptable banknotes are visible on the screen. If the user inserts a non-acceptable banknote, then it will be given back, and an error message will appear notifying the user of the error.

- **Successful transaction.** The ticket machine always shows the remaining amount necessary for the transaction, which is successful if the inserted money reaches or exceeds the required amount. In the latter case, the difference is given back to the user. After payment, the tickets are printed.

- **Inactivity.** After 20 seconds of inactivity, the initial screen appears again, and the previous ticket selection has been deleted.

- **Delete selection and error handling.** The transaction can be cancelled any time before finishing the payment. In this case, all the inserted money is given back. The situation is similar when something goes wrong, that is all the inserted money is given back. In the case of an error the ticket machine state will be 'faulty', and the start screen will appear with an error message.

- **Reduced mode.** If there is a chance that the ticket machine cannot return the change, then the machine will go into 'reduced' mode. In this case, only those coins and banknotes will be accepted that do not result in the amount inserted exceeding the required amount. The status 'reduced' will be visible on the screen.

We implemented the TVM, however, a little bit differently from the final version above because of the lack of hardware. For example, the reduced mode can be switched on/off in our implementation, but in the real solution, it will be set by the (lack of) money in the machine.

Considering the implementation, in the initial screen the '+' and '-' icons are enabled/disabled according to the specification. After setting the number of the selected ticket type, we can pay or reset (see the implemented version in Figure 2.1.).

Figure 2.1 Selecting five standard tickets in the TVM interface

	(Unit price)	(Max 10)		
Standard ticket	€2.10	5	+	-
Short distance ticket	€1.40	0	+	-
24-hour ticket	€7.60	0	+	-

Pay   Reset

Acceptable notes: €5, €10, €20, €50

Acceptable coins: 5c, 10c, 20c, 50c, €1, €2

After selecting 'Pay', only the acceptable banknotes are displayed. Since the necessary amount to be paid is EUR 2.1 x 5 = 10.50, the maximum banknote allowed is €20. Inserting the coins and banknotes is simulated by clicking on the enabled coins/banknotes; see Figures 2.2 and 2.3.

Figure 2.2 Payment process with different possibilities

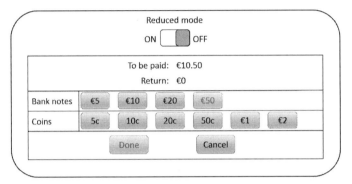

Figure 2.3 Payment snapshot after clicking the €5 in the previous screen

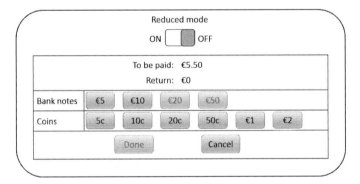

When the inserted money exceeds the tickets' price, the amount to be returned is displayed, and the 'Done' button is enabled (Figure 2.4).

Instead of printing the ticket, by clicking on the 'Done' button, a message 'Successful transaction' appears (Figure 2.5).

One can try the reduced mode by setting the 'OFF' button (Reduced mode) to 'ON' (see Figure 2.6).

You can see that in this case the selectable coins are restricted so that we cannot exceed the remaining amount to be paid (Figure 2.7).

Figure 2.4 Payment can be finished

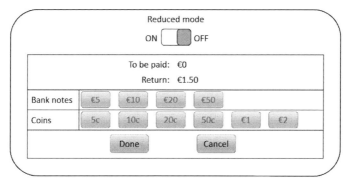

Figure 2.5 Successful transaction

Figure 2.6 'Reduced' mode

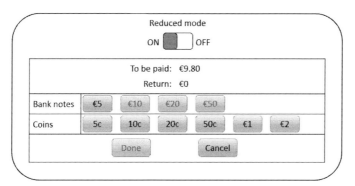

Figure 2.7 Payment in 'Reduced' mode

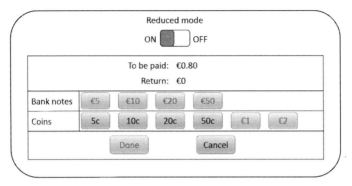

SUMMARY

In this chapter we described the TVM, our key example. We use it throughout the book. Some bugs are intentionally seeded into the code of it. In Chapter 14 we design test cases for it, evaluate the results and compare the different test design techniques.

PART I
NECESSARY STEPS BEFORE TEST DESIGN

3 RISK MANAGEMENT AND TEST OPTIMISATION

WHY IS THIS CHAPTER WORTH READING?

In this chapter, you will learn how to apply risk analysis. You will also learn why risk analysis is necessary and how to optimise project cost by applying more test design techniques in parallel, instead of using one costly combinatorial method. We also define a measure for cost-effective testing.

Risk elicitation is the starting point of test design. The output of risk analysis is the input of test design. We select test design techniques based on risks and complexity.

Everybody knows that there is no industrial-sized software without bugs. Bugs are everywhere. The case is similar with software production: the customer always wants more and more, cheaper and cheaper, with as high quality as possible. On the other side, managers and engineers try to optimise the time and the resources. The result is well-known: the Standish Group[1] and others regularly report the list of software risks and damages. Managing risks is an important part of software testing.

WHAT IS RISK?

Risk can be defined as the possibility of a negative or undesirable outcome or event. In other words, **'risk involves the possibility of an event in the future that has negative consequences. The level of risk is determined by the likelihood of the event and the impact (the harm) from that event'** (ISTQB, 2018b). The larger the impact or damage could be, the higher the risk we could face. Similarly, the higher the probability of a negative event, the higher the risk. Hence, the level of risk can be calculated as:

Level of risk = Impact if it did happen × Probability of the risk occurring

If there is a high probability of a software failure, then this failure certainly occurs during the product life cycle. The probability is measured by the frequency of usage, as we have no more information about potential bugs prior to coding. We can either fix the defect prior to release or it will cause undesirable behaviour for users later. Also, fixing the bug later costs more. This leads to another common-sense conclusion. Where the risk

---

[1] https://www.standishgroup.com/

is higher, we should test more thoroughly and more frequently. Risks can be kept low if they are recognised as early as possible, and countermeasures are initiated in time to lower the probability of occurrence or the extent of the damage.

> There can be other factors of risks, like levels of control or confidence; however, we do not deal with these factors in this book as these factors have no impact on test design.

A comprehensive risk management process describes the following activities:

- identify the risk;
- analyse the risk;
- evaluate and rank the risk;
- treat the risk;
- monitor and review the risk.

These activities need effective communication channels and all of them should start as soon as possible in the project's life cycle.

The most important risk content factors can be technical, corporate-specific, commercial, economic, political, legal, financial, environmental and so on. Some of them are relatively easy to predict (e.g. strategic risks), others are hard (e.g. external risks), while some of them are easy to influence (e.g. project risks) and others are more difficult (e.g. external).

One of the most important risk categories is product risk, which is closely connected to the possible deficiencies with the delivered product. They can be business-oriented (risks of some critical business functions) or technical (technology risks, non-functional risks, user experience risk (ISO 25010, 2011)).

During risk identification different techniques can be applied: interviews, questionnaires, independent assessments, risk workshops, brainstorming, risk poker, risk templates (general, corporate, project-specific), past experiences and so on. (Risk poker is an Agile method, where teams assess the quality risks for the user stories. The Agile team members individually score the risks, then try to reach a common score based on consensus.)

Risk analysis can be made quantitatively or qualitatively. The former can be applied if data are available, while the latter can be performed early in the project life cycle. The outcome of the risk analysis is a so-called *risk inventory*. The risk inventory contains the estimations on the probability and the impact of the expected damage from the risks identified.

SCORING THE RISKS

In most cases the probability of occurrence and the incurred damage is not accurately quantifiable, hence, quantitative estimations are used. In these cases, the risks can be classified into finite classes or categories. Unfortunately, the scoring results may depend on the experiences of the evaluators. There are two possible types of evaluation:

- **Individual evaluations**, where the different stakeholders evaluate the risks (individually) and then some weighted average is calculated.
- **Group-based evaluations**, where a group of experts exchange views and give estimates independently to the facilitator in two or more rounds. After each round the facilitator provides a summary of the experts' forecast and judgement from the previous round. Then, the group members discuss and review the summary report, and give an updated forecast to the facilitator. The process continues until all participants reach a consensus and the mean score of the final round determines the results.

The second method (sometimes called the Delphi technique) is the origin of risk poker (Black et al., 2017).

Independently of the evaluation types, various scoring categories exist in practice. One can use three, four, five or more classes for both impact and probability during risk estimation. In the case of inexperienced evaluators, we suggest using an even number (e.g. four) of possible scores, otherwise there is the possibility of scoring to the middle, saying perhaps 'I don't know, I'll leave the decision to others.' These classes are then mapped onto the natural numbers forming impact and probability values. In the case of having four categories the possible scoring hierarchy can be the following:

Impact:

1. **Negligible** (score 1) – the problem does not affect the correct functionality.
2. **Low** (score 2) – the issue can be solved easily by the user with some simple workaround.
3. **High** (score 3) – some of the key features do not work or function differently from expected. No workaround is possible (e.g. the search feature in a text editor does not work, data may be lost or corrupted, etc.).
4. **Extreme** (score 4) – the software does not work at all or causes serious damage to people or the environment.

Probability:

1. **Rare** (score 1) – users almost never use this function.
2. **Occasional** (score 2) – users occasionally use this function.
3. **Frequent** (score 3) – this function is used by most users frequently.
4. **Always** (score 4) – this function is (almost) always used.

In most cases we do not have information about the potential bugs prior to coding, therefore we estimate the usage frequency. The values above quantify the individual factors by which a risk diagram (or risk matrix) can be drawn (see Figure 3.1).

Note that the project stakeholders must agree and understand the scales. Moreover, note that the probability should not influence the impact and vice versa during the evaluation.

Figure 3.1 Risk diagram and risk matrix

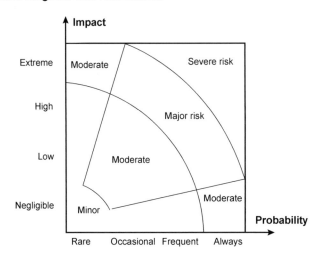

	Rare	Occasional	Frequent	Always
Extreme	Moderate	Major	Severe	Severe
High	Minor	Moderate	Major	Severe
Low	Minor	Moderate	Moderate	Major
Negligible	Minor	Minor	Minor	Moderate

The risk level is usually the multiples of the scores and can be obtained from the risk diagram or the risk matrix. Risks can be colour and size coded. Green and small may indicate low values, while red and large may mean that the value is above some threshold value. In between, there can be other colours in various shades. Please note that risk analysis and evaluation should be repeated periodically.

In our view the risk probability is mainly related to product risks. In general, the likelihood may depend on other factors such as training, contracts, team distribution, tools, technology, leadership, project constraints, change and so on. Similarly, the impact can be related to reputation, loss of business, legal sanctions, licences, negative publicity, safety and so on.

RISK MANAGEMENT

Risk control is critical in risk management. There can be different responses to the perceived risks. There is a wide range of possibilities that can be taken into account; however, we have mainly the following choices:

- We accept the risk and do nothing.
- We take preventive actions.
- We plan contingency actions.
- We outsource the risk.

The nature of the risk can be used to clarify further what, how and when to mitigate – the optimal test techniques shall be determined by the stakeholders.

We now provide a possible mitigation concept (all techniques will be explained in Chapters 4–9) in Table 3.1.

Table 3.1 Test design techniques applied for a given aggregated risk class

Aggregate risk	Risk level	Test techniques to apply
1–3	Low	• Exploratory testing (session-based testing).
4–6	Minor	*Test design is made only for interesting conditions in the related risk area, and only if it involves a small investment of time and effort.* • Exploratory tests • Structure-based tests, where additional test cases are generated based on some missing coverage of exploratory tests
7–10	Moderate	*A small number of tests are designed that sample the most interesting conditions in the related risk area.* • Defect prevention • Exploratory tests • The simplest specification-based tests (such as EP, BVA – see Chapter 5) • Structure-based tests, where additional test cases are generated based on some missing coverage
11–13	Major	*An average number of tests are designed that exercise many different interesting conditions in the related risk area.* • Defect prevention • Exploratory tests • Specification-based tests by applying combinative testing (see Chapter 9) • Structure-based tests, where additional test cases are generated based on some missing coverage • Static analysis

(Continued)

Table 3.1 (Continued)

Aggregate risk	Risk level	Test techniques to apply
14–16	Severe	*A large number of tests are designed that are both broad and deep in scope, where deep tests exercise many combinations of interesting conditions. The condition is split into simpler sub-conditions, if possible.*
		• Defect prevention
		• Review techniques
		• Exploratory tests
		• Specification-based tests by applying combinative/combinatorial testing (see Chapter 9)
		• Structure-based tests, where additional test cases are generated based on missing coverage
		• Static analysis

Note that the higher the risk level, the higher the level of formality during reviews. The final decision must always be documented.

Planning the contingency actions and the risk outsourcing are parts of the risk mitigation process, but they belong to the task of the test manager; we refer the interested reader to Spillner et al. (2014).

RISKS, COSTS AND QUALITY

In this section we explain why risk analysis is necessary, and how we can use it to select the appropriate test design techniques. Surprisingly, there is a joint optimum of the testing effort and the testing costs.

Why do we need risk management at all?

Why is risk management needed at all? The answer is short: because of the costs. Among others, the cost of a project is strongly influenced by two factors. One is the **cost of testing** (designing and executing the tests, building the testing environment, etc.), the other is the **cost of defect correction** (through the SDLC).

The cost of testing increases with the testing effort. This increase is polynomial when we design not too many test cases, but when increasing the tests may become exponential. The reason is that after a certain level we need to combine (and test) the elements of the input domain by combinatorial methods. For example, we first test some partitions, then their boundaries, then pairs or triples of boundary values and so on. There is no reason to design and execute too many tests since we are unable to find twice as many bugs with twice as many tests, when the number of test cases is not negligible.

The other factor is the cost of defect correction (bug fixing). Obviously, the later we find a bug in the software life cycle, the more costly its correction. IBM System Science Institute reported that defect correction cost is exponential in time (Dawson et al., 2010), but clearly over linear, most likely showing polynomial growth. Therefore, if we are able to find faults early enough in the life cycle, then the total correcting costs can drastically be reduced. As you can see in Figure 3.2, considering these two factors together, the total cost has an optimum value.

Figure 3.2 Optimum cost of testing. The optimal cost of testing (dotted curve) is the sum of the testing cost (solid line) and the late correcting cost (dashed curve)

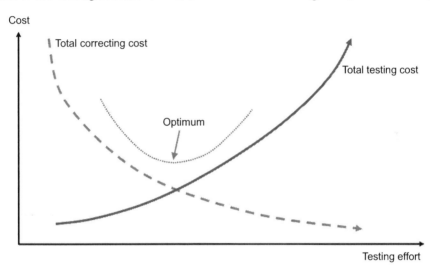

This optimum will differ in different situations depending on the risks and complexities.

As an example, let's examine two code bases of the same size (> 10 k lines of code (LOC)) developed and tested in the same way in the same environment, and assume that the **first one** is more complex (in some aspects). Hence, it contains more faults with high probability. If we test both at the same expense and thoroughness, then after testing, more faults will be left in the first code. It means that the total correcting cost will be higher.

We can use similar arguments for other test objects. Suppose that we have two functions with the same complexity and testing cost, but the first one is **riskier**. For example, this function is used more often. Therefore, more bugs will be detected and fixed in this function, and it will have a higher correcting cost during the life cycle. Note that we are speaking about **detection of bugs** here, not about the presence of bugs.

Roughly speaking, more complex code and higher risk raise the bug-fixing costs if the testing cost remains unchanged. Since this additional bug fixing occurs later in the life cycle, the code quality at release will be poorer. Therefore, it is important that a more risky or more complex code part should be tested with more thoroughness, that is with higher testing costs. This **higher testing cost is inevitable to achieve the optimal total**

cost, as shown in Figure 3.3. Note that in a wider sense we can add the cost of any damage caused by a bug to the defect correction cost. In this way, the cost minimisation results in an appropriate quality even for safety-critical systems.

Figure 3.3 Total cost optimum of a high-risk function. The total cost optimum of a high-risk function (HRF) is above the total cost optimum of a low-risk function (LRF). However, this optimum can be reached via spending more money on testing (multiple designs, etc.)

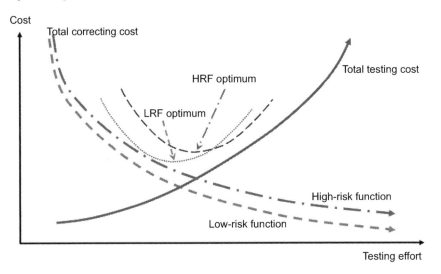

Now we have shown that the total testing and correcting cost together can be minimised. But how can we adjust the testing costs to reach this minimum?

If a function is simple and not risky, then in most cases only one single method (such as exploratory testing) for testing is enough. If the risk grows, then we can combine more test techniques (e.g. various design techniques, structural testing, static analysis and reviews) without creating pure combinatorial test cases. Of course, different techniques may detect the same bugs, but also may detect different ones. By combining more non-combinatorial testing techniques the testing costs will be below the testing costs of a single combinatorial technique. In this way, the optimum of the total cost decreases. If even this is not enough, then combinative or combinatorial testing becomes an option. Combinative and combinatorial testing (see Chapter 9) aim to determine input data combinations to be tested.

We have shown that optimising the cost of testing and defect correction should be done together. In many cases, cost optimisation and quality should have a trade-off, that is we want to achieve as high a quality as possible with the lowest cost. However, our presented cost optimisation is different. Let's assume that the sum of the correcting and testing cost is minimal but the quality of the released application is poor. In this case, the users will find lots of bugs, which should be fixed. However, this will increase the cost, hence, it could not be minimal, which is a contradiction. Therefore, we strongly believe that reaching a minimum cost also results in adequate quality. The conclusion is as follows.

- Risk analysis is necessary to decide the thoroughness of testing. The more risk the usage of the function/object has, the more thorough the testing that is needed.
- Complexity analysis is also necessary for cost optimisation.
- There is a minimum value in considering the testing costs and the defect correcting costs together, and the goal of good test design is to select appropriate testing techniques approaching this minimum. This can be done by analysing complexity, risk and using historical data.
- For more risky code we should first apply more non-combinatorial test techniques instead of one pure combinatorial one. For example, we can use specification-based test design, exploratory testing, defect prevention, static analysis and reviews together.
- Cost minimisation also results in appropriate code quality.

How can we make testing optimal?

In reading some books, blog posts and so on about the main goals of software testing, you always find goals like 'increasing bug detection', 'preventing bugs in the system', 'improving quality and user satisfaction' and 'reducing maintenance cost'. There can be different goals of testing. When, for example, the goal is finding defects, then a successful test is a test that makes the system perform incorrectly, and so exposes a defect in the system. However, when the goal is to show that the software meets its requirements, then a successful test shows that the system operates as intended. The testing community refers to them as negative tests and positive tests. In a test project, we usually target both. Remember that good tests must be reasonably capable of revealing information about bugs, information for managers (go/no-go), information about risks, technical support costs, quality, conformance to standards and so on.

The following question arises naturally: are we able to convert the various types of testing goals and test information requests into one measurable criterion of cost-effective testing? In the previous subsection, we saw that considering the testing and the defect correction costs together we can approach a minimum cost, and this minimum, in addition to the financial resources available, correlates with the software quality. This is because higher complexity and risks require more testing, resulting in higher quality and optimum costs in parallel.

> The cost of the project life cycle can be optimised by minimising the sum of the total testing and defect correction costs. This also results in adequate code quality. Hence, minimising this cost is one of the most important aspects of the test design.

The next question is about how to reach this optimum. This is not an easy task, and we have no complete answer. But we do think this is possible. First, risk and complexity analyses have to be done for each software element, and the assessed risk and complexity data should be stored. Second, the company should collect and store all the testing and defect correction costs. Third, the company must define and apply different strategies for optimising the costs based on the measured data on different levels of risks and complexities. This selection can be validated and improved periodically to approach the optimum. We suggest building the proposed model into the company's process improvement strategy.

Regarding the test design, the suggested approach supports the selection and improvement of the 'best set' of test techniques.

 RISK AND OPTIMISATION

In the previous section we analysed the effect of risk management on test design. Now we describe its effect on test execution.

Test case prioritisation

Risk management is closely connected with test case prioritisation. If the test resource and budget allocated for testing are limited, then the test cases should be prioritised. Test case prioritisation techniques (TCP) define an execution order for the test cases of a test suite according to the given goals.

Both code-based and model-based test suites may be handled by TCP techniques, although most techniques presented in literature have been defined and evaluated for code-based suites in the context of regression testing.

There are various techniques for prioritising test cases. Many of them are **risk-based** and suggest further classification of the probability and impact of risk (with visibility, frequency, time delay, complexity, etc.) and mapping some weight for them. Then, the prioritisation of the risks is used for the prioritisation of the tests by executing tests with large risks earlier. Gutjahr suggested extending it with test intensity computations to avoid the low priority entities remaining untested because of budget and time constraints (Gutjahr, 1995).

In some cases, the prioritisation is determined by the availability of the resources (right people, equipment, data, etc.). Note that such **resource-based** prioritisation has serious drawbacks working in any incremental life cycle model. One reason is that some test cases are dependent on others. Clearly, the known dependencies should always be documented to avoid the unnecessary failures.

To perform dynamic test case prioritisation, usually historical data is utilised. Remember that organising the tests is closely related to organising the test data. TCP is out of scope for test design; we refer the interested reader to Hao et al. (2016).

Test suite optimisation

Nowadays, living in the DevOps era, the lowest level test suites are executed several times a day. However, in large projects, it is not possible to execute all the test cases in each test execution process. One of the main objectives of test suite optimisation is to reduce the total execution time of the selected test cases while preserving the testing scope and the fault detection capability. In other words, the objective of the optimisation is to improve the effectiveness (fitness) of test cases in the test suite.

To improve test execution effectiveness, several factors should be considered. One of the most important among them is the risk. Unfortunately, these factors can be conflicting in nature. Most of the approaches in scientific literature target a single factor for optimisation. However, we want to achieve a maximum level of requirement coverage, code coverage, high fault detection capability and so on at the same time. Why is it so hard? The answer is because the test suite optimisation problem is computationally hard. But that is not all. When dynamic testing techniques are mixed with scripted techniques, it is not unexpected to discover new issues, so continuous reprioritisation is needed again and again during the project life cycle. And we need risk management for that.

Please note that risk-oriented testing guides not only the selection of test design techniques but the determination of test priority and the allocation of test effort as well.

EXAMPLE: RISK ANALYSIS OF TVM

In this section, we consider the full TVM, that is the machine with the software together, not only the software itself.

The physical parts requirements are:

- Ticket issuing system.
- Control unit (industrial PC-based, real-time operating system, connection to LAN, Ethernet network, TCP/IP protocol, GSM module, connection to Control Centre, etc.).
- Uninterruptible power supply, extremely resistant outer wrap.
- Fare collection support system (for coins, banknotes, smart cards, bank magnetic strip cards, etc.).
- User interface:

    - ergonomic design, TFT colour display, touchscreen;
    - specific input device;
    - single coin insertion slot;
    - single change return and note collection;
    - general information display, user's operation guide;
    - voice navigation system for visually impaired people;
    - identification of authorised operators by contactless card, magnetic card or code entering for maintenance purposes.

General features:

- For simplicity, the system should accept only coins and banknotes.
- The system should be easily configurable due to its modular design.
- The system should be easily handled due to its:

- effective and intuitive interface;

- support for impaired people;

- fast operation (ticket selection, charging and issuing);

- remote loading of configurations, fare schemes, specific software;

- maintenance utilities and statistical control possibilities (reports on the operation servicing by maintenance staff, coin box and consumables status, etc.);

- standalone operation function.

- The system should be secure against:

  - vandalism;

  - unauthorised entry and so on.

- And the system should be compliant with the General Data Protection Regulation (GDPR).

Now we concentrate only on some **specific** product feature risk items, mainly for demonstration purposes.

Risk items:

1. Inappropriate or missing information on the initial screen regarding the available ticket types.

   a. Probability: Always; Impact: Low.

   b. Reason: appropriate information is necessary for passengers.

2. When issuing the tickets the number of chosen and printed tickets differs. Note that this risk is related to both the software and hardware parts of the TVM.

   a. Probability: Always; Impact: Extreme for the customer and High for the supplier.

   b. Reason: if the number of the printed tickets is fewer than the number of the chosen tickets, legal problems may arise due to the customer's loss, and/or extra human maintenance interaction may be needed.

3. The ticket selection operation cannot be finished. This can happen if the payment operation in the selection screen does not work. In this case, the TVM cannot be used.

   a. Probability: Always; Impact: High

   b. Reason: without the correct payment mechanism the TVM is useless.

4. Inappropriate or missing transition to reduced mode.

   a. Probability: Occasional; Impact: Extreme for the customer and High for the supplier.

   b. Reason: reduced mode is occasional, as usually there are enough coins and banknotes for change. The biggest damage occurs if somebody wants to buy ten 24-hour tickets, inserts two €50 notes, and the system does not give their 24 EUR change back. Anyway, buying ten 24-hour tickets is very rare in any mode. However, here real financial loss can happen.

5. The acceptable banknotes are improperly displayed.

   a. Probability: Always; Impact: Low.

   b. Reason: if the acceptable banknotes are displayed faultily, and something is misinterpreted, the whole process can be deleted. However, the remaining money that appears shall be exact.

6. Neither the timeout nor the reset selection feature is working.

   a. Probability: Frequent; Impact: Extreme for the customer and Extreme for the supplier.

   b. Reason: during ticket selection, the customer sometimes changes their mind and leaves the machine or has not got enough money to buy the ticket. This happens several times a day, that is frequently. From the viewpoint of the supplier, the impact is high as in this case the machine will not work until it has been reset. The impact for the customer is high if they inserted some money, and cannot get it back.

Based on these considerations, the risk scores are shown in Table 3.2.

Table 3.2 Risk table for TVM ('W' is the weight on customers and supplier)

| Risk item | Probability | Impact | | |
		On customer $W = 0.7$	On supplier $W = 0.3$	Aggregate risk
1. Inappropriate or missing information on the initial screen.	4	2	2	8
2. When issuing the tickets, the chosen and the printed number of tickets differs.	4	4	3	14.8
3. The ticket selection operation cannot be finished.	4	3	3	12
4. Inappropriate/missing transition to reduced mode.	2	4	3	7.4
5. The acceptable banknotes are improperly displayed.	4	2	2	8
6. Neither the timeout nor the reset feature is working.	3	4	4	12

The next step is to decide how to manage these risks. Now we deal only with the three highest risk level items (those in bold in Table 3.2).

Risk item: when issuing the tickets, the chosen and the printed number of tickets differs.

Countermeasures:

- defect prevention;
- exploratory tests;
- specification-based tests by applying combinative testing;
- structure-based tests, where additional test cases are generated based on some missing coverage.

Risk item: the ticket selection operation cannot be finished.

Countermeasures:

- defect prevention;
- exploratory tests;
- specification-based tests such as equivalence partitioning (EP) and boundary value analysis (BVA);
- structure-based tests, where additional test cases are generated based on some missing coverage.

Risk item: neither the 'inactivity' nor the 'delete selection' feature is working.

Countermeasures:

- defect prevention;
- exploratory tests;
- specification-based tests by applying state transition testing;
- structure-based tests, where additional test cases are generated based on some missing coverage.

Risk management is not a test design technique, and it is not optional. Without risk analysis, you will not be able to select appropriate test design techniques and either the quality of testing will be low or the costs will be too high, usually both.

KEY TAKEAWAYS

- Risk management is an unavoidable prerequisite of test design.
- By applying risk and complexity analysis you can minimise project costs by applying appropriate testing techniques.
- Instead of applying a single and costly test design method you can apply simpler techniques together. With this you can reach the measurable goal of testing.
- You saw how risks were analysed for our TVM example.

4 DEFECT PREVENTION

WHY IS THIS CHAPTER WORTH READING?

In this chapter, you will learn why defect prevention (DP) is important and what the main techniques are regarding the test design. We also provide two examples of requirements refinement, which make the design of the systems to be implemented easier.

Prevention is applied in many areas of our world. We all know that prevention is better than cure. Consider medicine for example. A healthy way of life is not only cost-effective, but it makes living much more enjoyable. In IT we can prevent lots of bugs in many ways. In this chapter we consider defect prevention concerning test design.

It is widely believed that the cost of a defect rises significantly with the project progressing. The clear challenge in any software development process lies in minimising the number of defects. In the software industry, testers and other stakeholders are not just performing defect detection, but they also need to participate in defect prevention mechanisms as well.

The reason for applying DP is twofold. Firstly, if we apply DP by which the number of bugs in the implemented code decreases by 20 per cent, then in applying the same testing methods, the remaining bugs will also decrease by 20 per cent. In this way, code quality will be improved. Secondly, DP is cost-effective. As you saw in the previous chapter, if there are fewer faults in the code, then the correction cost will be lower, and as the testing code is the same, the overall test design plus the correction costs will be lower. Therefore, defect prevention is a critical activity as it has a direct, positive impact on costs and quality.

The typical process of DP includes the following major steps:

1. Analyse risky problems (defects) from (historical) database.

2. Identify the actual defects during the software requirements/specification/user story reviews and analysis meetings where preventive actions are proposed.

3. Fix the defects.

4. Validate the modifications.

By focusing on DP, one can work on improving the software quality from a very early stage. Existing DP emphasises software process improvement based on learning from historical faults/failures. This is where testers play an important role. Testers carefully read and try to understand requirement specification documents. They have to recognise different types of issues such as incompleteness, inaccuracy, inconsistency and so on. However, DP is not only for testers. Developers and business analysts also play a key role by participating in DP activities such as reviews, static code analysis, unit testing and so on.

Figure 4.1 shows the defect-prevention cycle (based on IEEE 1044, 2009):

Figure 4.1 Defect prevention cycle (source: IEEE Software Productivity Consortium, extended with test-related improvements)

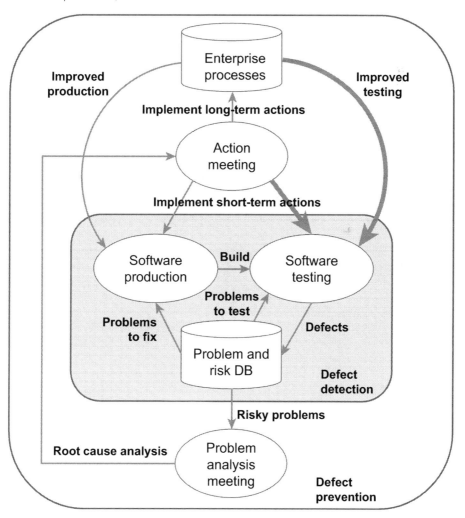

The efficiency of DP is difficult to measure; however, we have lots of historical data and analysis supporting the usefulness of DP (see Jones and Bonsignour, 2011).

DEFECT PREVENTION METHODS

There are a lot of defect prevention methods. In the following list, we only consider a few of them that are closely connected with test design.

- **Model-based testing** is a very efficient method for defect prevention. **Models are more understandable by testers and developers than any, sometimes unclear and inconsistent, textual specification.** Building the right models may help to understand the problem and avoid the use of faulty specifications that often result in faulty test cases.

- **Managing complexity by dividing and conquering.** Complex things are difficult to handle. Even a small part of a specification may be too complex. If possible, we should divide these parts into manageable portions. A smaller fraction of the specification can be handled more easily by both the testers and the developers. Maintenance of smaller chunks can also be simpler.

- Too many very simple parts may be problematic and unnecessary. Consider an average risky condition. A specification is well-refined if not more than 5-10 abstract test cases are enough to cover it. Note, however, that the complexity and size in any large-scale system have power law distribution, which means that there will always be complex or large cases that cannot be further refined.

- Reviews. **Review, Review, Review!**

  - **Standard reviews.** The most traditional and most common method that has been in use for a long time for defect prevention is review, for example requirements review, design review, code review. There are various types of reviews (see the IEEE 1028:2008 or ISO/IEC 20246:2017 standards), but basically, there are self-reviews and peer-reviews.

  - **Checklist-based reviews.** For beginners, a checklist offers a step-by-step process, which is much better to follow than relying entirely on memory to ensure that all steps are covered. The list includes verifications such as:

    - Is the source information complete, detailed and consistent?

    - Is the value of the items to be reviewed well understood?

    - Are the dependencies recognised?

    - Can the complexity be handled?

    - Is the test coverage well-defined?

    - And so on.

- **Specification by examples** (SBE). These techniques are applied mainly in Agile. They require a team to discuss the specification. This team is usually composed of the three amigos, a tester, a developer and a business analyst. A team with different knowledge and views:

1. reviews the specification very carefully;
2. asks questions and finds incompleteness, ambiguity, controversy and so on;
3. creates examples.

The result is a well-defined specification accepted by every team member and the designed test cases (the examples).

- **Implementation-independent test design**. The 'test-first' point of view is a special case of the divide and conquer approach. **Divide producing test cases into two parts: implementation independent (test design), and implementation dependent (test creation)**. Maintaining implementation-independent test cases is easier and more cost-effective since no modification is needed when the implementation changes. Well-designed implementation-independent test cases can be considered as an extended specification by examples. Based on it, the developers can implement code with much fewer defects.

These types of defect prevention methods should be applied before any test design. However, this is not a completely separate task. Defect prevention and test design require full understanding of the specification. Understanding the specification is a joint activity, and the deeper the understanding of the specification, the more efficient defect prevention and test design can be.

FROM REQUIREMENTS TO SPECIFICATION ('TWO LIFTS IN A 10-STOREY BUILDING' EXAMPLE)

In this section we should like to draw attention to the importance of requirements' feasibility. Approximately half of software faults emerge because of incompleteness, inaccuracy and ambiguities in requirements. Clearly, DP must start with requirements analysis.

Here we begin with some general requirements on an elevator system and at the end we get a refined specification. We demonstrate only one refinement cycle; we skip explaining the inspection, elicitation and analysis parts, as well as the validation. Note that there are processes and techniques on requirements engineering; we refer to Wiegers and Beatty (2013), Cockburn (2001), and Leffingwell (2011).

Part of the following specification will be used later to demonstrate aspects of test design techniques.

Mr Newrich plans to build a 10-storey, many-starred luxury hotel. He thinks that two lifts will be enough to transfer the guests. He obviously does not know much about algorithms and specifications. Basically – regarding the lifts – he has three main requirements, where 'F' denotes Functional requirement and CMC denotes Cabin Movement Controlling (System):

F-CMC-1   Every user request should be eventually served if it is not prohibited by emergencies and/or blocked doors. This is the most important requirement.

F-CMC-2   The waiting time and the transferring time should be as minimal as possible, independently of the calling position of the users. This is the second most important requirement.

F-CMC-3   The unnecessary movements of the lifts should be minimised, assuming requirements 1 and 2 hold.

After the first meeting with Mr Newrich, the engineering staff (requirements engineers, lift experts, etc.) reviewed and discussed the possible approaches. They gave Mr Newrich an overview of lift systems (types of lifts, design issues such as cost, speed, capacity requirements, safety, reliability, etc.). They drew attention to the fact that lift users are responsible for operating the lifts according to the safety specifications laid out, and the building owners are responsible for the maintenance of the lifts and for assuring the lifts are compliant before use (via a certificate). The IT staff remarked that in the design, installation and usage a lot of communications have to be done between the various stakeholders, especially with regulators (there are fire regulations, disability acts, design regulations, architectural regulations, etc.). The staff submitted a fourth basic requirement, and the hotel owner accepted it:

F-CMC-4   There will be two types of calling buttons on each level, the 'Up' and the 'Down'; however, on the ground floor only 'Up', and on the 10th floor only 'Down' will be available. The selected button is displayed.

We can see that these requirements do not involve any implementation details. Of course, we can add more requirements; however, it is not necessary, and for simplicity, we do not do that. Based on these initial requirements the following specification can be given.

Initial specification

The first draft of the specification is the following:

Guests can call the lifts on all floors. If the empty lift is on the same floor as the guest, then the lift door opens (the door of a vacant lift is closed). Guests can call a lift by pressing the button in the desired direction. On the top floor only down, and on the ground floor, only the upward direction is available. If both lifts are empty and a guest calls one, then the closer one starts. If their distance is equal then **either of them** can start. If the lift moves up or down to a floor where other guests plan to go up or down, then the lift stops and the other empty lift does not start to go to the guests. This means that the lift collects the guests if their moving direction is the same.

If one of the two lifts is moving away from the caller, the empty lift starts for the guest. When a guest enters the lift, they can press the destination. If a guest in the lift presses the opposite direction as outside the lift and other calls are in the original direction, the lift will only go to the desired floor when the other guests have been served.

When a guest calls a lift, the light indicates the desired direction. If the lift arrives, the light goes out. However, if the lift is full and the guest cannot enter the lift, their call remains intact. The lift can measure the weight of the passengers and validate when someone is on board. If the weight does not change, the lift assumes no one has entered, even if a guest left and someone with the same weight boarded. When a lift becomes vacant, and there are registered calls in its memory, then it starts to serve them.

Refined specification

The previous specification has some shortcomings:

- Who is the guest?
- Who presses which button and when?
- What happens when the weight of the guests exceeds the permitted?
- What about emergencies?
- And so on.

The following refinement tries to clarify the deficiencies above. To keep our example simple, we do not detail the following requirements: power system, energy buffers, safety measures, enclosures, dimension, lift entrance measures, door closing time, door opening time, passenger transfer time, speed for normal travel, acceleration time, jerk rate, peak handling capacity time to various destinations, fire services, barrier-free access and so on.

Figure 4.2 shows the basic usage (and actors) of the lift system.

Figure 4.2 Basic usage of the lifts in the 'Two lifts in a 10-storey building' example

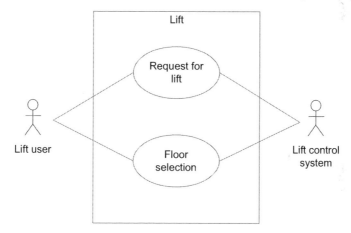

The lift user is the guest and the lift control system (LCS or controller) is a device that controls the movements of the lifts. Besides the functional (F) requirements we consider only some sample non-functional requirements.

Cabin Request (CR) by user:

F-CR-1   Users can request lifts on each floor via a lift request panel (LR-panel).

F-CR-2   Users can request lifts by selecting the direction they want to go in the LR-panel. On the top floor only 'Down' and on the ground floor only the 'Up' direction is available.

F-CR-3   User requests are processed by the LCS.

Cabin Control (CC) by user:

F-CC-1   When the user enters the lift they can select the destination floor in the LC-panel.

F-CC-2   When users press buttons for their desired destinations in the LC-panel inside the cabin, the lift will schedule its movement to those floors.

F-CC-3   When the user selects a destination in alignment with the lift movement, the lift will stop when it arrives at the selected floor; when the user selects a destination opposite to the lift movement, it will not be served until all the requests in alignment with the actual movement are served. Then the lift direction will change and the destination will be served as described.

F-CC-4   When users select the destination floor, it should be highlighted in the LC-panel. When a user presses the 'Door Open' or 'Door Close' button, the door will react as conditions permit.

F-CC-5   When a user stops the lift (by pushing the Stop button), it ceases its movement.

Cabin Movement Display (CMD) System:

F-CMD-1   When a user requests a lift (by pushing the button 'Up' or 'Down' or both in the LR-panel) the required direction will be displayed.

F-CMD-2   If a lift stops at a floor, and a guest enters the lift (measured by weight change), the display of its next movement direction is switched off (if it was on) in the LR-panel and the system sends a message to the LCS that the guest request has been satisfied.

F-CMD-3   If no guest enters when a lift stops for them, then the display is switched off, and the system sends a message to the LCS that the guest request has been satisfied.

F-CMD-4   When a lift stops at a level, then the direction of the next movement is displayed (there are four possibilities, None, Up, Down, Up/Down).

Cabin Movement Controlling (CMC) System:

F-CMC-1   If both lifts are vacant and a user requests one, then always the closer lift will start to the caller's direction. **In the case of equality, Lift-1 is chosen**.

F-CMC-2   If one of the lifts is vacant and the other one is moving then the vacant one starts for them.

F-CMC-3   When no lift is available then the user request is scheduled.

F-CMC-4   When a lift becomes vacant, the oldest pending request must be handled first.

F-CMC-5   The lift measures the weight of the passengers and validates when someone is on board.

F-CMC-6   The lift does not start when it is overloaded. In this case, a safety message is displayed to the user.

F-CMC-7   The serving order depends on the location of the lifts, on their moving directions and on their request queues.

F-CMC-8   The non-empty lift stops for users when an up/down call is received from them while the lift is moving up or down as well, and is approaching the user.

Example: Empty Lift-1 is standing at floor 2. Non-empty Lift-2 is moving from floor 6 downwards to the ground floor. At present it is between floors 5 and 4. Then, there is a down call on floor 3 and an up call on floor 1. Lift-2 will stop at floor 3 and pick up the passengers. It does not stop at the first floor. Lift-1 starts to pick up the passengers in floor 1.

F-CMC-9   The empty lift goes for the user first in the queue and does not stop for other users.

Some non-functional (NF) emergency requirements:

NF-1   The buttons for the lift request system (Up/Down) must be distinguishable.

NF-2   The buttons for the lift control system (Floors, Door Open/Close, Start/Stop) should be easy to use.

NF-3   When the lift's travelling plan is empty, but the lift is not empty (meaning that somebody is in the lift), after a certain timeout an emergency sign will be sent to the dispatcher.

The Cabin Movement Controlling System gets messages from the users when they push some buttons in the LR-panel. The CMC also gets messages when the requests are satisfied. The task of the CMC is to control the travelling plans of the lifts.

We can see that after the refinement, the specification is more structured, much clearer and more complete. We suggest the reader validate the requirements by examining the following attributes: necessity, completeness, correctness, unambiguity, technical availability, verifiability and implementation independence (see Pohl and Rupp, 2016). Based on good requirements both the test design and the implemented code will be better.

REFINEMENT OF THE TICKET VENDING MACHINE SPECIFICATION

In this section, we apply the defect prevention based on SBE. In Chapter 2 we gave a specification of the ticket vending machine. Both authors reviewed this and believed it was OK. Later on, they organised an Agile meeting including a developer whose task was the implementation of the TVM. One of the authors read one bullet point at a time, and the team tried to find bugs in the specification. In the case of an issue, the team discussed it and made a decision based on consensus. A significant number of issues were found:

1. Ticket prices may change; the text omits any reference to it.

2. In some places, the text contains implementation-related elements ('Reset' button, '+', '-').

3. Payment is only possible if the number of selected tickets is greater than zero.

4. It can happen that the machine does not operate properly and there is no error message. The requirements description should also include these cases.

5. The time limit should also be considered during the money insertion phase.

We improved the specification as follows. New text in the specifications is denoted by *italics*; the deleted text by 'deletedtext':

The ticket vending machine is a vending machine that produces tickets. The typical transaction consists of a user using the display interface to select the type and quantity of tickets. After successful payment, the ticket or tickets are printed and dispensed to the user.

- **Ticket types**. There are three types of tickets:

  a. standard ticket valid for 75 minutes on any metro, tram or bus line;

  b. short-distance ticket valid within five stations on a single line of any metro, tram or bus;

  c. 24-hour ticket for unlimited metro, bus, and train travel for 24 hours from validation.

  The price of the tickets can only be modified by the system administrator of the TVM company. It is impossible for any users to modify the prices. Currently (a) is EUR 2.10, (b) is EUR 1.40 and (c) is EUR 7.60.

- **Initial screen:** Coins to be accepted: 5c, 10c, 20c, 50c, €1, €2. Banknotes to be accepted: €5, €10, €20 and €50. Initially, the three types of tickets are shown with the quantity to be bought, which is at the beginning set to 0. A 'Reset' button is also found on the screen by which the number of tickets can be reset to 0. Buttons '+' and '-' are beside the ticket types for increasing and decreasing the number of tickets to be purchased. *The number of tickets can be reset to 0 at any time.*

- **Selecting tickets.** The customer can buy tickets of one type only. If all the amounts of the tickets are zero, then any of them can be increased. After that, the ticket type with the non-zero number can be increased or decreased by clicking on '+' or '-'. The maximum number of tickets to be chosen is 10. '+' and '-' are unavailable when the number of tickets is 10 or 0, respectively. *The customer can increase the number of tickets to be purchased by one up to 10. The customer can reduce the number of tickets to be purchased by one but not below 0.* If the selected amount of tickets is greater than 0, then the buying process can start.

- **Buying process.** Payment is possible *if the customer has selected at least one ticket.* Payment is made by inserting coins or banknotes. The ticket machine always shows the remaining amount necessary for the transaction. For the remaining amount to be paid, the machine only accepts those banknotes for which the selection of the smaller banknote does not reach the required amount. €5 is always accepted. For example, if the necessary amount is EUR 21, then the machine accepts €50 since EUR 20 will not exceed EUR 21. If the user inserts €10 and then €2, then even €20 is not accepted since the remaining amount is EUR 9; EUR 10 would exceed the necessary amount. The remaining amount and currently acceptable banknotes are visible on the screen. If the user inserts a non-acceptable banknote, then it will be given back, and an error message will appear notifying the user of the error.

- **Successful transaction.** The ticket machine always shows the remaining amount necessary for the transaction, which is successful if the inserted money reaches or exceeds the required amount. In the latter case, the difference is given back to the user. After payment, the tickets are printed.

- **Inactivity.** After 20 seconds of inactivity, the initial screen appears again and the previous ticket selection has been cancelled. *If money has been inserted and nothing happens for 20 seconds, the money the customer put in is returned and the start screen is displayed.*

- **Delete selection and error handling**. The transaction can be cancelled at any time before finishing the payment. In this case, all the inserted money is given back. The situation is similar to when something goes wrong, that is all the inserted money is given back. In the case of an error the ticket machine state will be 'faulty', and the start screen will appear with an error message. *If the TVM goes wrong, then any inserted money should be given back. If this does not happen, the customer can get the money from the TVM company in another way.*

- **Reduced mode.** If there is a chance that the ticket machine cannot return the money exceeding the ticket price *(which process is specified by a third party algorithm)*, then the machine will go into 'Reduced mode'. In this case, only those coins and banknotes will be accepted that do not result in the amount inserted exceeding the required amount. The status 'reduced' will be visible on the screen. *The largest usable banknote is displayed.*

  - *(**Other issues.** It can happen that the machine does not operate properly and there is no error message. For example, the user's inserted money is absorbed. The TVM must know this amount. This money must be returned; the complaint can be made by the customer via telephone. To keep our example simple, the testing of this part is not covered by our book.)*

With this improvement, the specification became more precise, lowering the probability of bugs due to the incomplete specification. Our defect prevention work has been done successfully.

In this book, we will use **parts of** these specifications in various examples to present the various testing techniques.

KEY TAKEAWAYS

- Use defect prevention to improve quality and decrease costs.
- Specifications and user stories are almost always incomplete and ambivalent – this can be fixed by different DP methods such as:
  - SBE;
  - review techniques;
  - reducing complexity;
  - model-based testing.
- Similarly to risk analysis, DP is a pre-test design activity which cannot be neglected.

PART II
TRADITIONAL TEST DESIGN

5   DOMAIN-BASED TESTING

WHY IS THIS CHAPTER WORTH READING?

In this chapter, you will learn how to apply equivalence partitioning (EP), boundary value analysis (BVA) and domain analysis. We show that for simple borders only three test cases (ON, OFF, IN/OUT) points are enough. We present how to use these methods through our TVM and other non-trivial examples.

Everybody knows that there can be different goals for testing. For example, if the goal is finding defects in a software system, then a successful test is a test that makes the system perform incorrectly, hence exposing a defect. However, when the goal is to show that the software meets its requirements, then a successful test shows that the system operates as intended. In both cases, we need appropriate test data. Unfortunately, the entire input domain (the set of all inputs) is often infinite or extremely large, and we can conclude with the well-known fact that exhaustive testing is impossible.

Domain-based testing is a functional testing technique, in which the test design aims to reduce the number of test cases into a possibly small finite set, preserving the error detection or correctness retention capabilities. In domain testing, we view the program as a set of functions and test it by feeding it with some inputs and evaluating its outputs.

An (input) domain is a set of input data that is surrounded by boundaries. The sections of the boundaries are called borders. A domain boundary is closed with respect to a domain if the points on the boundary belong to the domain. If the boundary points belong to some other domain, the boundary is said to be open.

There are three techniques discussed in this chapter. The first is **equivalence partitioning** (EP). Here the input domain is divided into equivalence partitions, that is, into disjoint, non-empty, finite subsets. The test cases then cover each partition and verify the expected and unexpected computations.

Boundary value analysis (BVA) is another functional test technique in which the test case design concentrates on the boundary values between equivalence partitions. This technique checks if there are any faults at the boundaries of the domains.

The third technique, **domain analysis**, is an analytical way of computing the boundaries in those cases when the boundaries are functions of the input variables.

You may notice that these techniques are three aspects of the same domain investigation. That is why we group them and in practice use them together. You cannot select borders without knowing the equivalence partitions, which can be obtained by domain analysis.

EQUIVALENCE PARTITIONING

In domain testing, the first step is to partition a domain D into subdomains (equivalence classes) and then design tests with values from the subdomains. The equivalence classes (or partitions) are non-empty and disjoint, and the union of the partitions covers the entire domain D.

Mathematically speaking, we devise an equivalence relation on D (which is reflexive, symmetric and transitive), which produces the equivalence classes.

Test designers produce equivalence classes based on the specification. The equivalence classes are constructed in a way that inputs a and b belong to the same equivalence class if and only if the code for inputs a and b test the same computation (behaviour) of the test object (which states that the program handles the test values from one class in the same way).

Sometimes, during equivalence partitioning, the borders are determined from the code, where the variables in the predicates are computed from input variables. At this point domain analysis can be applied. However, the analysis here happens on the actual code, which turns the specification-based technique into a structured one. Hence, the technique can be applied in the test generation phase as well.

When the EPs are determined, it is mainly enough to select one input data from each equivalence class (see Figure 5.1).

In practice, we always start with determining first the **valid, then the invalid partitions**. This is especially important for BVA (see the section on boundary value analysis later in this chapter). Sometimes the given domain can be partitioned in different ways.

Fault models in EP

Selecting the test data from the partitions follows the rule: 'A best representative of an equivalence class is a value that is at least as likely as any other value in the class to expose an error' (Kaner, 2003). In practice, the input domain is in many cases multidimensional. In these cases, the test data selection depends strongly on the risk

Figure 5.1 Equivalence partitioning and test data selection

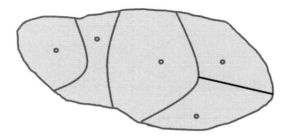

and the chosen fault strategy. In equivalence partitioning, we have two basic strategies: single vs multiple fault assumption.

Example for EP – multiple fault assumption

Let's assume that we have two (independent) input variables X and Y. Assume further that variable X has three EPs, X1, X2 and X3, while variable Y has four EPs, Y1, Y2, Y3 and Y4. We can test the system with four test cases, selecting a single pair of values from each EP, for example:

$$T1 = [x1, y1], T2 = [x2, y2], T3 = [x3, y3], T4 = [x1, y4].$$

Observe that one test case includes data from two EPs. If some test fails, we have to create additional tests to decide whether x_i or y_j is faulty. In some cases, we can solve the problem by applying special (e.g. null) values. For example, if X is a weight and Y is a size, both influencing the price of the delivery, then zero is a special value. In this case, we can create seven test cases.

Example for EP – single fault assumption

We have two (independent) inputs X and Y, where X has three EPs, X1, X2 and X3, while Y has four EPs, Y1, Y2, Y3 and Y4. We can test the system with seven test cases, selecting a single x_i or y_j value considering the EPs separately:

$$T1 = [x1, null], T2 = [x2, null], T3 = [x3, null],$$

$$T4 = [null, y1], T5 = [null, y2], T6 = [null, y3], T7 = [null, y4].$$

The single fault assumption is better for selecting concrete fault types and is more maintainable. The multiple fault assumption may result in fewer test cases. The right choice depends on the risks, which determine the chosen fault model.

Partitions exist in many areas of our software. It is the test designer's task to safely and significantly reduce the testing effort by identifying and testing these partitions.

An example – authorisation

Authorisation version 1

Specification: A valid password must contain at least 8 and at most 14 American Standard Code for Information Interchange (ASCII) characters. Among the characters there has to be at least one lower case letter (a–z), at least one upper case letter (A–Z), at least one numeric character and at least one of the following special characters: ':', ';', '<', '=', '>', '?' and '@'. In the case of less than 8 characters the error message 'The number of characters is less than 8' appears. In the case of more than 14 characters, the error message 'The number of characters is more than 14' appears. In the case of a missing character type, the error message 'Missing character type' appears, showing one of the four types (lower, upper, numerical, special).

For this example, it is reasonable to focus on a single fault model.

Equivalence partition 1

The first test is always the happy path test, for which the password is correct. According to the specification, a password is correct if and only if:

- the number of characters is between 8 and 14; and
- it contains at least one lower case character from a to z; and
- it contains at least one upper case character from A to Z; and
- it contains at least one numeric character; and
- it contains at least one of the following characters: ':', ';', '<', '=', '>', '?', '@'.

The valid equivalence partition contains the passwords with properties above.

Equivalence partition 2

What are the other (invalid) equivalence partitions? Obviously, another partition can be when the number of characters in the password is less than eight, like 'babE1='. This can be our second equivalence partition. Also, this partition contains all the necessary characters, that is, upper and lower case character(s), number(s) and a special character(s) as well. This is because this partition then tests exclusively the passwords which are too short. A partition, which contains passwords having both too short and non-numeric characters, were inappropriate for the chosen model.

The test case selected from this invalid partition works in a way that for a short password, the result should be an error message 'The number of characters is less than 8'. If the code were wrong, then instead of this message, the password would have been accepted (or an incorrect error message would appear).

Equivalence partition 3

The third – invalid – partition can be when the number of characters is greater than 14, such as 'asdf1234ABC<?>@'. Also, similar to the first partition, this partition should contain all the necessary characters, that is upper and lower case characters, numbers and special characters as well.

Now, consider the next invalid partition. Starting from the error message 'Missing character type', we construct an equivalence partition where at least one of the character types is missing, while the number of characters is between 8 and 14. However, this partition is not appropriate. We have to separate the cases where lower case characters, upper case characters, numbers or special characters are missing. Therefore, we must have exactly four more equivalence partitions.

Equivalence partition 4
It contains upper case characters, lower case characters and numeric characters, but not any special characters from ':', ';', '<', '=', '>', '?', '@'. Also, the number of all the characters is between 8 and 14. An example is 'Qwerty43'.

Equivalence partition 5
It contains upper case characters, lower case characters, special characters from ':', ';', '<', '=', '>', '?', '@', but not any numeric characters. Also, the number of all the characters is between 8 and 14. An example is 'Man>=Boy'.

Equivalence partition 6
It contains upper case characters, numeric characters, special characters from ':', ';', '<', '=', '>', '?', '@', but not any lower case letters. Also, the number of all the characters is between 8 and 14. An example is 'WOMAN=42'.

Equivalence partition 7
It contains lower case characters, numeric characters, special characters from ':', ';', '<', '=', '>', '?', '@', but not any upper case letters. Also, the number of all the characters is between 8 and 14. An example is 'rose11;;'.

Equivalence partition #8
A partition for inputs outside all of the partitions above.

Clearly, the first seven equivalence partitions do not result in full partitioning. It is easy to see that there are other partitions in the domain space, but these contain data violating our fault model. Such an example is 'aaaa2222', which is not in any EPs of those listed (it is not on the happy path, it contains neither an upper case character nor a special character). Hence, the tester either gives up the single fault model or does not choose test data from the remaining invalid partition(s). In the first case there are 11 other partitions to consider (with sample data '########', 'aaaabbbb', 'QWERTYUI', '66666666', '=<>??@:;', 'aaaa2222', 'LADYemma', 'dady@com', 'PAWN1234', 'BOY?GIRL', ':::;9876'). In the second case, insisting on the fault model, we do not choose data from the 8th partition.

> In practice, according to the quality requirements (fault models) and risks, stop refining the equivalence partitioning process where the fault detection capability falls below a certain level.

Insisting on the single fault model, Table 5.1 shows the equivalence partitions.

Table 5.1 Equivalence partitioning for the authorisation example

Equivalence partitions	Password attributes				
1	Number of characters >= 8 and <= 14	At least one lower case character	At least one upper case character	At least one numeric character	At least one character: ':', ';', '<', '=', '>', '?', '@'
2	**Number of characters < 8**	At least one lower case character	At least one upper case character	At least one numeric character	At least one character: ':', ';', '<', '=', '>', '?', '@'
3	**Number of characters > 14**	At least one lower case character	At least one upper case character	At least one numeric character	At least one character: ':', ';', '<', '=', '>', '?', '@'
4	Number of characters ≥ 8 and ≤ 14	At least one lower case character	At least one upper case character	At least one numeric character	**No special character: ':', ';', '<', '=', '>', '?', '@'**
5	Number of characters ≥ 8 and ≤ 14	At least one lower case character	At least one upper case character	**No numeric character**	At least one character: ':', ';', '<', '=', '>', '?', '@'
6	Number of characters ≥ 8 and ≤ 14	At least one lower case character	**No upper case character**	At least one numeric character	At least one character: ':', ';', '<', '=', '>', '?', '@'
7	Number of characters ≥ 8 and ≤ 14	**No lower case character**	At least one upper case character	At least one numeric character	At least one character: ':', ';', '<', '=', '>', '?', '@'
8	Inputs outside all of the partitions above				

In Table 5.1, bold represents the error-revealing partitions assuming the single fault model. If a test fails, then the bug relates to exactly one of the partitions.

Finally, based on the equivalence partitions we design the test cases. We simply select one test from the first seven partitions. A possible solution can be the following (test cases for EPs in the authorisation example):

T1 = [6sG?B7u;j]

T2 = [a:B51]

T3 = [anm@@9A8B8Cdfdff]

T4 = [avAQ9821]

T5 = [SwDy:@JJ]

T6 = [weo8712:]

T7 = [=?0P34JK]

The authorisation example also shows that the fault model determines the partitions, and hence, the number of tests.

> Even if the single fault model is not prescribed, and the multiple fault model can be used for some reason, do not combine several invalid partition tests into one test case at the beginning of testing. If possible, test the invalid partitions separately.

BOUNDARY VALUE ANALYSIS

Equivalence partitioning is rarely used in isolation. Potential bugs occur 'near to the border' of the partitions with higher probability. As Boris Beizer said, 'Bugs lurk in corners and congregate at boundaries' (Beizer, 1990). The reason is that the implemented and the correct borders are often different. The question is how to select the test cases concerning the boundaries. Note that different textbooks suggest different solutions. We show in this section why the test selection criterion presented here is worth applying.

Before we continue, let's define some important notions:

- A test input on the closed boundary is called an ON point; for an open boundary, an ON point is a test input 'closest' to the boundary inside the examined domain.
- A test input inside the examined domain ('somewhere in the middle') is called an IN point.
- A test input outside a closed boundary and 'closest' to the ON point is called an OFF point; for an open boundary, an OFF point is on the border.
- A test input outside the boundary of the examined domain is called an OUT point.

The ON and OFF points have to be 'as close as possible'. This means that if an EP contains only integers, then the distance of the two points is one; for example, if an EP contains book prices, where the minimum price difference is EUR 0.01, then the distance between the points is also EUR 0.01.

> Mathematically speaking, there must be a **metric space or an ordering defined on the domain D.** We have to know what 'close to' or 'neighbour' means. The ordering determines the accuracy, which has to be defined in any boundary value analysis first.

For example, in the TVM specification, the minimum price shift is EUR 0.1.

Fault models in BVA

There are two types of fault models in BVA: **predicate faults and data (variable, operator) faults**.

Predicate faults

Assume that a valid equivalence partition contains integer values greater than 42. A correct implementation of this partition can be:

if Age > 42 then ...

The potential error can be any other implementation of the predicate. Table 5.2 shows the error detection capabilities of BVA for various predicates (shaded boxes mean that an error has been detected for a given test case).

Table 5.2 Test design against predicate faults. BVA for predicate Age > 42

Program version no.	Correct/wrong predicate	Test data 1	Test data 2	Test data 3	Test data 4
	Age	Specific values of the variable Age			
		43 (ON)	42 (OFF)	20 (OUT)	50 (IN)
		Output			
1 (correct)	> 42	T	F	F	T
2	>= 42	T	T	F	T
3	< 42	F	F	T	F
4	<= 42	F	T	T	F
5	= 42	F	T	F	F
6	<> 42	T	F	T	T
7	> 43	F	F	F	T
8	> 41	T	T	F	T

We can see that the first three test data are necessary to detect all possible errors, while the fourth one is superfluous. We can also see that for program version 7, test data 1 will detect the bug for > 44, > 45 and so on. Similarly, for program version 8, test data 2 reveals the bug for > 40, > 39 and so on. Therefore, the BVA requires three test cases (see Figure 5.2).

Figure 5.2 Equivalence partitioning with ON/OFF/OUT points for open boundary

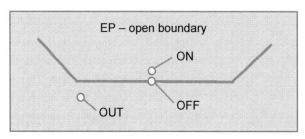

In practice, we have to test the neighbour partitions as well. The OUT point can be any 'middle' point outside the boundary. The ON point of the neighbour is just the OFF point of our original partition, therefore one ON and one OFF point is enough. But what about the 'extreme' partitions, where no neighbour partitions are serving ON points in this way? In this case, we have to consider the 'limit' values, bounded by some (specification or computer hardware) constraint. For example, if the valid partition is bounded by $x < 5$, where x is an integer, then the limit value is the smallest negative integer representable by the programming language or hardware architecture. Obviously, it can be implementation or architecture dependent, which has to be considered in the implementation phase.

> Be careful with implementation-dependent test cases. Your code probably has to be maintained long term, and technology changes rapidly.

Let's consider the case when the correct implementation is a 'greater than or equal to' border:

if Age >= 43 then ...

Table 5.3 demonstrates this point.

In this case, also three test cases are required (for test data 1, 2 and 4, see Figure 5.3). However, they are different from the ones previously seen.

Table 5.3 Test design against predicate faults. BVA for predicate Age >= 43

Program version no.	Correct/wrong predicate	Test data 1	Test data 2	Test data 3	Test data 4
	Age	Specific values of the variable Age			
		43 (ON)	42 (OFF)	20 (OUT)	50 (IN)
		Output			
1 (correct)	>= 43	T	F	F	T
2	> 43	F	F	F	T
3	<= 43	T	T	T	F
4	< 43	F	T	T	F
5	= 43	T	F	F	F
6	<> 43	F	T	T	T
7	>= 44	F	F	F	T
8	>= 42	T	T	F	T

Figure 5.3 Equivalence partitioning with ON/OFF/IN points for closed boundary

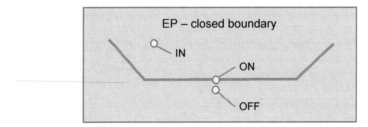

Similar to the previous case, one ON and one OFF point are enough, since an IN point is an OFF point of a neighbour partition.

Now let's consider the following predicate:

if Age == 43 then ...

This is demonstrated by Table 5.4.

Table 5.4 Test design against predicate faults. BVA for predicate Age == 43

Program version no.	Correct/wrong predicate	Test data 1	Test data 2	Test data 3	Test data 4	Test data 5
	Age	Specific values of the variable Age				
		43 (ON)	42 (OFF)	44 (OFF)	20 (OUT)	50 (OUT)
		Output				
1 (correct)	== 43	T	F	F	F	F
2	> 43	F	F	T	F	T
3	>= 43	T	F	T	F	T
4	< 43	F	T	F	T	F
5	<= 43	T	T	F	T	F
6	<> 43	F	T	T	T	T
7	== 44	F	F	T	F	F
8	== 42	F	T	F	F	F

In this case, three test cases are required as well. All of the following triples are reliable (test data 1, 2 and 3), (test data 1, 2 and 5), (test data 1, 3 and 4), (test data 1, 4 and 5). This means that one ON and two OFF/OUT points are reliable when the two OFF/OUT points are on the opposite side of the border (see Figure 5.4).

Figure 5.4 Equivalence partitioning with ON/OFF/OUT points for closed boundary from both sides

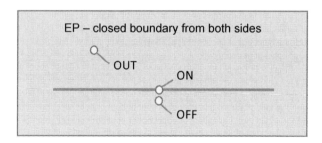

For simplicity, we can use the same solution as above, that is requiring an ON–OFF pair and a third point, which can be an ON point of another border (or limit value) on the other side of the OFF point.

Finally, for the predicate

if Age <> 43 then ...

the reliable solution is as per Figure 5.5.

Figure 5.5 Equivalence partitioning with ON/OFF/IN points for open boundary from both sides

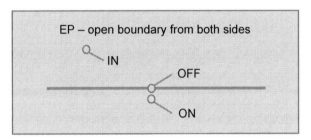

Observe that one ON–OFF pair and one IN/OUT point is reliable for all the examined predicate faults above. The IN/OUT point can be the OFF/ON point of the neighbour partition.

Data faults
Let's consider the following data fault, where **badVariable** is used instead of **Age**:

if badVariable >= 43 then ...

If **Age** is incorrectly changed to **badVariable**, then an ON–OFF pair is reliable for revealing the fault (see Table 5.5).

The only additional requirement is that we have to keep all the other variables (except Age) unmodified. You can see that the ON point reveals the defect of badVariable being 42 and 20 (diagonal), while the OFF point reveals the other incorrect values of badVariable (darker grey).

Now let's consider the fault:

if badVariable == 43 then ...

Again, an ON–OFF pair is enough to detect the bug, and it is true for all other cases when only one variable is wrong in a predicate (see Table 5.6).

Table 5.5 Test design against data faults. BVA for badVariable >= 43

Program version no.	Correct/wrong predicate	Value of badVariable	Test data 1	Test data 2	Test data 3	Test data 4
			Specific values of the variable Age			
			43 (ON)	42 (OFF)	20 (OUT)	50 (OUT)
1 (correct)	**Age** >= 43		T	F	F	T
2 (incorrect)	**badVariable** >= 43	43		T		
3 (incorrect)	**badVariable** >= 43	44		T		
4 (incorrect)	**badVariable** >= 43	42		F		
5 (incorrect)	**badVariable** >= 43	20		F		
6 (incorrect)	**badVariable** >= 43	50		T		

Table 5.6 Test design against data faults. BVA for badVariable == 43

Program version no.	Correct/wrong predicate	Value of badVariable	Test data 1	Test data 2	Test data 3	Test data 4
			Specific values of the variable Age			
			43 (ON)	42 (OFF)	20 (OUT)	50 (OUT)
1 (correct)	**Age** == 43		T	F	F	F
2 (incorrect)	**badVariable** == 43	43		T		
3 (incorrect)	**badVariable** == 43	44		F		
4 (incorrect)	**badVariable** == 43	42		F		
5 (incorrect)	**badVariable** == 43	20		F		
6 (incorrect)	**badVariable** == 43	50		F		

Similar is the case for predicates with more variables. Consider this correct predicate:

if Age + otherVariable >= 43 then ...

One variable mistake can happen as a result of a change, for example replacing **otherVariable** with **wrongVariable**. This case is similar to the one above. Another variable error is omitting **otherVariable**. To test this case reliably, we should avoid degenerate values of variables, here **otherVariable** = 0. Therefore, set all the variable values to non-zero, non-empty string and so on.

Finally, let's consider the case when the correct predicate is:

if Age >= 0.5 then ...

Let the accuracy of the data type of the variable be 0.01. If the incorrect implementation is

if 1.01 x Age >= 0.5 then ...

then Table 5.7 applies.

Table 5.7 Test design against data faults. BVA for bad constant

Program version no.	Correct/wrong data	Test data 1	Test data 2	Test data 3	Test data 4
		Specific values of the variable Age			
		0.5 (ON)	0.49 (OFF)	0.51 (IN)	0.48 (OUT)
		Output			
1 (correct)	**Age** >= 0.5	T	F	T	F
2 (incorrect)	1.01 × **Age** >= 0.5	T	F	T	F
			(0.495 > 0.5) -> F		

No test case reveals this 'bug'. However, this is not a real bug as for each value of **Age** the same branches will be executed; therefore here the two implementations are 'identical'. When the incorrect implementation is

if 1.05 x Age >= 0.5 then ...

then our tests become reliable (Table 5.8).

Here the OFF point reveals the bug, that is the ON–OFF pair is error revealing in this case as well (or the jumps to branches are identical).

Testing a boundary requires setting other input data, which is not related to that boundary. If we follow the single fault assumption, we will set these variables as IN points of the related domains.

Table 5.8 Test design against data faults. BVA for other bad predicate

Program version no.	Correct/wrong data	Test data 1	Test data 2	Test data 3	Test data 4
		Specific values of the variable Age			
		0.5 (ON)	0.49 (OFF)	0.51 (IN)	0.4 (OUT)
		Output			
1 (correct)	**Age** >= 0.5	T	F	T	F
2 (incorrect)	1.05 × **Age** >= 0.5	T	T	T	F
			(0.515 > 0.5) -> T		(0.42 > 0.4) -> F

The test selection criterion of boundary value analysis requires testing an ON, an OFF and an IN/OUT point for each border so that the (ON, IN) points are on different sides of the boundary. Similarly, the (OFF, OUT) points should be on the other side of the boundary. Note that the IN/OUT points can be the OFF/ON points of adjacent borders. When setting the ON–OFF pairs for a border, the variables (data) that are not related to that border have to be unchanged. Set the variables to be non-degenerate.

EP and BVA together

Equivalence partition testing and boundary value analysis are used together. The former is weak without the latter, while boundary value analysis can only be used if we know the equivalence partitions. When designing the test cases, we explore equivalence partitions first, and then, knowing the boundaries, we design the tests to fulfil both methods together.

We mentioned earlier that differentiating valid and invalid partitions is very important for boundary value analysis. The reason is that it is superfluous to test a boundary between two invalid partitions. Consider Figure 5.6 where we separate the valid and invalid partitions.

In Figure 5.6 'I' denotes invalid and 'V' denotes valid partitions. We can see that we test the borders between (valid, valid) and (valid, invalid) partitions. However, we never test a border between (invalid, invalid) partitions.

Since test cases on or near to the boundary may reveal more defects than test cases of inner points, ON points may detect multiple defects, that is both computation and domain errors.

We have seen that for BVA an ON–OFF pair is enough since the necessary IN/OUT points are usually covered by other partitions. However, when we need an ON, OFF, OUT triple,

Figure 5.6 Valid and invalid partitions with ON-boundary points

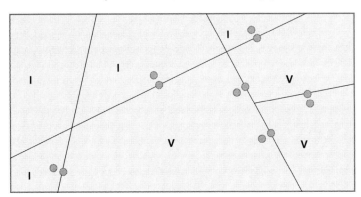

we have no IN point. The question is whether in this case the ON point is enough or not. In the case of a single ON point we do not always know whether it is a computation error (erroneous computation resulting in an incorrect result) or a predicate error (due to an erroneous condition). Selecting a single ON point, our testing satisfies the multiple fault assumption. However, in many cases, we still know which of the error types occurred. In the case of a predicate/domain error, the control (execution) goes along another input domain, and we know the expected result of the neighbour domain. Therefore, except for some coincidences, it is superfluous to design two test cases, that is one ON and one IN point.

Example

```
if x > 10 then   // correct would be x ≥ 10
    a = x + 2
else
    a = x * x     // correct would be 2 * x
```

In this case, testing with input x1 = 10 (ON) and x2 = 9.9 (OFF), the results are a = 100 and 98.01. Therefore, the ON point shows a predicate error since 12 is expected, which is computed in a different branch. The OFF point (a = 98.01) shows a computation error since 19.8 is expected.

This knowledge permits us to design minimal but still reliable tests. Other test selection criteria found in textbooks or blogs may result in significantly more test cases. Let's consider the most frequent case when we have linearly ordered partitions (see Figure 5.7).

In this case, our test selection criterion requires 4 ON, 4 OFF and one IN/OUT points. If we have N domains in this simple arrangement, then the number of test cases is 2N − 1, which can be extended by special test cases containing special values.

Summarising, we have a test selection criterion for the combined EP and BVA method that is identical with the test selection criterion for BVA.

Figure 5.7 Linearly ordered partitions

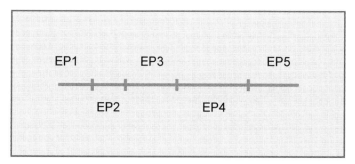

Some data is especially important, independent of which domain it belongs to. What happens if you perform a bank transfer of EUR 0? A system crash? Some developers try to divide by zero, mishandle null pointers and so on (of course, inadvertently). Imagine that you want to buy something in an ecommerce portal. You put the article into the basket, then change your mind, and put it back on the shelf, so your basket is empty. Then, you order the content of the basket. After a few days, you get an empty box from the store. Of course, this is unrealistic... or perhaps not. Please do not forget to test zero as a number, as a pointer and so on.

Example for BVA (continued from EP)

Now let's consider the equivalence partitions in our previous example. For clarity, we start with the test cases other than the happy path:

Equivalence partition 2	**Number of characters < 8**	At least one lower case character	At least one upper case character	At least one numeric character	At least one character: ':', ';', '<', '=', '>', '?', '@'

The ON-boundary value here is 7, the OFF-boundary is 8 and the OUT point is 14. The OFF-boundary and the OUT point will be the boundary of the happy path. Here, we consider only one input characteristic, that is the length, while the others remain unchanged. Since we intend to test whether the length of the password is not too short, all other characteristics are irrelevant. That is, we can select any characters that meet the related characteristic, for example 'aa' + 'BB' + '33' + ':'. These strings fulfil the above characteristics, respectively. Considering EP3:

Equivalence partition 3	**Number of characters > 14**	At least one lower case character	At least one upper case character	At least one numeric character	At least one character: ':', ';', '<', '=', '>', '?', '@'

The ON-boundary is 15, while the OFF-boundary is 14, and the OUT point is 8, which are also located on the boundary of the happy path. Let's go on:

Equivalence partition 4	Number of characters > 8 and < 14	At least one lower case character	At least one upper case character	At least one numeric character	**No special character: ':', ';', '<', '=', '>', '?', '@'**

At first sight, all the special characters seem to be equivalent. However, a professional developer does not consider these characters one by one. Instead, they know the ASCII code of these characters, which makes it possible to handle all these characters together. Here, ':' has the smallest, while '@' has the highest, ASCII code, that is 58 and 64, respectively, which are the OFF-boundary characters of EP4. These OFF-boundary values are just ':' and '@', which are also the boundary of the happy path.

These points can also be considered as OUT points. When ':' is the OFF point, then '@' is the OUT point and vice versa. Here we would just like to demonstrate our assertions that an ON–OFF pair is enough; the OUT/IN points are ON/OFF points of the neighbour partitions. From here we only consider the ON–OFF pairs.

The boundaries are 57 and 65, which are the closest non-special characters. These are just the ASCII codes of 9 and A, respectively.

Equivalence partition 5	Number of characters > 8 and < 14	At least one lower case character	At least one upper case character	**No numeric character**	At least one character: ':', ';', '<', '=', '>', '?', '@'

In EP5 the OFF-boundary values are 0 and 9, which are the boundary values of the happy path. The boundary values, that is the closest non-numeric characters, are '/' and ':', respectively. The second is a boundary value of the happy path.

Equivalence partition 6	Number of characters > 8 and < 14	At least one lower case character	**No upper case character**	At least one numeric character	At least one character: ':', ';', '<', '=', '>', '?', '@'

In EP6 the OFF-boundary values are A and Z, respectively, which are the boundary values of the happy path. The boundary values, that is the closest non-upper case characters, are '@' and '[', respectively. The first is a boundary value of the happy path.

Equivalence partition 7	Number of characters >8 and <14	**No lower case character**	At least one upper case character	At least one numeric character	At least one character: ':', ';', '<', '=', '>', '?', '@'

In EP7 the OFF-boundary values are 'a' and 'z', respectively, which are the boundary values of the happy path. The boundary values, that is the closest non-lower case characters are '`' and '{', respectively.

Since the OFF-boundary values of the non-happy path test cases are just the boundary values of the happy path, considering equivalence partitions 2–7 gives all the necessary boundaries.

Based on these ON-boundary and OFF-boundary values the complete test set can be constructed. We aim to minimise the number of the test cases. Unfortunately, we have to do this optimisation manually. Note that the different sub-boundaries are independent, hence, we can set more ON-boundaries in one test case.

Table 5.9 contains the test design of the above example. Here, the table contains the type and the ID of the test cases with their descriptions, and the OFF-boundary pairs of the (boundary) test. Here 'V' means valid, 'I' means invalid, 'C' relates to the partition (class) and 'B' relates to the boundary, for example 'VB' is a valid boundary test (ON point).

Table 5.10 contains the test case IDs, the input, the expected output and some comments. Here we only consider boundary test cases. It is cost-effective since if a test, whose probability is low, fails, we can add a 'mid-boundary' test case to help the developer to know whether the bug is due to a faulty border or a computation defect.

Table 5.9 Test design for the 'Authorisation' example

Test design item no. 1234		Trace: Req. authorisation	
Based on: Input		**Assumption:** Length is a non-negative integer	
Type	**Description**	**ID**	**Belongs to**
VC	Happy path	1234-1	–
VB	Happy path with 8 characters containing ':', '@', 0 and 9	1234-2	1234-5, 1234-9, 1234-11

(Continued)

Table 5.9 (Continued)

Test design item no. 1234		Trace: Req. authorisation	
Based on: Input		**Assumption:** Length is a non-negative integer	
Type	**Description**	**ID**	**Belongs to**
VB	Happy path with 14 characters containing A, Z, a and z	1234-3	1234-7, 1234-13, 1234-15
IC	Short passwords	1234-4	–
IB	Password one character shorter than the minimum 8 character limit	1234-5	1234-4, 1234-2
IC	Long passwords	1234-6	–
IB	Password one character longer than the maximum 14 character limit	1234-7	1234-6, 1234-3
IC	Missing only special characters from ':', ';', '<', '=', '>', '?', '@'	1234-8	–
IB	Missing only special characters from ':', ';', '<', '=', '>', '?', '@' but containing 9 and A, the ASCII neighbours of ':' and '@'	1234-9	1234-8, 1234-2
IC	Missing only numerical characters	1234-10	–
IB	Missing only numerical characters but containing '/' and ':' the ASCII neighbours of 0 and 9	1234-11	1234-10, 1234-2
IC	Missing only upper case characters	1234-12	–
IB	Missing only upper case characters but containing '@' and '[', the ASCII neighbours of A and Z	1234-13	1234-12, 1234-3

(Continued)

Table 5.9 (Continued)

Test design item no. 1234	Trace: Req. authorisation
Based on: Input	**Assumption:** Length is a non-negative integer

Type	Description	ID	Belongs to
IC	Missing only lower case characters	1234-14	–
IB	Missing only lower case characters but containing '`' and '{', the ASCII neighbours of a and z	1234-15	1234-14, 1234-3

Table 5.10 Test cases for the 'Authorisation' example

ID	Input: string	Expected output	Comment
1234-2	A0a@z9Z:	ACCEPT	Length = 8 containing ':' and '@'
1234-3	@43zG:A2a=s7FZ	ACCEPT	Length = 14
1234-5	B2a=s7F	REJECT	Length = 7
1234-7	<43zG:B2a=s7FT9	REJECT	Length = 15
1234-9	A0aHKz9ZbK	REJECT	Length = 10, containing A and 9
1234-11	/cdHU:tGaaV	REJECT	Length = 11 containing '/' and ':'
1234-13	j5@k9[6hx0	REJECT	Length =10 containing '@' and ' ['
1234-15	QH5`7{J2W2'	REJECT	Length = 11 containing '`' and '{'

We can see that the number of test cases is increased only by one. This is because 1234-2 involves many independent boundaries and since passwords contain multiple characters, we can cover more boundary characteristics in one test case. One exception is the length of the happy path, which cannot be 8 and 14 at the same time.

Example: Authorisation Version 2

Specification: A valid password must contain at least 8 and at most 14 ASCII characters. Among the characters there has to be at least one lower (a–z), at least one upper case letters (A–Z), at least one numeric and at least one of the following special characters: ':', ';', '<', '=', '>', '?' and '@'. In the case of less than 8 characters, the error message 'The number of characters is less than 8' appears. In the case of more than 14 characters the error message 'The number of characters is more than 14' appears. In the case of a missing character type, the error message 'Missing character type' appears showing one of the four types (lower, upper, numerical, special).

Version 2 is very similar to the original, therefore even taking into account the competent programmer hypothesis, a developer may implement it incorrectly. This specification has to be tested by a slightly different test case set. Namely, test case T1234-11 = {/cdHU:tGaaV} would be superfluous for Version 2, since it would test the same equivalence partition (the happy path) as T1234-2. Therefore, we justified the necessity of T1234-11 by this alternative specification.

On the other hand, if T1234-11 were missing, then Version 2 would reveal it.

Similarly, you can easily imagine alternative specifications for all test cases from T1234-5 to T1234-13, while the tests for a happy path are obvious.

This example shows the essentials of black-box mutation testing, which is a method for validating whether our test cases are well designed without executing the test cases. If you are not sure whether a given test case is necessary or not, just imagine a slightly modified specification, which makes this test necessary in the original, and superfluous in an alternative one. If you could not find it, maybe it is superfluous. If you could imagine a slightly alternative specification for which you believe that the EPs, the boundaries and thus the test cases are just the same, then you have probably missed some tests.

It is not necessary to construct all the EPs and boundaries; just consider the modified part and the EPs related to this modification, for example modifying the specification part from

- it contains at least one upper case character from A to Z; **AND**
- it contains at least one numeric character; and

to

- it contains at least one upper case character from A to Z; **OR**
- it contains at least one numeric character; and

you have to investigate only EP5 and EP6.

The specification has to contain the EP to be validated in such a way that only a test case from this EP would detect the defect. If the alternative specification is far from the original, then it can be ignored. If the specification is close to the original, the EP has to be considered. Fortunately, black-box mutation analysis can be used for both cases.

DOMAIN ANALYSIS

We have considered so far the cases when EPs can be generated based on one input variable directly. In practice, however, predicates are functions of more variables, such as 2x + 5y + k, where k = z/4 +1, and x, y, z are input variables. White and Cohen (1980), who introduce domain testing, investigated the types of predicates. Their result is language independent since the predicates reflect the specification. They found that more than 10 per cent of the predicates contain more than one variable.

In the case of more complex predicates, the domains are determined by domain analysis. In the simplest cases, the domain analysis is straightforward and can be done at the test design phase. In complex cases, the task may be unsolvable.

Example: taxi driver's decision – go/no go

The taxi driver knows the following:

- The starting time, when the driver has a call and makes a decision – denoted by t-start (in hours).

- The elapsed time before they arrive to pick the passenger – denoted by t-pick (in hours).

- The distance from the place of pick up to the destination – denoted by d (in km).

- The elapsed time from the place of pick up to the destination – denoted by t-ride (in hours).

- The duration of working – denoted by t-full (in hours, ≤ 10 according to the law).

We assume that the driver wants to earn at least EUR 20 for each ride, the precision of measuring d is 0.1 km, the time accuracy is 0.1 hour. Then, the fare of a ride is 2 + 16 x t-ride (hour) + d (km). The driver cannot accept a reservation that would exceed t-full = 10. The starting time is calculated by the engine, and should be between zero and t-full. The program computes whether the driver should go or wait for another call.

For example, if the ride takes 45 minutes and the distance is 5 km (huge traffic jam), then they earn 2 + 12 + 5 = 19 EUR, which is below the limit, and thus, they reject this passenger.

The input variables d, t-start, t-pick and t-ride have to be non-negative. These conditions seem to be borders. However, at the current state-of-the-art of development, input handling is addressed by applying existing frameworks. It means that when we apply the chosen framework correctly, we do not have to test the predicate d >= 0 (since it is the framework). As a consequence, this condition has to be tested only with two values: (1) d = 0; (2) d < 0. Value (2) is necessary because the developer may set the framework incorrectly, so that negative values may occur.

Test for (1) is just an ON point, and test for (2) is an OUT point, but here OUT means 'outside the input domain'. To test this OUT point, checking the existence of the sign '–' may be enough. **No IN point is required when testing these conditions**. With one ON and one OUT point, we are able to test the integration of our application with the framework. All these necessary tests can be done by two test cases: T2 involves the testing of non-enabled negative values, while T1 involves zero for all inputs (see Table 5.11). This is a real case, for example when somebody stops a taxi but changes their mind.

The border with regards to the necessary income is:

$$2 + 16 \times \text{t-ride} + d >= 20.$$

The border with regards to the time limit is:

$$\text{t-start} + \text{t-pick} + \text{t-ride} <= 10.$$

Considering the first border, the ON point (T3 in Table 5.11) can be determined by solving this equation:

$$16 \times \text{t-ride} + d = 18.$$

A realistic and simple solution is when t-ride is 0.5 (30 minutes) and

$$d = 18 - 16 \times 0.5 = 10.$$

The OFF point (T4) is when we reduce either the distance by 0.1 km or the time by 0.1 hour. Considering these cases we obtain:

OFF1: $2 + 16 \times 0.4 + 10 = 18.4$

OFF2: $2 + 16 \times 0.5 + 9.9 = 19.9$

where the latter is a valid OFF point. According to our test selection criterion we need an IN point (T5), since our partition, 16 x t-ride + d >= 18, is an edge partition. Let's select a very large IN point: t-ride = 9.8, and d = 500; since t=ride < 10, t-start = 0, t-pick = 0. The result is 656.8.

We determine the values of the other variables later. Now consider the other border.

$$\text{t-start} + \text{t-pick} + \text{t-ride} <= 10.$$

For a realistic solution let the pickup time t-pick be 0.2 and the paid time t-ride be 0.8 and d =15. With this, t-start = 9 resulting in an ON point (T6): (9 + 0.2 + 0.8 = 10). The OFF point (T7) has to be 10.1 and we can increase t-ride to 0.9.

We have to test the IN point as well; however, this has been tested by T5.

The variables, which are outside a predicate, are used satisfying the single fault assumption. For example, in the case of testing the OFF2 point, t-start and t-pick is selected in a way that t-start + t-pick + t-ride << 10.

A domain test matrix is used to make the choice of the boundary values more convenient and easier. Here the necessary information is represented in the form of a table. This helpful technique was suggested by Binder (2000).

You can see that in selecting ON/OFF points for a given border we always select IN points for the other border to satisfy single fault assumption.

Table 5.11 Test design for the 'Taxi driver' example

Variable			Tests						
Input	condition	Type	T1	T2	T3	T4	T5	T6	T7
d	≥ 0	ON	0						
		OUT		-1					
		IN			10	9.9	500	15	15
t-ride	≥ 0	ON	0						
		OUT		-1					
		IN			0.5	0.5	9.8	0.8	0.9
t-pick	≥ 0	ON	0						
		OUT		-1					
		IN			0.2	0.2	0	0.2	0.2
t-start	≥ 0	ON	0						
		OUT		-1					
		IN			5	5	0	9	9
Output	**border**								
income = 2 + 16 × t-ride + d	2 + 16 × t-ride + d ≥ 20	ON			20				
		OFF				19.9			
		IN	2				656.8	29.8	31.4
t-full = t-start + t-pick + t-ride	t-current + t-pick + t-ride ≤ 10	ON						10	
		OFF							10.1
		IN	0		5.7	5.7	9.8		
	Expected result		Acc.	N/A	Acc.	Rej.	Acc.	Acc.	Rej.

Extending this example, we easily get non-linear borders. We can assume that the driver wants to earn EUR 20 in one hour instead of gaining EUR 20 for a ride. In this case, the border is non-linear – the interested reader can easily determine the predicate for this case. According to our knowledge, there is no accepted theoretical result for this rare case; we suggest applying more ON/OFF/IN data.

CHALLENGES IN DOMAIN-BASED TESTING

The fault assumption for domain-based testing is that the computation is correct, but the domain definition is wrong. An incorrectly implemented domain means that the boundaries are wrong, which may induce incorrect control flow. In this section we summarise the possible domain problems.

Possible domain problems:

- Overlapping domains. Overlapping domain specification means that at least two supposedly distinct domains overlap.

- Incomplete domains. Incomplete domains mean that the union of the domains is incomplete, that is, there are missing subdomains or holes in the specified domains.

- Boundary problems:

  - Open–closed boundary exchange. Typically, the predicate is defined in terms of > and the developer implements an open border >= incorrectly instead. For example, x > 0 is incorrectly implemented as x >= 0. The closed -> open exchange can also occur.

  - Boundary reversal. Typically, the predicate is defined in terms of >= and the developer implements the logical complement incorrectly and uses <= instead. For example, x >= 0 is incorrectly negated as x <= 0.

  - Other boundary exchange. For example, instead of >=, the developer implements == or <>.

  - Boundary obfuscation. If complex, compound predicates define domain boundaries incorrectly and faulty logic manipulations may occur.

As you can see, the partitioning questions raise the problems of deeper boundary analysis. That is why we have to discuss it in more detail.

TVM EXAMPLE

Let's select specification 'Buying process' from our TVM example. For this chapter, extending it with the acceptable banknotes:

> Banknotes to be accepted by the machine: EUR 5, EUR 10, EUR 20, EUR 50. The remaining amount is the starting amount minus the inserted one. *For the remaining amount to be paid, the machine accepts only those banknotes for which selecting a smaller value banknote would not reach the necessary amount. €5 is always accepted.*

For example, if the necessary amount is EUR 21, then the machine accepts €50 since EUR 20 will not exceed EUR 21. If the user inserts €10 and then €2, then even €20 is not accepted since the remaining amount is EUR 9; EUR 10 would exceed the necessary amount. The remaining amount and *current acceptable banknotes are visible on the screen.* If the user inserts a non-acceptable banknote then it will be given back and an error message appears notifying the user of the mistake.

Note that in the previous chapter we extended the specification so that the admin of the ticket machine company will be able to modify the ticket prices. Therefore, we assume that the ticket prices can be set to any amount. We also consider the granularity of the ticket price of 0.1 EUR.

Let's consider the text in italics first. The examples in this specification help us in selecting the equivalence partitions. We have two inputs: (1) the remaining ticket price and (2) the set of available banknotes. It is very important that the set of acceptable banknotes is constant and not a variable. Therefore, though we have to consider it when constructing the EPs, we can create the partitions without involving this set, since every partition will contain the same elements. Let's start with the partitions of the ticket prices.

Let the remaining amount to be paid (RAP) be:

1. less than or equal to EUR 5;

2. EUR > 5 and EUR <=10;

3. EUR > 10 and EUR <=20;

4. EUR > 20 and EUR <=50;

5. greater than EUR 50.

Considering the acceptable banknotes, we can construct Table 5.12. We assume here that the remaining amount to be paid is always positive.

Table 5.12 Acceptable banknotes for TVM

EP	RAP in EUR	Acceptable banknotes
1	<= 5	€5
2	> 5 and <= 10	€5, €10
3	> 10 and <= 20	€5, €10, €20
4	> 20 and <= 50	€5, €10, €20, €50
5	> 50	€5, €10, €20, €50

We can easily observe that EP5 can be merged with EP4 since the acceptable banknotes are the same. The table has been updated as Table 5.13.

Table 5.13 Acceptable banknotes for TVM – improved

EP	RAP in EUR	Acceptable banknotes
1	<=5	€5
2	> 5 and <=10	€5, €10
3	> 10 and <=20	€5, €10, €20
4	> 20	€5, €10, €20, €50

Instead of selecting one test case from each partition, we move forward to include boundary value analysis. According to Table 5.13 we have four EPs and according to our test selection criterion we design three test cases for each EP – we restrict them to the input values only:

EP1: 0.1 (IN), 5 (ON), 5.1 (OFF)

EP2: 5 (OFF1), 5.1 (ON1/IN2), 0.1 (OUT1), 10 (ON2), 10.1 (OFF2)

EP3: 10 (OFF1), 10.1 (ON1/IN2), 5.1 (OUT1), 20 (ON2), 20.1 (OFF2)

EP4: 20 (OFF), 20.1 (ON), 10.1 (OUT)

We selected the first IN point as the minimum possible amount. Considering EP2 and EP3, they have two ON/OFF points and one IN/OUT point because of the two borders. Because of the same values in different EPs, we have 7 test cases instead of 14. To make our tests complete, we extend the test cases with the ticket price and the inserted amount of money; see Table 5.14 for the designed test cases.

Table 5.14 Test cases for TVM

Test	EP	Ticket price	Inserted amount	RAP in EUR	Acceptable banknotes
T1	1	1.4	1, 0.2, 0.1	0.1	€5
T2	1	7 (5 × 1.4)	2	5	€5
T3	2	6.2 (3 × 2.1)	1, 0.1	5.1	€5, €10
T4	2	10.5 (5 × 2.1)	0.5	10	€5, €10

(Continued)

Table 5.14 (Continued)

Test	EP	Ticket price	Inserted amount	RAP in EUR	Acceptable banknotes
T5	3	10.5	0.2, 0.2	10.1	€5, €10, €20
T6	3	21	1	20	€5, €10, €20
T7	4	21	0.5, 0.2, 0.2	20.1	€5, €10, €20, €50

Note that here we only test the software of the machine and we cannot test the 'hardware' by inserting non-acceptable banknotes. Of course, the hardware has to be tested by inserting non-acceptable banknotes and other banknotes, for example smaller value foreign banknotes such as HUF 500 (< 2 EUR).

What we can learn from this example is the following:

1. We should always start with the core part of the specification.
2. Inputs and outputs have to be carefully considered.
3. Boundaries should be carefully investigated. We had to select those OFF-boundary values that resulted in a modification in the output domain. To avoid superfluous work and additional cost, we had to analyse whether test cases for similar partitions could be put together or not.

Summarising, applying EP and BVA is not an easy task but is challenging and interesting for testers.

Finally, let's consider inserting coins: payment is possible by inserting **coins or banknotes**. There is not too much information on inserting coins. Since there is not any restriction, we can select a unique happy path where the input is a set of all the acceptable coins and where each coin type is inserted more than once. Another possibility is that coins are tested for another specification (user story), where coin insertion is more relevant.

METHOD EVALUATION

Domain-based testing is perhaps the most widely used test design technique. This is because it is easy to use and lots of real specifications require the application of it. In this section we summarise its applicability, advantages and limitations.

Applicability

These techniques are applicable at any levels of testing. Moreover, the presented domain testing methods can rarely be used in isolation, and are applicable mainly in stateless cases. Roughly speaking, we can apply them if all the inputs are available at the initial state, and no input can be entered into a special state.

However, we show that different test design methods can be used together for some specifications. If the program is in a given state, we can apply EP and BVA as in the case of a stateless code.

Types of defects

The methods are especially useful for domain errors, that is when predicates in the conditional statements are faulty. The methods are also beneficial for detecting simple computational errors, which may occur along the execution paths inside the equivalence partition.

Advantages and shortcomings of the method

The advantages of EP, BVA and the domain analysis methods are the following:

- They reduce the number of test cases. One equivalence partition may contain a huge number of possible inputs, but it is enough to use only one test case when all the members of a set of values to be tested are expected to be handled in the same way and where the sets of values used by the application do not interact. Boundary value analysis improves the method significantly and usually requires only a few additional test cases.

- Reliable test cases. The methods result in test cases that reveal lots of bugs, such as slightly erroneous predicates, erroneous assignments and so on.

- Cost-effectiveness. Test cases can be designed in a relatively short time. Therefore, these methods are cost-effective.

- Simple to learn and easy to use. The learning curve is short and testers can use it without programming knowledge.

The limitations and shortcomings of EP, BVA and the domain analysis methods are the following:

- In cases when the partitions cannot be determined based on the specification, we have to construct the EPs by intuition. However, this is sometimes difficult or not reliable. Consider a sorting algorithm. In this case, the partitions are unknown and strongly depend on the algorithm. What can we do then? For example, we can construct EPs in the following way: consider the function $f(n)$ as the sum of the distance of the elements from their original positions after sorting, where n is the number of elements. For sorted input $f(n)$ is just zero; for the reverse order $f(n)$ is $(n^2 - 1)/2$ (if n is odd). For $n \geq 9$ we can select EPs where $f(n)$ is less than n, between n and $(n^2 - 1)/4$, and between $(n^2 - 1)/4 + 1$ and $(n^2 - 1)/2$. However, this seems to be ad hoc (and it is). Similarly, it is very difficult to determine EPs for testing programming languages.

- The method is applicable for stateless cases (see Chapter 6). Unfortunately, we know that most of the applications are stateful. However, if the application has stateless parts, the method is applicable. We have to apply different methods in combination.

- Sometimes it is difficult to minimise the test sets, for example if there are equivalence partitions with common boundaries. Even in our simple example, we had to combine the test cases into one test case carefully. Finding non-reliable EPs is not an easy task either.

- In many cases there is no hierarchical solution. In complex cases, with many equivalence partitions and boundaries, no straightforward way exists for simplification by dividing the equivalence partitions into smaller groups and applying the method in a hierarchical manner.

- These methods do not support preconditions. We can either neglect these inputs or consider the related equivalence partitions and boundaries in a similar way to other partitions and boundary values.

- These methods are difficult to maintain. If the specification changes, then we should modify the partitions and the boundary values, and we should modify the test cases accordingly. Unfortunately, we have to search for the test cases from the whole test set, which may be time-consuming.

- If the code implements processes where the ordering of the events is important, then these methods are difficult to use. These methods are mainly for specifications where all the inputs have to be available at the beginning of the execution.

- What should be done if the number of EPs is very large? In these cases, the related specification is probably large as well. It is not possible that a four-line requirement requires 1000 EPs. The size of the specification and the number of EPs are in correlation. In the case of a large specification, it has to be broken down. However, if we have a large non-linear boundary, we may be in trouble. In this case, we have to select the sensitive boundaries very carefully. Historical data may help.

THEORETICAL BACKGROUND

The theory of domain-based testing dates back to the 1970s, when testing research started. Unfortunately, testing theory in general is rarely used in practice, but domain-based testing is a refreshing exception.

Partition Testing

Partition testing is one of the oldest testing methods, first mentioned in a paper by Goodenough and Gerhart (1975). EP is a special case of partition testing where the partitions are disjoint. In EP testing, we call a domain partitioning homogeneous if either all of its members cause the program to pass or all cause it to fail. Weyuker and Ostrand (1980) used the term 'revealing' for homogeneous partitions. A very good description about partition testing comes from Hamlet and Taylor (1990). They state that 'specification-based subdomains are particularly good at detecting missing logic faults, which are the most common programmer mistakes'.

In general, partitions are not necessarily disjoint; they may overlap. In this case, we cannot call them partitions, but rather overlapping subdomains. This is the case for statement testing, which is a white-box testing strategy, where the program statements have to be covered. Here the subdomain relation is the following: two inputs are in the same subdomain if they cause the same set of statements to be executed. Since one input may cover many (different) statements, the subdomains are overlapping. The case for mutation testing is similar.

The reliability of equivalence partitioning was investigated in different case studies. Reid (1997) investigated EP, BVA and random testing for real code with real bugs. He found that BVA was much more reliable than EP. However, the number of test cases were three times more in BVA than that of EP. We considered these methods together and suggest not using EP in isolation.

In Arnicane (2009) the author described several test selection criteria for EP and BVA. She referred to the original single fault solution as weak equivalence class testing. She considered the combinatorial extension of EP as strong equivalence class testing. The paper differentiates between inner and outer OFF points, where inner OFF points are actually ON points close to the border. With this, the author introduced weak IN and OFF boundary testing, where each (ON–inner OFF), (ON–outer OFF) pair is tested, extended by an inner value of the EP. When both IN and OFF boundaries are tested with an inner test case, she calls it 'robust weak boundary value testing'. It is not clear which out of the test selection criteria have to be applied in which situation. This author prefers single fault solution with one ON–OFF pair of test cases.

Domain testing in general

One of the basic errors in software is **domain error** (Howden, 1976), which occurs when a specific input follows a wrong path because of an error in the control flow of a program. This type of error can be revealed by applying a domain testing method introduced by White and Cohen in 1980. Since the faulty domain can be very close to the correct one, input data near the boundary of a domain partition are therefore more sensitive to program faults and should be carefully tested.

The idea of domain testing is to detect these types of faults by carefully selecting data that are on and near the boundary of the path domain. White and Cohen's method requires two ON and one OFF points for a simple linear two-dimensional border. Jeng and Weyuker (1994) presented a simplified domain testing strategy where a linear border in any dimension is tested by one ON and one OFF point.

The design for domain testing can be supported by automatically generating the ON and OFF points. However, generally, it is very costly. A heuristic approach published by Jeng and Forgács (1999) addresses this difficulty.

We can see that domain testing may offer a white-box alternative to boundary value analysis. BVA intends to find particular domain errors. Domains have to be (implicitly or explicitly) described in the specifications. Since a significant portion of bugs are domain errors, we can now understand why this method is very successful (see Reid, 1997).

KEY TAKEAWAYS

Any software can be viewed as a function mapping from an input domain to the output domain. Domain-based testing focuses on the classification aspect of the input and explores incorrect boundaries and computations.

- If domain testing is based on specifications, the interpretation is specific to the specification data-flow. If domain testing is based on code structure, the interpretation is specific to the control flow through the set of predicates defining the domain.

- Determine the valid and the invalid partitions first. Take care with the fault model you want to apply.

- When possible, apply EP, BVA and (in complex cases) domain analysis together using ON, OFF, IN/OUT triple for test selection criterion.

- Every domain boundary has a closure that specifies whether boundary points are or are not in the domain. Examine carefully those boundaries.

- Almost all domain boundaries found in practice are based on linear inequalities. The rest can often be converted to linear inequalities by a suitable linearisation.

- Domain testing is easy for one dimension, more difficult for two and tool-intensive for more than two. Analyse risks, think and use appropriate tools before you attempt to apply domain testing to the general situation.

- Test your tests.

EXERCISES

E5.1 Identify the EPs and one ON, OFF and IN/OUT point for each EP in the following specification.

Payment: for online shopping, the shipment fee is the following. If the final price is below EUR 50, then the shipment is not possible. If the price is below EUR 100, then the shipment fee is 10 per cent of the final price, in the case where the price is below EUR 500 the shipment fee is five per cent, and if the price reaches or exceeds EUR 500, the shipment is free. If the weight surpasses 10 kg, then EUR 1 is paid for each kilogram (where weight is rounded up to the next integer). Finally, if the shipment comes from abroad, the extra fee is doubled except for neighbouring countries, where the extra fee is only 1.5 times more. The price shift is EUR 0.1; the minimum non-zero weight shift is 0.1 kg. No negative or non-numeric cases should be considered.

E5.2 Produce a test design for the specification above.

6   STATE TRANSITION TESTING

WHY IS THIS CHAPTER WORTH READING?

State transition testing models the behaviour of an application or system for different input conditions. Behaviour here means the full expected functionality. In this chapter you will learn the difference between stateless and stateful applications, the main concepts of describing states and transitions and how to apply state transition testing (STT) in test design. You will learn how to use STT on its own, or together with EP and BVA. We introduce two test selection criteria: all-transition-state coverage and all-transition–transition coverage, which are relatively 'cheap' with high defect detection capability.

STATEFUL AND STATELESS SYSTEMS

In the previous chapter, we considered test techniques for **stateless** software. Statelessness means computational independency on any preceding events in a sequence of interactions. A stateless application decouples the computations from the states; it is dependent **only** on the input parameters that are supplied. Simple examples are:

- a search function in a text editor with a given search pattern;
- a sort function with given items to be sorted;
- a website that serves up a static web page (each request is executed independently without any knowledge of the previous requests) and so on.

In these cases, a stateless system/function returns the same value for the same arguments. The computations are replaceable without changing the behaviour of the application.

On the other hand, **stateful** applications have internal states. These internal states need some place for storage (allocated memory, database, etc.). When a stateful function is called several times, then it may behave differently. From the test design point of view, it is more difficult to test since it must be treated together with the preceding events. An operating system is stateful. If you set your screen resolution, next time you switch on your machine, this resolution is preserved.

Printed by Amazon POD

STATES, TRANSITIONS, CONDITIONS

Most complex systems are stateful. Many of them are event-driven (or reactive) in which they wait continuously for some external or internal event (mouse click, time tick, data packet, button press, etc.), and after recognising the event, react to them by performing some computation or by triggering other software components. Such systems can have more than one state and exhibit different behaviours in different states. There can be various transitions between the states.

There are two main ways to represent stateful systems: using state transition diagrams (graphs) or state transition tables. In the first case, the nodes represent states and the edges represent transitions. If the system is in state s1, and an input event/trigger E occurs, then the system changes its state to s2 via the transition t, producing the output action O (see Figure 6.1).

Figure 6.1 State transition diagram. A transition t occurs from state s1 to s2, which is triggered by some input event E and resulting in an output action O

Roughly speaking, a transition consists of a start state + an input event + an action + a next state. In an extended model, the transition and the resulting state may also depend on some conditions. For example, by clicking on the '+' button next to some food to be ordered, if the maximum number of the ordered item has been reached, then nothing happens, while in other cases the ordered amount is incremented. Such **guard conditions** are usually denoted by Event/[**condition**]/Action.

It is important to note that for any given state an event can cause an action (or set of actions), but the same event – from a different state – may cause a different action and transitions to a different state. In practice, an action set may include programming elements, that is code.

There are two common ways to arrange state transition data in a table.

1. All the states are listed on the left side, and the events are enumerated on the top. Each cell in the table represents the next state and the action list of the system after the event has occurred (see Table 6.1).

2. All the originating states are listed on the left side and the resulting states on the top. Each cell in the table represents the event/action list of the system (see Table 6.2).

Table 6.1 State–event notation for a state transition table

	event$_1$	...	event$_N$
start state	next state / action	...	next state / action
s$_1$	s$_i$ / a$_k$	...	–
...	...	...	...
s$_n$	s$_j$ / a$_l$	...	s$_p$ / a$_q$

Table 6.2 State–state notation for a state transition table

	s$_1$	...	s$_n$
states	event / action	...	event / action
s$_1$	e$_i$ / a$_k$	...	–
...	...	...	...
s$_n$	e$_j$ / a$_l$	...	e$_p$ / a$_q$

Note that an action may consist of independent, simple actions. **Valid transitions** are transitions described in the model (see Figure 6.1 and Tables 6.1 and 6.2). However, there can be some **undefined** ('–') **transitions** in both tables. These transitions may mean that the specification is incomplete; therefore the tester should analyse undefined transitions thoroughly.

In practice, incomplete specifications can be handled in two ways: (1) the system does not change its state, and there is no output (the undefined transition meets the specification) or (2) there should be a transition to an error state (each event should be handled). An **invalid transition** refers to the transition that transforms the system into a state that causes the incorrect or undefined behaviour of the system, indicating that such transitions are not feasible. In some cases, it is useful to use a transition **without** any output (e.g. allocating a resource that is not available, or a timeout happens). We call these **null transitions**. Null transitions can have guards (for example, [timer = 3]). Note that undefined or null transitions are not necessarily invalid.

A state transition graph always has a **start** and may have one or more **end nodes**. Each node has to be accessible from a start node, and loops in the graph are allowed.

Mathematically speaking, a state transition diagram (state diagram) for a finite-state machine (FSM, finite automaton) is a directed graph with (S, E, O, δ, q$_0$, F), where S denotes the finite set of states, E denotes the finite set of input symbols (events), O denotes the finite collection of output symbols, $\delta : S \times E \rightarrow S \times O$ (the transition function), q_0 is the start state, and F denotes the set of final states (if used).

A **Mealy Machine** is an FSM whose output depends on the actual state as well as the actual input. A **Moore machine** is an FSM whose output depends on only the actual state. The finite automaton is **deterministic** (DFA) if each transition is uniquely determined by its source state and input symbol, and reading an input symbol is required for each state transition. Otherwise we call it **non-deterministic**. DFAs are used in formal language theory in describing regular languages. The deterministic and the non-deterministic automaton have the same 'power', that is they both recognise the same formal language.

State machine minimisation (reduction) identifies and combines all states that have equivalent behaviour. Two states have equivalent behaviour if, for all input combinations, their outputs are the same and they change to the same or equivalent next states. Hopcroft's algorithm finds the **minimal** deterministic automaton in $O(n \log n)$ time complexity with n states (Hopcroft, 1971). The 'big oh' notation here means the upper bound performance or complexity of the algorithm.

Extended finite-state machine (EFSM) extends the classical Mealy or Moore automaton with input and output parameters, context variables, operations (update functions), timers and predicates defined over the context variables and parameters (Lee and Yannakakis, 1996; Broy et al., 2005). The EFSM architecture consists of three major blocks: (1) the evaluation block evaluates the trigger conditions associated with the transitions, (2) the conventional FSM block computes the next-states and (3) the arithmetic block performs data operations and data movements associated with the transitions.

EXAMPLE: ROBODOG

Imagine a robot dog that barks, wags its tail and sometimes interacts with a robot cat. We will demonstrate the usage of state transition testing with the behaviour analysis of such an item.

RoboDog is an interactive puppy that is able to react to commands and touch. Its functionality has the following specification. When it hears the command 'speak' it starts barking. While barking, the RoboDog waits for the command 'quiet', then stops barking, or waits to get petted. For this latter event, RoboDog stops barking, wags its tail for 5 seconds, then starts barking again. When the silent RoboDog is getting petted, it wags its tail for 5 seconds. When the RoboDog sensors spot a RoboCat, then the RoboDog starts barking. (We do not consider the switching on and off process. During an action the RoboDog does not accept/sense any other events.)

Preconditions: the RoboDog is switched on, all of its sensors are functioning.

States:

- s1: Normal (which is both the initial and the final state);
- s2: Flustered.

Input (events):

- e1: Giving the command 'speak' (speak);
- e2: Giving the command 'quiet' (quiet);
- e3: Sensed petting (pet);
- e4: Spotting a RoboCat (cat).

Output (actions):

- a1: Starts barking (barks);
- a2: Stops barking (quiets);
- a3: Wags tail for 5 seconds (wags tail).

Transitions:

- t1: In the normal state, for the event **speak**, the RoboDog starts barking and goes to the flustered state (speak / barks);
- t2: In the normal state, if the RoboDog is getting petted, it wags its tail for 5 seconds, and remains in a normal state (pet / wags tail);
- t3: In the normal state, if the RoboDog spots a RoboCat, it starts barking and goes to the flustered state (cat / barks);
- t4: In the flustered state, for the event **quiet**, the RoboDog stops barking and goes to the normal state (quiet / quiets);
- t5: In the flustered state, if the RoboDog is getting petted, it stops barking, wags its tail for 5 seconds and starts barking again (and remains in the flustered state) (pet / quiets, wags tail, barks).

The state diagram and the associated state table are in Figure 6.2 and Table 6.3, respectively.

The state transition table (Table 6.3) shows some undefined transitions. If the RoboDog barks (the automaton is in state s2), the command 'speak' or spotting a RoboCat have nothing to activate. If the RoboDog is in a normal state, the command 'quiet' has no effect either. We extend the state machine with null transitions (Table 6.4).

Figure 6.2 State diagram for the 'RoboDog' example

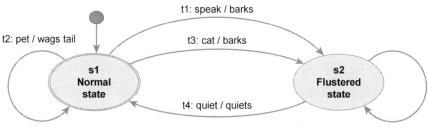

Table 6.3 State–event notation for the 'RoboDog' example with undefined transitions

	input: speak	input: quiet	input: pet	input: cat
start state	end state / action	end state / action	end state / action	end state / action
normal	flustered / barks	–	normal / wags tail	flustered / barks
flustered	–	normal / quiets	flustered / quiets, wags tail, barks	–

Table 6.4 State–event notation for the 'RoboDog' example

	input: speak	input: quiet	input: pet	input: cat
start state	end state / action	end state / action	end state / action	end state / action
normal	flustered / barks	normal	normal / wags tail	flustered / barks
flustered	flustered	normal / quiets	flustered / quiets, wags tail, barks	flustered

Let's alter the RoboDog specification with the following:

EXAMPLE: ROBODOG (EXTENSION)

When the RoboDog barks and is getting petted, it stops barking, wags its tail for 5 seconds and starts barking again, as before. **However, after the third time petting the flustered RoboDog, it stops barking, wags its tail for 5 seconds and then goes quiet.**

The state table changes (as shown in Table 6.5) where there are new actions, namely

- a4: PettingNo is set to zero (:= 0), (setzero);
- a5: Increments PettingNo (incr).

Table 6.5 State–event notation for the extended 'RoboDog' example

start state	input: speak	input: quiet	input: pet	input: cat
	end state / action	end state / action	end state / action	end state / action
Normal	flustered / barks, setzero	normal	normal / wags tail	flustered / barks, setzero
Flustered	flustered	normal / quiets	flustered / [PettingNo < 3] / incr, quiets, wags tail, barks, normal / [PettingNo = 3] / quiets, wags tail	flustered

We note that PettingNo should be global for the system and initiated to zero at the beginning (precondition). See the resulting state diagram (Figure 6.3).

Figure 6.3 State diagram for the extended 'RoboDog' example

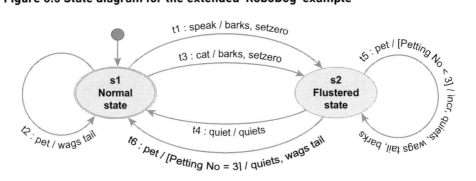

Altogether we have two states, four events and five possible actions. Observe that the guard conditions for the petting number cover the whole domain, that is $0 \leq$ PettingNo < 3 or PettingNo $= 3$; other values are not possible.

VALIDATE YOUR STATE TRANSITION GRAPH

When the state transition graph (or table) has been created the **test designer must carefully analyse and validate it.**

The following guidelines help in analysing the completeness and consistency of the state transition graph model.

- State, event and action names must be unambiguous and meaningful in the context.
- There must be an initial state and at least one final state in the automaton. If the latter does not exist, the termination condition should be made explicit.
- Every state must be reachable from the initial state (not necessarily in one step).
- Every state shall have at least one ingoing and one outgoing transition except the initial and the final states. (Anther exception can be an 'error collector' node. If this rule is violated, the tester has to know why.)
- Every defined event and action shall come up in at least one transition.
- The actions cannot influence the behaviour of the state machine; their implementation does not contain 'teleports'.
- The state machine shall be complete, that is,

  - All state/event pairs have a transition. If not, check the specification for correctness. Implicitly given completeness is allowed (null transitions).
  - The error (exception) handling shall be explicitly or implicitly given.

- The state machine should be minimal (with a minimal number of states) or well hierarchised. Sometimes the latter is more important if it supports human readability better.

Practically speaking:

- Naming conventions are important. For example, a name for an action should refer to an action to be performed (in 'ing' form, reading, writing, updating, petting, etc.).
- When there is no initial state then it is not clear when to start.
- When a state is not reachable, then something is missing and so on.

When we test a stateful system (system under test, SUT), sometimes it is desirable to fulfil certain properties:

- Status messages. The tester wants to ask the implementation of the SUT's current state (without changing its state).
- Reset capability. The tester wants to bring the SUT to the initial state. In automated test execution after a blocking event, it can be useful in continuing the testing. Then, the reset capability can be practical.
- Set-state capability. The tester wants to bring the SUT to any given state.

All of these properties can be present reliably or unreliably. The following checklist extends the previous guidelines:

- Completely specified? The state transition graph is complete if no states, transitions, events and actions are missing.
- Deterministic or non-deterministic? In a given state, the system returns similar or different results for the same input.
- Strongly connected? All nodes are reachable from each node.
- Reduced or minimal? The same behaviour exists with a smaller state machine.
- Reliable/unreliable reset? Or reset capability does not exist?
- Reliable/unreliable status message? Or status message capability does not exist?
- Reliable/unreliable set-state? Or set-state capability does not exist?

Satisfying a test selection criterion, we shall cover the nodes/edges/paths of the state transition graph. Also we have to consider the semantics of the graph (the specification) as well. For example, in the extended RoboDog example, the transition t6 can happen only after petting twice the flustered RoboDog.

There are different fault models available to the stateful systems.

Validating the state machine against control faults

When testing an implementation against a state machine, the following typical control faults should be examined.

- **Missing transition** (nothing happens as a consequence of an event). In the RoboDog example, if t2 (if the RoboDog is getting petted, it wags its tail for 5 seconds, and remains in a normal state) is missing, then petting the RoboDog has no consequence in the normal state (there is no tail wagging).
- **Extra transition**. The extra transition may mean incorrect behaviour.
- **Incorrect transition** (the resulting state is incorrect). For example, if t2 were incorrect (t2 goes from s1 to s2), then by petting the RoboDog two times it would behave incorrectly (the RoboDog starts barking unexpectedly).
- **Missing event**. The system is unable to handle some events.
- **Extra event**. The implementation accepts undefined events. Avoiding extra events is especially important for analysing security or safety criteria (trap doors).
- **Incorrect event**. The system behaves incorrectly. For example, giving the command 'quiet' to the RoboDog in the normal state it starts barking (in transition t1 the event 'speak' has been changed to 'quiet').
- **Missing, extra or incorrect action**. As a result of a transition, nothing or inappropriate actions happen. For example, the RoboDog begins to wag its tail for the command 'speak'.
- **Missing, extra or incorrect state**. These kinds of faults can be interpreted together with transition faults belonging to that state.

TEST SELECTION CRITERIA FOR STATE TRANSITION TESTING

State transition testing is measured mainly for **valid transitions**. There are many different test selection criteria regarding the transition-based method. First, we explain only the methods, then we show their thoroughness.

Test selection criteria for transition-based models

The examples in this subsection come from Figure 6.2, and we always aim to achieve full (100 per cent) coverage. We use the usual 'big oh' notation for describing the time complexities for calculating the tests.

Classical criteria
The following criteria are related to the states, events and transition sequences:

- **All-states criterion**, in which each state is visited at least once by some test case in the test suite.
  - The transition sequence t1–t4 is appropriate. The test sequence can be [speak, quiet].
  - Complexity: *O(number of states).*
- **All-events criterion**, in which each event of the state machine is included in the test suite (all events are part of at least one test case).
  - The test can be [cat, quiet, pet, speak].
  - Complexity: *O(number of events).*
- **All-actions criterion**, in which each action is executed at least once.
  - The test [speak, quiet, pet] results in the RoboDog barking, quieting and wagging its tail for 5 seconds.
  - Complexity: *O(number of actions).*
- **All-transitions criterion**, in which every transition of the model is traversed at least once (called Chow's zero-switch coverage) (Chow, 1978). It implies (subsumes) all-events, all-states and all-actions criteria.
  - The transition sequence t1-t5-t4-t3-t4-t2 is appropriate, for which the test is [speak, pet, quiet, cat, quiet, pet].
  - Complexity: *O(number of transitions).*

    Considering the extended RoboDog example (Figure 6.3), we need a different test for the same criterion: [pet, cat, quiet, speak, pet, pet, pet]. Here we used an EFSM, hence, the time complexity depends on the maximal boundary values of the guard condition variables as well.

- **All-transition-pairs criterion** (called Chow's one-switch coverage), in which every pair of adjacent transitions are traversed at least once.
  - The following two transition sequences satisfy the criteria: t2-t2-t1-t4-t1-t5-t4-t3-t5-t4 and t3-t4-t2-t3-t4, for which the tests are {[pet, pet, speak, quiet, speak, pet, quiet, cat, pet, quiet], [cat, quiet, pet, cat, quiet]}.

- Complexity: $O(transitions^2)$.

- **All-n-transitions criterion** (called Chow's n-switch coverage), in which every transition sequence generated by n+1 consecutive events is exercised at least once. The all-n-transitions criterion implies (subsumes) all-(n-1)-transitions criteria.

  - Complexity: $O(transitions^{n+1})$. Observe that this is exponential in the number of transitions.

    Besides the complexity, there is another shortcoming of this criterion. Namely, it produces too many infeasible paths. It is important to note that in practice most of the faults regarding consecutive states in a state machine are mainly 1-switch or 2-switch faults; 3 or more switch faults are very rare.

- **All configurations criterion**, in which parallel systems are modelled in a way that every configuration is visited at least once. A configuration is a 'snapshot' of the active states of the parallel processes. If no parallelism exists, then it is equivalent to the all-states coverage.

The following criteria are related to traversing the possible loops:

- **All loop-free paths criterion**, in which every loop-free path is traversed at least once.

  - Complexity: $O(states \times log(transitions))$ (spanning tree searching).

- **All-round-trip paths criterion**. We need some definitions: a **simple path** is a path in which any node cannot appear more than once except maybe the starting and the ending nodes. A **prime path** is a simple path that does not appear as a sub-path of any other simple path. A **round-trip path** is a prime path of non-zero length that starts and ends with the same node. A complete round-trip coverage means that every round-trip path for each reachable node should be taken.

- **All-one-loop paths criterion**, in which all loop-free paths are traversed plus all the paths that loop once.

- **All-path criterion**. Every path should be traversed in the state diagram at least once. Similar to exhaustive testing, in general, it is impossible to satisfy.

The following is not really a criterion, but it is a useful non-deterministic technique for traversing a graph.

- **Random walking**. A random walk is a trajectory that consists of successive random steps in the graph model. For more details see the GraphWalker section in Chapter 13.

We have to discuss the 'minimality' of the constructed sets. Before optimising the test sets, a target function should first be determined. This can be the expected running time, some restrictions on the number of the test cases, the number of transitions in a test case, the average length of the tests and so on. This optimisation can be hard, as with pairwise testing, whose task is nondeterministic polynomial (NP)-complete (Lei and Tai, 1998). In practice, however, it is enough to approach close to the optimum value.

Please do not underestimate the importance of the random walk coverage. Many test design automation tools use this approach since for small–medium state transition graphs it works effectively (the GraphWalker section in Chapter 13). For simpler state diagrams the test cases can even be created manually.

All-transition-state and all-transition–transition criteria

Unfortunately, simple criteria are sometimes weak; strong criteria may lead to exponential explosion. The main question is as follows: Is there any criterion between them that is both reliable and manageable? Here we introduce two criteria, which we think of as both reliable and 'cheap enough' to use in practice.

The rationale behind these criteria is the following:

1. When there is a faulty computation in an action through a transition t, and the erroneous data is used later at a transition belonging to the state s, then the program fails. Therefore, it is reasonable to test each transition-state pair (t, s).

2. Let's assume that erroneous data is defined in a transition; however, the same data is defined correctly in another transition t. If a test case traverses t, avoids the other one, and is used later at an action belonging to s, then the bug remains undetected. Therefore, we shall omit the path from t to s, and we will denote these paths by (!t, s).

3. Now let's assume that there is a guard condition related to a transition t. The guard condition determines a boundary value and we shall test this boundary with ON and OFF points by traversing the transition t as many times as is needed. For example, in our TVM we can buy a maximum of 10 tickets. We shall test the boundary point by trying to traverse the transition beyond the limit, that is 11 times.

With these three requirements the first test selection criterion is the following:

ALL-TRANSITION-STATE CRITERION

For a given transition t let's denote the set of all reachable states by RS(t) for which there is a path via the transition t to any element of RS(t). Then, satisfying the criterion means that

1. The test set must cover at least one path via t to S for all transition t and S $\in$ RS(t),

2. There is at least one path to all S $\in$ RS(t) that does not include the transition t (if possible),

3. When there is a boundary value guard condition for a transition t in path P then P should be extended in a way that the number of traversing t reaches the boundary value of that guard condition (if feasible). Informally, the given transition should be traversed multiple times, till the boundary value of the guard condition is reached.

Note that reachability mainly means available paths in the state transition graph, but may mean feasibility (executability) in the case of test generation. Note as well that satisfying the all-transition-state criterion also satisfies the all-transitions criterion.

Now let's consider our RoboDog example and investigate the test (steps) to satisfy this criterion. The graph is strongly connected; moreover, by deleting any transition except t4, it remains strongly connected. Hence, the sequence

s1-t2-s1-t1-s2-t5-s2-t4-s1-t3-s2-t4-s1

covers the (t, s) paths for all transition t and s ∈ RS(t), and the sequences

s1-t1-s2-t4-s1, s1-t3-s2-t4-s1

cover the (!t, s) paths. The appropriate test set is

{[pet, speak, pet, quiet, cat, quiet], [speak, quiet], [cat, quiet]}.

Sometimes even this test selection criterion is weak. For a stronger criterion, we have to consider each (t, t') pairs. The related definition is the following:

ALL-TRANSITION–TRANSITION CRITERION

For a given transition t let's denote the set of all reachable transitions from t by RT(t) for which there is a path via the transition t to any element of RT(t). In the case of looping, t ∈ RT(t). Then, the coverage means that

1. The test set must cover at least one path via t to t' for all transition t and t' ∈ RT(t),

2. There is at least one path to all t' ∈ RT(t) that does not include the transition t (if possible),

3. When there is a guard condition for transition t in path P then the path should be extended in a way that the number of traversing t reaches the boundary value of that guard condition (if feasible).

Complexity: without the third condition, the number of test cases is quadratic in the worst case since we shall cover pairs of transitions. The existence of boundaries may increase the complexity proportionally to their maximal value.

How can we satisfy this stronger criterion for the extended RoboDog? Since the state transition graph of the RoboDog is Eulerian, that is we start from s and traversing each edge only once we can go back to s, the path

s1-t1-s2-t4-s1-t2-s1-t3-s2-t5-s2-t4-s1-t2-s1-t1-s2-t4-s1-t3-s2-t5-s2-t4-s1

satisfies the first criterion, and partly the second, that is

(!t1, t1), (!t2, t1), (!t3, t1), (!t4, t1), (!t5, t1), (!t2, t4), (!t3, t4), (!t4, t4), (!t5, t4), (!t2, t2), (!t3, t2), (!t5, t2), (!t3, t3), (!t5, t3), (!t5, t5).

The rest can be satisfied with the paths

s1-t2-s1-t3-s2-t4-s1-t1-s2-t4-s1, s1-t3-s2-t5-s2-t4-s1 and s1-t1-s2-t5-s2-t4-s1

since in these cases the following pairs are valid:

(!t1, t2), (!t4, t2), (!t4, t3), (!t1, t3), (!t2, t3), (!t1, t4), (!t1, t5), (!t2, t5), (!t4, t5), (!t3, t5).

The test set is

{[speak, quiet, pet, cat, pet, quiet, pet, speak, quiet, cat, pet, quiet], [pet, cat, quiet, speak, quiet], [cat, pet, quiet], [speak, pet, quiet]}.

Recall that the Chow coverage test set becomes exponentially larger with growing n. We note that the all-transition-state and the all-transition–transition criteria measures may serve as a bridge between the linearity and the exponentiality. These two criteria aim at examining defects that cannot be unfolded by Chow's switching criteria, that is when the defects are 'far away' from each other. The boundary value guard is related to boundary value analysis.

Thoroughness of the criteria

Recall that the extended RoboDog state transition graph contains two states, four events, and six transitions. The extra precondition of this state transition diagram is that the global variable PettingNo is defined as zero. Let's suppose that the behaviour shown in Figure 6.4 has been implemented.

There are three changes (faults) compared to the specified behaviour. In transition t3 there is a missing initialisation, and instead of three, after the fourth time petting, the flustered RoboDog stops barking, wags its tail and goes quiet (these faults are in the transitions t5 and t6). Of course, the black-box tester does not know about this. Suppose that the tester designs the test cases for satisfying the all-states, all-events, all-actions, all-transitions criteria according to the model shown in Figure 6.3.

Figure 6.4 Programmed behaviour of the 'RoboDog'. The difference from the specified behaviour is underlined

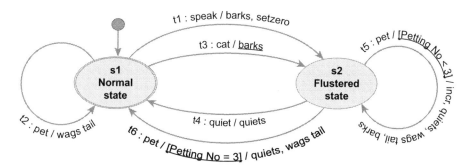

103

Table 6.6 shows a simple short test. The test does not show any faults. The faults are in combination, that is the missing initialisation causes RoboDog to quiet at step 8. OK, we think, very good, let's check the 1-switch criterion by Chow. The clever tester observes that the transition pairs t1–t6 and t3–t6 are impossible (because of the specification), therefore they omit them from the test design. To spare time, the tester divides the previous test into two parts: ShortTest = [t2, ShorterTest]. Then, their result is the following test:

Table 6.6 Short test for the extended 'RoboDog' example

Name: ShortTest

Steps	1	2	3	4	5	6	7	8
Events	pet	speak	pet	quiet	cat	pet	pet	pet
Trans. no.	t2	t1	t5	t4	t3	t5	t5	t6
States (from/to)	s1/s1	s1/s2	s2/s2	s2/s1	s1/s2	s2/s2	s2/s2	s2/s1
Expected result	wags tail for 5 sec.	barks	quiets, wags his tail for 5 sec., barks again	quiets	barks	quiets, wags his tail for 5 sec., barks again	quiets, wags his tail for 5 sec., barks again	quiets, wags his tail for 5 sec.
Observed result	wags tail for 5 sec.	barks	quiets, wags his tail for 5 sec., barks again	quiets	barks	quiets, wags his tail for 5 sec., barks again	quiets, wags his tail for 5 sec., barks again	quiets, wags his tail for 5 sec.

{[ShortTest-ShorterTest-t3-t4], [t2-t3-t4-t1-t4-t2], [ShorterTest-t2]}.

It is easy to check that this test set fulfils the 1-switch coverage criteria, but does not find the faults. The reason is that we have a 2-switch fault, hence, only the 2-switch criteria would be able to find it.

Kuhn et al. (2008) determined that up to 97 per cent of software faults can be detected by at most two variables interacting. These criteria consider pairs, which influence each other. Chow's switch coverage considers only adjacent transitions, but erroneous influence may come from remote transitions as well. The all-transition-state criterion considers arbitrary (transition, state) pairs; the all-transition–transition criterion arbitrary (transition, transition) pairs. The method could be extended to triples, but pairs are usually enough.

Let's summarise why the proposed criterion is useful. Regarding EFSMs, in some cases, guard condition variable assignments (initialisations) are in the wrong places. To detect this problem, we should cover an execution path excluding a transition with this assignment. Traversing every (!t, s) or (!t1, t2) will reveal the bug. Considering the last criterion, guard condition boundaries should be handled with boundary value analysis techniques.

EXAMPLE: COLLATZ CONJECTURE

Finite-state machines are used to model complex logic in dynamic systems, such as automatic transmissions, robotic systems and mobile phones. This complex logic includes operations like scheduling tasks, supervising how to switch between different modes of operation, recovery logic and so on.

The following example presents complex logic with elementary operations. We show how to model it with a state transition graph, and we analyse some loop-related test selection criteria.

EXAMPLE: COLLATZ

The Collatz conjecture concerns a sequence in number theory defined as follows: starting with any positive integer n, each term is obtained from the previous term as follows: if the previous term is even, the next term is half of the previous term. If the previous term is odd, the next term is 3 times the previous term plus 1. The conjecture is that no matter what the value of n is, the sequence will always reach 1. We checked the validity of the conjecture for 2, 3, 4, 5, by hand, and for those cases the computation terminates. We model the computations with a state machine.

Preconditions: there is a global integer variable n, initially set to zero. The variable n can arbitrarily be large. The input is a positive integer.

States:

- s1: Initial state;
- s2: Even state;
- s3: Odd state;
- s4: Final state.

Input (event):

- e1: Getting the input;
- e2: Changing the value of n.

Output (action):

- Result: print('the process terminates').

Transitions:

- t1: e1 / [input is odd] / n := input;
- t2: e2 / [n = 1 OR n = 3 OR n = 5] / Result;
- t3: e1 / [input is even] / n := input;
- t4: e2 / [n = 2 OR n = 4] / Result;
- t5: e2 / [n ≠ 1 AND n ≠ 3 AND n ≠ 5] / n := 3n + 1;
- t6: e2 / [n ≠ 2 AND n ≠ 4 AND n := n/2 is odd] / <>;
- t7: e2 / [n ≠ 2 AND n ≠ 4 AND n := n/2 is even] / <>.

The Collatz machine is in Figure 6.5.

Figure 6.5 Collatz machine

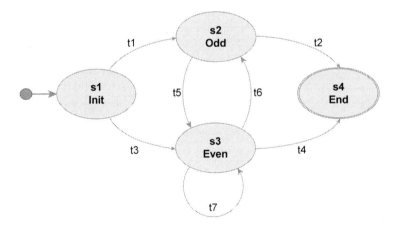

Let's check the functioning. When the input is 1, 3 or 5 the processing goes through s1-t1-s2-t2 and the output is a message about termination. When the input is 2 or 4, the processing is via s1-t3-s3-t4 and there is a termination message again. Let the input be the magic number 42. Then the processing is the following: s1-t3(n = 42)-s3-t6 (n = 21)-s2-t5(n = 64)-s3-t7(n = 32)-s3-t7(n = 16)-s3-t7(n = 8)-s3-t7(n = 4)-s3-t4 and the output is the termination message. The termination was checked for integers up to 87×2^{60} by Roosendaal (2018).

The test data 2 (traversing t3-t4) and 3 (traversing t1-t2) traverses **all** loop-free paths since t1-t5-t4 and t3-t6-t2 are impossible to get around without looping. Let's analyse the all-round-trip paths criterion. The only simple paths in the graph are t1-t2, t3-t4, t3-t6-t2 and t1-t5-t4. Hence, the tests for this criterion are identical to the all-loop-free paths tests. To get tests for the all-one-loop path criterion, we have to add one loop for the possible loop-free paths. The transition sequence t3-t7-t4 is reliable; the test data is (for example) 8. The sequence t3-t6-t5-t4 is unreliable. The sequence t3-t7-t6-t2 is reliable with test data = 6. The sequence t1-t5-t7-t4 is unreliable as well as the sequence t1-t5-t6-t2.

WHEN MULTIPLE TECHNIQUES ARE USED TOGETHER

This may be a surprise, but it's difficult to find any description or examples on how to apply more test design techniques together. Here is a short introduction where we demonstrate using multiple techniques through our example. Usually we combine two techniques, therefore we will demonstrate this case; however you can easily extend it.

- Make the test design for the two techniques separately.
- Select the one that has more test cases.
- Map the test cases of the other technique to these test cases.
- If some test cases cannot be mapped, try to refactor the test cases for better mapping.
- Map the refactored test cases again.
- Validate the test cases.

In this section we consider a specific, simplified part of the specification 'Two lifts in a 10-storey building' described in Chapter 4. The slightly reduced specification can be tested independently from the other parts. The most important requirement in this case says that all the guests should be served (sooner or later). For example, if the lift goes down from the upper floor, and the guest – who called it first – is standing on the fifth floor, but after a few seconds a family calls the lift at the sixth floor, then the lift may become full, and the guest at five cannot enter. The specification guarantees that a similar situation cannot happen (except when the lifts never become empty, but this case is unrealistic).

I have frequently noticed when checking out from a hotel with my luggage that some lift specifications consider cost-effectiveness more important than guests. For instance, the lifts went first to the guests on the higher floors, then collected the other guests on their way down. Unfortunately, because of the huge morning traffic, the lifts almost always became full at the higher levels, and I could not enter. After 2–3 attempts I changed my mind and took the stairs.

Here we have omitted some of the steps in the original specification (see Chapter 4).

F-CMC-1 If both lifts are vacant and a user requests one, then the closer lift will always start in the caller's direction. In the case of equality, Lift1 is chosen.

F-CMC-2 If one of the lifts is vacant and the other one is moving, then the vacant one starts for the requester.

F-CMC-3 When no lift is available then the user request is scheduled.

F-CMC-4 When a lift becomes vacant, the oldest pending request must be handled first.

F-CMC-5 The serving order depends on the location of the lifts, on their moving direction and on their request queues.

F-CMC-6 The non-empty lift stops for users when an up/down call is received from them while the lift is moving up/down as well and approaching the user.

F-CMC-7 The empty lift goes for the guest first in the queue and does not stop for other guests.

Here we do not consider priorities.

This is a good example as different test design techniques are applied together. Clearly, the model is reactive since it contains states such as vacant, moving or standing lifts (waiting for the guests to leave and/or enter).

For this example, we show you step by step how to design test cases involving STT, EP and BVA together. The first step is to create the state transition diagram.

Preconditions: the starting state is when both lifts are vacant.

States:

- s1: Lift1, Lift2 vacant;
- s2: Only Lift1 is vacant;
- s3: Only Lift2 is vacant;
- s4: Lift1 is moving;
- s5: Lift2 is moving;
- s6: Lift1 is standing;
- s7: Lift2 is standing.

Inputs (event)

- e1: Guest calls from outside the cabin (up/down);
- e2: Guest requests from inside the cabin in Lift1 (pushing target level number);
- e3: Guest requests from inside the cabin in Lift2 (pushing target level number);
- e4: Lift1 weight control notices that all guests leave it (empty lift signal);
- e5: Lift2 weight control notices that all guests leave it (empty lift signal).

Note that if not all the guests leave a lift, then there shall be a guest request. Here we do not consider the non-functional requirement when a guest is not able to get out or press a button. Remember an outside guest **calls** a lift; a guest inside the cabin **requests** the lift to stop at a chosen floor.

Outputs:

- o1: Lift1 starts according to the inside request, or if it is empty, then to the floor of the oldest pending guest;
- o2: Lift2 starts according to the inside request, or if it is empty, then to the floor of the oldest pending guest;
- o3: Lift1 stops and opens door, the queue of the pending callers is updated, if needed;
- o4: Lift2 stops, opens door, the queue of the pending callers is updated, if needed;
- o5: Lift1 opens door, the queue of the pending callers is updated, if needed;
- o6: Lift2 opens door, the queue of the pending callers is updated, if needed.

Transitions:

- When Lift1 and Lift2 are vacant, and there is an outside guest call (first in the queue) closer or equal to Lift1,
  - **t1**: Lift1 serves the guest by moving for them if the caller and Lift1 are on different levels (o1),
  - **t2**: Lift1 serves the guest by opening its door if they are at the same level (o5).

  Lift2 remains vacant in both cases.

- When Lift1 and Lift2 are vacant, and there is an outside guest call (first in the queue) closer to Lift2, then
  - **t11**: Lift2 serves the guest by moving for them if they are on different levels (o2), Lift1 remains vacant.
- **t3**: When Lift1 is approaching the next floor and there is an acceptable guest call then the lift stops and opens door (o3),
- **t13**: When Lift2 is approaching the next floor and there is an acceptable guest call in the request database, then the lift stops and opens door (o4),

- **t4**: When Lift1 is approaching the next floor and there is a guest request to that floor, the lift stops and opens door (o3),
- **t14**: When Lift2 is approaching the next floor and there is a guest request to that floor, the lift stops and opens door (o4),
- **t5**: When (the non-empty) Lift1 is standing and there is a guest request in it, then Lift1 starts and goes towards the requested floor (o1),
- **t15**: When (the non-empty) Lift2 is standing and there is a guest request in it, then Lift2 starts and goes towards the requested floor (o2),
- **t6**: When all guests leave Lift1 (no guest request remains), it is vacant,
- **t16**: When all guests leave Lift2 (no guest request remains), it is vacant,
- When only Lift1 is vacant, and there is an outside guest call non-acceptable for Lift2, then
  - **t7**: Lift1 serves the guest by moving for them if the caller and Lift1 are on different levels (o1),
  - **t8**: Lift1 serves the guest by opening its door if they are on the same level (o5),
- When only Lift2 is vacant, and there is an outside guest call non-acceptable for Lift1, then
  - **t17**: Lift2 serves the guest by moving for them if the caller and Lift2 are on different levels (o2),
  - **t18**: Lift2 serves the guest by opening its door if they are on the same level (o6),
- **t9**: When Lift1 is vacant, and Lift2 becomes empty, Lift1, Lift2 are vacant,
- **t19**: When Lift2 is vacant, and Lift1 becomes empty, Lift1, Lift2 are vacant.

Note that 'acceptable call' means that:

- If the lift is non-empty then:

  (1) a guest (outside the cabin) pushed UP/DOWN at a level; and

  (2) the lift is moving towards the guest.

- If the lift is empty then the only acceptable call is the first pending call.

The system is concurrent since 'it includes a number of execution flows that can progress simultaneously, and that interact with each other' (Bianchi et al., 2017). Extension of state diagrams are Harel (and Unified Modelling Language (UML)) statecharts (see the 'Theoretical background' section later in this chapter). Concurrency in statecharts can be shown explicitly using 'fork' and 'join'. A fork is represented by a bar with more outgoing arrows; a join is represented by a bar with more incoming arrows.

Here we have two parallel sub-systems: one for Lift1 and the other for Lift2. For simplicity we cut the state transition diagram into two parts (Lift1 and Lift2 are L1 and L2, respectively, see Figures 6.6a and 6.6b). The figures are almost symmetric (t2 does not have a 'pair').

Figure 6.6a State transition graph for 'Two lifts in a 10-storey building' – Lift1

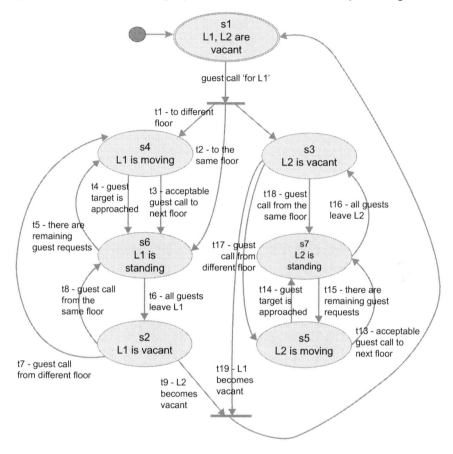

Let's consider some examples.

- Lift1 is non-empty and moving upwards approaching floor 3. Lift2 is vacant. The first pending call is upwards at floor 5. Lift2 will start.

- Lift1 is non-empty and moving upwards approaching floor 3, Lift2 is not vacant and moving down from floor 9. The first pending call is up at floor 5, the second is down at floor 3 and the third is up at floor 4. Lift1 will stop at floor 4, then at floor 5 but it will not stop at floor 3. Lift2 will stop at floor 3.

Up to now we have not considered testing concurrent systems. There are several test selection criteria for concurrent systems (Bianchi et al., 2017). Here we consider a very simple criterion that requires all states to be held in parallel. For example, if Lift1 is moving, then Lift2 shall (1) stand (2) move, (3) remain vacant.

Figure 6.6b State transition graph for 'Two lifts in a 10-storey building' – Lift2

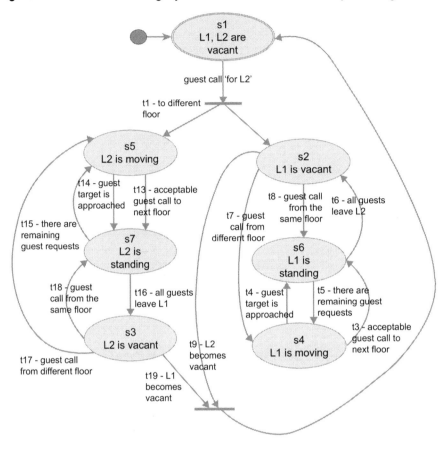

We can extend the all-state-transition criterion for concurrent systems in a way that each (transition, state) pair is executed for all concurrent execution flows.

According to this criterion we have the following test steps for Figure 6.6a, and remember that the two sub-diagrams are similar as L1 → L2 and L2 → L1.

The test path for the concurrent case (ST-Tpath2) is described by two parallel sequences containing the states such as *s6 L1 is standing* and transitions such as *t5 – there are remaining guest requests.*

ST-Tpath1: simple, see Table 6.7.

ST-Tpath2: both lifts are vacant at the beginning and the end of this test path, see Table 6.8.

Table 6.7 State transition test for 'Two lifts in a 10-storey building', ST-Tpath1

s1 L1, L2 are vacant
t1 – to different floor
s4 L1 is moving
t4 – guest target is approached
s6 L1 is standing
t5 – there are remaining guest requests
s4 L1 is moving
t4 – guest target is approached
s6 L1 is standing
t6 – all guests leave L1
s1 L1, L2 are vacant

Table 6.8 State transition test for 'Two lifts in a 10-storey building', ST-Tpath2

Lift1	Lift2
s1 L1, L2 are vacant	
t1 – to different floor	
s4 L1 is moving	**s3 L2 vacant**
t3 – acceptable guest call to next floor	
s6 L1 is standing	
t5 – there are remaining guest requests	
s4 L1 is moving	
t3 – acceptable guest call to the next floor	
s6 L1 is standing	
t5 – there are remaining guest requests	
s4 L1 is moving	
t4 – guest target is approached	*t18 – guest call from the same floor*
s6 L1 is standing	s7 L2 is standing
t6 – all guests leave L1	*t15 – there are remaining guest requests*

(Continued)

Table 6.8 (Continued)

Lift1	Lift2
s2 L1 is vacant	s5 L2 is moving
	t14 – guest target is approached
t7 – guest call from different floor	s7 L2 is standing
s4 L1 is moving	*t16 – all guests leave L2*
t3 – acceptable guest call to next floor	**s3 L2 vacant**
s6 L1 is standing	
t5 – there are remaining guest requests	*t17 – guest call from different floor*
s4 L1 is moving	s5 L2 is moving
t4 – guest target is approached	*t13 – acceptable guest call to next floor*
s6 L1 is standing	s7 L2 is standing
t6 – all guests leave L1	*t15 – there are remaining guest requests*
s2 L1 is vacant	s5 L1 is moving
	t13 – acceptable guest call to the next floor
	s7 L2 is standing
	t15 – there are remaining guest requests
t8 – guest call from the same floor	s5 L2 is moving
s6 L1 is standing	*t14 – guest target is approached*
t5 – there are remaining guest requests	s7 L2 is standing
s4 L1 is moving	*t16 – all guests leave L1*
t4 – guest target is approached	**s3 L2 is vacant**
s6 L1 is standing	
t6 – all guests leave L1	
s2 L1 vacant	*t19 – L1 becomes vacant*
t9 – L2 becomes vacant	
s1 L1, L2 are vacant	

Here, the left column contains the movement of Lift1 (L1) and the right one contains the movement of Lift2 (L2). Lift1 is vacant four times (1) at the beginning, (4) at the end and (2), (3) to test guest calls from different floors (2), and a guest call from the same floor (3). Lift2 is vacant three times (1) for testing guest calls from the same floor, (2) testing a guest call from different floors and (3) when both lifts become vacant. The vacancies happen at different times, hence the concurrent test selection criterion is satisfied.

We can see that except for *t2*, all the transitions are covered. We traverse ST-Tpath2, then ST-Tpath4 in a similar way, which result in the 'traditional' all-state transition criterion being satisfied. This is because in traversing ST-Tpath4, all the states are covered after *t2* and all other transitions in ST-Tpath2. We have the 4th test path ST-Tpath3, which is symmetric with ST-Tpath1.

Now let's consider the EP and BVA part. We have two lifts, Lift1 and Lift2. The third 'participant' is the guest calling them. There are several different locations of this {Lift1, Lift2, guest} triple. There are several elements of this triple; however, we can classify them. For example, the cases (Lift1=2, Lift2=9, guest=3) are similar to (Lift1=2, Lift2=8, guest=4) as in both cases Lift1 shall start. In this way the elements in the triple can be classified into four EPs:

EP1: Guest is in between the lifts and Lift1 is not further than Lift2 from the guest.

EP2: Lift1 is between the guest and Lift2 (including the case when Lift1 and Lift2 are on the same level) – obviously, Lift1 is not further.

EP3: Guest is in between the lifts and Lift2 is closer.

EP4: Lift2 is between the guest and Lift1 – obviously, Lift2 is closer.

Let's extend the EPs with boundary values. Though three points are required for each EP, because of overlap, eight test cases are enough. The test inputs are shown in Table 6.9.

Table 6.9 BVA test input for 'Two lifts in a 10-storey building', ST-Tpath1

	ON	OFF	IN
EP1	Lift1 – 1, Lift2 – 9, guest – 5	Lift1 – 1, Lift2 – 8, guest – 5	Lift1 – 1, Lift2 – 9, guest – 2
EP2	Lift1 – 1, Lift2 – 8, guest – 5	Lift1 – 1, Lift2 – 9, guest – 5	Lift1 – 1, Lift2 – 9, guest – 8
EP3	Lift1 – 1, Lift2 – 1, guest – 7	Lift1 – 1, Lift2 – 2, guest – 7	Lift1 – 6, Lift2 – 1, guest – 8
EP4	Lift1 – 1, Lift2 – 2, guest – 7	Lift1 – 1, Lift2 – 1, guest – 7	Lift1 – 1, Lift2 – 6, guest – 7

There are also equivalence partitions related to the guests: whether they can be picked up or not by a moving lift. These EPs shall be tested in a way that if a guest cannot be picked up, then the other lift shall start. There are other EPs to test whether the moving lift stops or the other will start:

> EP11: Non-empty Lift1 is approaching up/down to the guest who pushed up/down – Lift1 stops.

> EP12: Non-empty Lift1 is approaching up/down to the guest who pushed up/down – vacant Lift2 starts.

> EP13: Non-empty Lift1 is moving up/down, the guest pushed up/down, but Lift1 is moving away from this guest – vacant Lift2 starts.

> EP14: Lift1 is empty and approaching the guest who first called it. Another guest called a lift – Lift2 starts.

> EP15: Non-empty Lift2 is approaching up/down to the guest who pushed up/down – Lift2 stops.

> EP16: Non-empty Lift2 is approaching up/down to the guest who pushed up/down – vacant Lift1 starts.

> EP17: Non-empty Lift2 is moving up/down, the guest pushed up/down, but Lift2 is moving away from this guest – vacant Lift1 starts.

> EP18: Lift2 is empty and approaching the guest who first called it. Another guest calls a lift – Lift1 starts.

Note that 'approaching' floor x means moving to floor x and possibly standing between moving to y and moving from y to x. We do not consider the EPs when one lift is vacant, and the guest is on the same or different level. This is because we have covered these cases by covering the related transitions.

The next step is to combine the test design techniques. Here we start from STT and map a BVA test to it. We design our first test case based on ST-Tpath2 (see Table 6.10). Here the events occurring at a state are to the right of the state, for example Lift1 is standing at (floor) 7 when Guest1 pushes (floor) 1.

Table 6.10 BVA test input for 'Two lifts in a 10-storey building', ST-Tpath2

State: Lift1	Event for Lift1	State: Lift2	Event for Lift2	Covered EP
Lift1 – 1, Lift2 – 1, both vacant	Guest1 ↓ at 7	Lift1 – 1, Lift2 – 1, both vacant	(Guest1 ↓ at 7)	EP3/ON point
Lift1 moves to 7	Guest1 ↓ at 7	Lift2 vacant		
Lift1 is standing at 7	Guest1 pushes 1			
Lift1 moves to 1	Guest2 ↓ at 3			EP11

(Continued)

Table 6.10 (Continued)

State: Lift1	Event for Lift1	State: Lift2	Event for Lift2	Covered EP
Lift1 is standing at 3	Guest1 pushes 1			
Lift1 moves to 1	Guest1 pushes 1	Lift2 vacant	Guest11 ↑ at 1	
Lift1 is standing at 1	Guests leave Lift1	Lift2 is standing at 1	Guest11 pushes 6	
		Lift2 moves to 6	Guest11 pushes 6	EP16
Lift1 is vacant	Guest3 ↑ at 4	(Lift2 left floor 4)		EP12
Lift1 moves to 4	Guest3 ↑ at 4			
Lift1 is standing at 4	Guest3 pushes 7	Lift2 is standing at 6	Guest11 leaves L2	
Lift1 moves to 7		Lift2 is vacant	Guest12 ↓ at 9	
Lift1 is standing at 7	Guest3 leaves L1	Lift2 moves to 9	Guest12 ↓ at 9	
		Lift2 is standing at 9	Guest12 pushes 4	
		Lift2 moves to 4	Guest13 ↓ at 7	EP15
Lift1 is vacant	Guest4 ↓ at 7	Lift2 is standing at 7	Guest12 pushes 4	
Lift1 is standing at 7	Guest4 pushes 5	Lift2 moves to 4	Guest12 pushes 4	
Lift1 moves to 5		Lift2 is standing at 4	Guests leave L2	
Lift1 is standing at 5	Guest4 leaves L1	Lift2 is vacant		
Lift1, Lift2 vacant		Lift1, Lift2 vacant		

Besides the EP3 ON point, we have covered EP11, EP12, EP15 and EP16. We can easily cover the EP1 ON point, EP13, EP14, EP17 and EP18 in ST-Tpath4. We can cover the remaining two ON points by ST-Tpath1 and ST-Tpath2. Finally, we should test the remaining four IN points by four simple test cases avoiding concurrency.

Summarising, when combining more techniques, a possible process is the following:

1. Design the test cases for the selected techniques separately.
2. Work out a plan on how to integrate the tests from the different techniques.
3. Select the larger set of test cases related to a test design technique, and map the test cases of the other technique to them (if possible).
4. Design additional integrated test cases for which the mapping is not possible.
5. Review and validate the result.

STATE TRANSITION TESTING IN TVM EXAMPLE

Let's consider the following part of the example TVM specification.

EXAMPLE: TVM TICKET SELECTION

There are three types of tickets:

    a. Standard ticket valid for 75 minutes on any metro, tram or bus line.

    b. Short distance ticket valid within five stations on a single line of any metro, tram or bus.

    c. 24-hour ticket for unlimited metro, bus and train travel for 24 hours from validation.

The price of the tickets can be modified, currently (a) is EUR 2.10, (b) is EUR 1.40 and (c) is EUR 7.60.

Selecting tickets: the customer can buy tickets of one type only. If all the amounts of ticket types are zero, then any of them can be increased. After that, the ticket type with non-zero can be increased or decreased by clicking on '+' or '-'. The maximum number of tickets to be bought is 10. '+' and '-' are unavailable when the number of tickets is 10 or 0, respectively. If the selected amount of tickets is greater than 0, then the buying process can start.

We model the ticket selection process of the TVM with a state transition graph. The first step is to create the state transition diagram. Usually, this is the simplest task. To do this, you must read the specification at least twice, maybe more times, and very carefully. You cannot create the correct graph until you really know this part of the specification.

> It is not enough to simply understand the specification on a basic level; it needs to be understood in depth!

If you know it well, you can start the design.

First, make a draft version by considering all the states, events and actions, then the 'forward' and 'backward' transitions one by one. The design is always an iterative process – it is not a problem if the draft version is not complete or is inconsistent. Approach the final version step by step. Finally, validate the graph.

Precondition: the TVM shows the initial ticket selection screen. The number of tickets is set to zero (NrT := 0) and the ticket type value is empty (TicketType := ' ').

States:

- s1: Initial state (Init);
- s2: Standard ticket selection (Stan);
- s3: Short distance ticket selection (Short);
- s4: 24-hour ticket selection (24h);
- s5: Payment (final state) (Pay).

Input (events):

- e1: Increasing the number of standard tickets (incStan);
- e2: Increasing the number of short distance tickets (incShort);
- e3: Increasing the number of 24-hour tickets (inc24);
- e4: Decreasing the number of standard tickets (decStan);
- e5: Decreasing the number of short distance tickets (decShort);
- e6: Decreasing the number of 24-hour tickets (dec24);
- e7: Selecting for payment (selectPay).

Output (actions):

- a1: Increments the number of standard tickets (NrT := NrT + 1)(Stan+);
- a2: Increments the number of short distance tickets (NrT := NrT + 1)(Short+);
- a3: Increments the number of 24-hour tickets (NrT := NrT + 1)(24+);
- a4: Decrements the number of standard tickets (NrT := NrT − 1)(Stan-);
- a5: Decrements the number of short distance tickets (NrT := NrT − 1)(Short-);
- a6: Decrements the number of 24-hour tickets (NrT := NrT − 1)(24-);
- a7: Goes to the payment screen (payment), passing the global data value NrT.

119

Transitions:

- t1: incStan / Stan+;
- t2: incShort / Short+;
- t3: inc24 / 24+;
- t4: decStan / [NrT = 1] / Stan-;
- t5: decShort / [NrT = 1] / Short-;
- t6: dec24 / [NrT = 1] /24-;
- t7: incStan / [NrT < 10] / Stan+;
- t8: incShort / [NrT < 10] / Short+;
- t9: inc24 / [NrT < 10] / 24+;
- t10: decStan / [NrT > 1] / Stan-;
- t11: decShort / [NrT > 1] / Short-;
- t12: dec24 / [NrT > 1] / 24-;
- t13: selectPay / <A7, TicketType := 'Standard'>;
- t14 – selectPay / <A7, TicketType := 'Short Distance'>;
- t15 – selectPay / <A7, TicketType := '24 hour'>.

The state transition graph of the TVM can be seen in Figure 6.7.

The next task is to choose the test selection criterion and to create the test cases based on the graph. In our case, the **all-transition-state** criterion seems to be the most promising. The others have either too weak fault-detection capabilities or need too many test cases.

We can see that the graph is symmetric for the ticket types available to buy. Clearly, for all transitions t, except t13, t14 and t15, the reachable states are RS(t) = {s1, s2, s3, s4, s5}. The following three tests cover those (t, s) pairs for which from each transition t there is a path to all the elements of RS(t). For clarity, we use the names of the transitions and the abbreviation of the states as follows: **St, 24, Short, Success** and **Init**:

Tpath1 = **Init** – incStan – **St** – incStan – **St** – decStan – **Init** – incStan – **St** – decStan – **Init** – incShort – **Short** – decShort – **Init** – inc24 – **24** – selectPay – **Payment**

Tpath2 = **Init** – incShort – **Short** – incShort – **Short** – decShort – **Init** – incShort – **Short** – decShort – **Init** – inc24 – **24** – dec24 – **Init** – incStan – **St** – selectPay – **Payment**

Tpath3 = **Init** – inc24 – **24** – inc24 – **24** – dec24 – **Init** – inc24 – **24** – dec24 – **Init** – incStan – **St** – decSt – **Init** – incShort – **Short** – selectPay – **Payment**

From the first test only (t13: selectPay, s5: Payment), (t14: selectPay, s5: Payment), from the second only (t14: selectPay, s5: Payment), (t15: selectPay, s5: Payment), from the third only, the pairs (t13: selectPay, s5: Payment), (t14: selectPay, s5: Payment) are

Figure 6.7 Ticket selection transition graph for the TVM

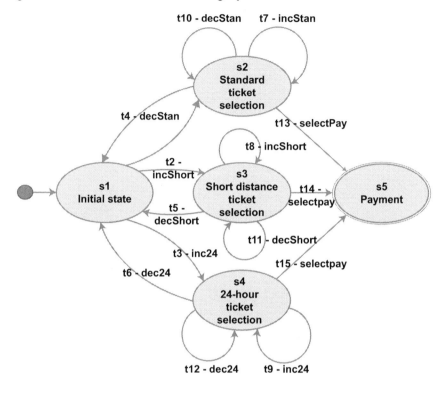

missing. Considering all these three paths, we satisfied (1) in the definition. Regarding the second criterion, it is easy to see that the path (t1: incStan-s2: St-t13: selectPay-s5: Payment) avoids all transitions except t1: incStan and t13: selectPay and reaches s2: St and s5: Payment. Extending the three tests above with the following basic paths, criterion (2) fulfils in the all-transition-state definition:

Tpath4 = **Init** – incStan – **St** – selectPay – **Payment**

Tpath5 = **Init** – incShort – **Short** – selectPay – **Payment**

Tpath6 = **Init** – inc24 – **24** – selectPay – **Payment**

Now we concentrate on the boundary values and extend our tests. This means, for example, that we try to increment the number of tickets above 10 and decrement it below 0. Even if it was successful, we could continue the testing. For automated tests, after the failed code is fixed, it is re-executed.

When the same event E happens n-times consecutively, we will shorten it by nx, for example E7x (apply the event E seven times). The six test cases are in Tables 6.11a–6.11f. Within these tables, Stan ticket stands for Standard ticket.

Table 6.11a State transition tests for the TVM-Test-1

Name: TVM-Test-1

Steps	1	2	3	4	5	6	7	8	9	10	11	12
Events	incStan	incStan 10x	decStan 9x	decStan	decStan	incStan	decStan	incShort	decShort	inc24	inc24 9x	select Pay
Trans. no.	t1	t7	t10	t4	–	t1	t4	t2	t5	t3	t9	t15
States (from/to)	s1/s1	s2/s2	s2/s2	s2/s1	s1/s1	s1/s2	s2/s1	s1/s3	s3/s1	s1/s4	s4/s4	s4/s5
Expected result	1 Stan ticket	10 Stan tickets	1 Stan ticket	0 ticket	0 ticket	1 Stan ticket	0 ticket	1 Short ticket	0 ticket	1 24h ticket	10 24h tickets	10 24h tickets
Observed result												

Table 6.11b State transition tests for the TVM-Test-2

Name: TVM-Test-2

Steps	1	2	3	4	5	6	7	8	9	10	11	12
Events	incShort	incShort 10x	decShort 9x	decShort	decShort	incShort	decShort	inc 24	dec 24	incStan	incStan 5x	select Pay
Trans. no.	t2	t8	t11	t5	–	t2	t5	t3	t6	t1	t7	t13
States (from/to)	s1/s3	s3/s3	s3/s3	s3/s1	s1/s1	s1/s3	s3/s1	s1/s4	s4/s1	s1/s2	s2/s2	s2/s5
Expected result	1 Short ticket	10 Short tickets	1 Short ticket	0 ticket	0 ticket	1 Short ticket	0 ticket	1 24h ticket	0 ticket	1 Stan ticket	6 Stan tickets	6 Stan tickets
Observed result												

123

Table 6.11c State transition tests for the TVM-Test-3

Name: TVM-Test-3

Steps	1	2	3	4	5	6	7	8	9	10	11	12
Events	inc24	inc24 10x	dec24 9x	dec24	dec24	inc24	dec24	incStan	decStan	incShort	incShort	select Pay
Trans. no.	t3	t9	t12	t6	–	t3	t6	t1	t4	t2	t2	t14
States (from/to)	s1/s4	s4/s4	s4/s4	s4/s1	s1/s1	s1/s4	s4/s1	s1/s2	s2/s1	s1/s3	s3/s3	s3/s5
Expected result	1 24h ticket	10 24h tickets	1 24h ticket	0 ticket	0 ticket	1 24h ticket	0 ticket	1 Stan ticket	0 ticket	1 Short ticket	2 Short tickets	2 Short tickets
Observed result												

Table 6.11d State transition tests for the TVM-Test-4

Name: TVM-Test-4		
Steps	1	2
Events	incStan	selectPay
Trans. no.	t1	t13
States (from/to)	s1/s2	s2/s5
Expected result	1 Stan ticket	1 Stan ticket
Observed result		

Table 6.11e State transition tests for the TVM-Test-5

Name: TVM-Test-5		
Steps	1	2
Events	incShort	selectPay
Trans. no.	t2	t14
States (from/to)	s1/s3	s3/s5
Expected result	1 Short ticket	1 Short ticket
Observed result		

Table 6.11f State transition tests for the TVM-Test-6

Name: TVM-Test-6		
Steps	1	2
Events	inc24	selectPay
Trans. no.	t3	t15
States (from/to)	s1/s4	s4/s5
Expected result	1 24h ticket	1 24h ticket
Observed result		

This example will be extended in the Gherkin-based test design chapter (Chapter 12) by paying for the tickets. In that case, STT and EP and BVA shall also be applied together.

METHOD EVALUATION

In this section we evaluate the state transition test design technique from various perspectives.

Applicability

The state transition testing technique can be applied when the system is defined in terms of a finite number of states and the transitions between the states are triggered by the rules of the system. Practically, the technique is usable for real applications involving states and transitions. This method is especially good for end-to-end testing of large systems, testing embedded systems, web applications, compilers, telecommunication protocols and so on.

Types of defects

The technique can detect integration and system errors even in large systems. Typical defects include incorrect or unsupported transitions, unreachable or non-existent states, omissions (there is no information about what the automaton should do in a certain situation) and inconsistent model descriptions. State transition testing can reveal some predicate errors as well.

Advantages and shortcomings of the method

The advantages of the state transition testing method are:

- State transition diagrams can be created for many applications, hence this testing technique is widely applicable.
- Other test design methods can be involved in state transition testing.
- There exist numerous test selection criteria, from linear up to exponential.
- State machines can be easily used for automated test design (such as model-based testing).
- In large systems, the models can be built up in a hierarchical manner.

The limitations and shortcomings of the method are:

- Constructing the state model is not always easy. If the graph is complex, then even a professional tester may make mistakes.
- The tests have to be carefully validated, which is not always simple.
- At the time of writing, there is no tool for automating test case generation based on all of the featured test selection criteria.

- Achieving high switch coverage levels implies almost always combinatorial explosion in the number of test cases.

- Sometimes it is difficult to include negative tests. The tester shall consider these tests additionally.

- Complex event-driven systems, where various data structures have to be handled concurrently (stack, FIFO, i.e. first in, first out, etc.), are hard to describe by FSMs because of the state space explosion. In such cases other modes are suggested, for example pushdown automaton.

THEORETICAL BACKGROUND

A state machine is a mathematical model of computation. The roles of state machines in software testing are: (1) before starting the actual implementation, an executable state machine may simulate the model with event sequences as test cases, (2) supports testing against the specification and (3) supports automatic test generation (there should be an explicit mapping between the state machine elements and the elements of the implementation, e.g. classes, objects, attributes, etc.).

The behaviour of discrete systems can be described by different models. **Labelled or unlabelled transition systems** are used to describe dynamic processes with configurations representing states and transitions prescribing how to go from state to state. Transition systems are mathematically equivalent to abstract rewriting systems or with directed graphs. Finite-state machines differ from them in several ways, namely, FSMs have a finite set of states and transitions, and have start nodes and so on. FSMs have less computational power than Turing machines or pushdown automatons since their memories are limited by their finite number of states. State machines are used to give an abstract description of the system's behaviour. This behaviour is analysed and represented as a series of events that can occur in one or more possible states. State diagrams are used to graphically represent those (finite-state) machines. Many forms of state diagrams exist, which are all slightly different.

Statecharts refer to Harel's notation described in Harel (1987), which was proposed as a significant notational extension over traditional finite-state machines. Statecharts have been incorporated in the UML by introducing the concept of hierarchically nested states (logically connected subgraphs can cluster into a new super-state) and orthogonal regions (orthogonality means compatibility and independency in the given context). With this hierarchical clusterisation, the state transition testing becomes possible even for large systems. UML state machines have the characteristics of both Mealy and Moore machines.

Specification and Description Language (SDL) state machines from the ITU (International Telecommunication Union) include graphical symbols to describe the actions in the transitions (timers, sending, receiving messages, etc.). SDL combines together abstract data types, an action language and an executing semantic to make the machine executable.

While using an FSM for embedded system design, the inputs and outputs are Boolean data types, and the functions represent Boolean functions with Boolean operations. This model is enough to describe control systems without involving input or output data. When data is to be dealt with, EFSM is needed.

The applicability of state diagrams in testing was observed in the 1970s. One of the first and the most cited papers is the work of Chow (1978), who proposed a method of testing the correctness of control structures that can be modelled by a finite-state machine. Test results derived from the design are evaluated against the specification. No 'executable' prototype was required. Clearly, his testing method was an early test-first method. You can read more on this topic in Chapter 11.

KEY TAKEAWAYS

- **Stateful systems** are able to 'memorise' the preceding user interactions or events; the remembered information is the **state** of the system. They exhibit different behaviours in different states. **State transition diagrams** are used to describe the behaviour of stateful systems. **State transition testing** is used for testing them.

- There are several test selection criteria available for state transition testing by which the test design can often be automated.

- For real specifications, **various test design methods** (like EP, BVA and STT) can be applied **in combination**.

- To catch data-flow defects among transitions and states the all-transition-state and all-transition–transition criteria were suggested.

EXERCISES

E6.1 Construct test paths applying the all-transition–transition criterion for 'TVM ticket selection' (see TVM example earlier in the chapter and Figure 6.7).

E6.2 Ordering water from an online shop. The types of water can be still or sparkling. We can buy bottles of one type only. If nothing is selected, then the quantity of either of them can be increased. After one has been selected, only one of the water types with a non-zero amount can be increased or decreased by one. The maximum number of bottles to be ordered is five. If the selected number of bottles is greater than 0, then the buying process can start. The output is the type and number of the selected bottles.

Model the buying process for this example with a state transition graph and design tests for the following test selection criteria:

1. All-transition criterion.
2. All-2-transitions criterion.
3. All-transition-state criterion.

7 BUSINESS RULE-BASED TESTING

WHY IS THIS CHAPTER WORTH READING?

In this chapter, you will learn how to apply decision table testing and cause–effect graph testing by applying non-trivial examples. You will also learn when to use, and when not to use, these methods. We also show how these methods and EP and BVA can be used in combination.

A business rule is a rule that describes certain aspects of the business and either it is fulfilled or it is not. Business rules are intended to assert business structure or to control or influence the behaviour of the business.

In this chapter, we introduce two basic business rule-based testing strategies, **decision table-based** and **cause–effect graph-based**.

DECISION TABLE TESTING

Decision table testing is a black-box test design technique used to determine test scenarios and test cases for **business logic**. Recall that we can apply equivalence partitioning and boundary value analysis techniques only to specific conditions or inputs. However, sometimes we have business rules to test with a **different combination of inputs**, resulting in different actions. To test these kinds of rules or logical conditions, we can use decision tables.

Why are decision tables important?

A decision table contains two main parts. The first is the conditions, which are the inputs; the second is the actions, which are the outputs. The possible values of the conditions are the 'condition entries' (condition alternatives). The actions contain action entries that are used to find out which action is taken corresponding to a particular condition alternative. Decision tables may vary widely depending on how these 'condition entries' and 'action entries' are represented. Sometimes we use simply TRUE/FALSE values to represent the condition alternatives; in other cases numbered alternatives or even probabilistic representations are applied. Action entries may represent whether an **action set** (checking the actions) or a **list of actions** is performed (numbering the actions). In special cases, even a state machine can be used to determine which actions to apply.

In a **limited-entry** decision table (see Table 7.1 below), the condition alternatives are simple Boolean values connected by logical AND, and the action entries are check-marks, representing which of the actions in a given rule have to be executed. We use Y for Yes, N for No and X for check-marks.

EXAMPLE: REDSHOE

Company RedShoe sells shoes to wholesale and retail outlets. Wholesale customers receive a 3% discount on all orders. RedShoe encourages both wholesale and retail customers to pay by cash on delivery by offering a 2% discount for this method of payment. Another 2% discount is given on orders reaching Limit1 or more units and 1% extra discount above or equal to Limit2 > Limit1.

Table 7.1 Limited-entry decision table – first step

Conditions	R1	R2	R3	R4	R5	R6	R7	R8	R9	R10	R11	R12
Fewer than Limit1 units ordered	Y	Y	Y	Y	N	N	N	N	N	N	N	N
Fewer than Limit2 units ordered	Y	Y	Y	Y	Y	Y	Y	Y	N	N	N	N
Paid by card	Y	Y	N	N	Y	Y	N	N	Y	Y	N	N
Retail outlet	Y	N	Y	N	Y	N	Y	N	Y	N	Y	N

Actions												
Discount rate is 0%	X											
Discount rate is 2%			X		X							
Discount rate is 3%		X							X			
Discount rate is 4%							X					
Discount rate is 5%				X		X					X	
Discount rate is 6%										X		
Discount rate is 7%								X				
Discount rate is 8%												X

In the first column, the first four rows below the head row represent the **condition stubs**, the rest are the **action stubs**. Similarly, from the second column, the first four rows contain the **condition entries**, the rest are the **action entries**. Each entry column represents a specific **business rule** such as '**fewer than Limit1 units ordered**'. Based on this compound, rules or assertions can be made: 'WHEN fewer than Limit1 units ordered AND fewer than Limit2 units ordered AND paid by card AND customer type is retail THEN the discount rate is zero per cent'.

Condition entries can be interpreted as input or equivalence classes of inputs. Action entries are interpreted as output or major functional processing portions. Each rule in the decision table gives at least one test case. Based on the decision structure of the program a complete decision table results in a complete set of test cases.

The careful reader may observe that our limited-entry decision table is not complete and that something is missing. The reason for this is that there are dependencies in the input domain: since Limit1 < Limit2, the situation that 'fewer than Limit1 units are ordered AND the number of orders is more than or equal to Limit2' is impossible. Those conditions must be placed into the decision table as well.

How many rules are in a complete limited-entry decision table? Having n conditions, the number of such rules is 2^n. You can check that our second decision table (Table 7.2) is complete, having 4 conditions and 16 rules.

Would it be possible to simplify large decision tables? Fortunately, in most cases, the answer is yes. We can extend the decision tables in condition alternatives with 'don't care' symbols denoted by '–'. Don't care entries reduce the number of explicit rules by implying the existence of non-explicitly stated rules. 'Don't cares' can simplify decision tables especially when a given condition does not influence the actions. In our example, the last four columns can be simplified in a straightforward way with don't cares. For further simplification, we have to check those rules that have similar action sets (Table 7.3). Some authors call these simplified decision tables **collapsed**. In our example, other simplifications with don't cares are not possible (analyse it!).

Moreover, there are other types of simplification possibilities, for example we can simplify the discount rate appearances, giving them explicit discount percentage values in an **extended-entry decision table** (see Table 7.4).

At this point it is good advice to refactor the table, if possible, making it more readable for the stakeholders. For example, our table can be refactored in the following way by introducing MAX, the maximal number of orders (making the equivalence partitions real and proper, see Table 7.5).

The last step is to check the table for consistency (no contradictory rules), redundancy (e.g. similar columns do not exist) and completeness (we have covered all possibilities). You can easily see that the number of different rules is 13, so we need to develop at least 13 test cases, at least one test case for each rule.

Now we can turn our decision table into test cases. In general, the condition values used in each rule (causes) will serve us as the different inputs for the test cases, and the values (effects) used in the actions will serve us as the expected results. We note

Table 7.2 Limited-entry decision table – second step

Conditions	R1	R2	R3	R4	R5	R6	R7	R8	R9	R10	R11	R12	R13	R14	R15	R16
Fewer than Limit1 units ordered	Y	Y	Y	Y	N	N	N	N	N	N	N	N	Y	Y	Y	Y
Fewer than Limit2 units ordered	Y	Y	Y	Y	Y	Y	Y	Y	N	N	N	N	N	N	N	N
Paid by card	Y	Y	N	N	Y	Y	N	N	Y	Y	N	N	Y	Y	N	N
Retail outlet	Y	N	Y	N	Y	N	Y	N	Y	N	Y	N	Y	N	Y	N

Actions

Actions	R1	R2	R3	R4	R5	R6	R7	R8	R9	R10	R11	R12	R13	R14	R15	R16
Disc. rate is 0%	X															
Disc. rate is 2%			X		X											
Disc. rate is 3%		X														
Disc. rate is 4%							X									
Disc. rate is 5%				X		X										
Disc. rate is 6%										X	X					
Disc. rate is 7%								X								
Disc. rate is 8%									X			X				
Impossible number of orders													X	X	X	X

Table 7.3 Limited-entry decision table – third step

Conditions	R1	R2	R3	R4	R5	R6	R7	R8	R9	R10	R11	R12	R13
Fewer than Limit1 units ordered	Y	Y	Y	Y	N	N	N	N	N	N	N	N	Y
Fewer than Limit2 units ordered	Y	Y	Y	Y	Y	Y	Y	Y	N	N	N	N	N
Paid by card	Y	Y	N	N	Y	Y	N	N	Y	Y	N	N	–
Retail outlet	Y	N	Y	N	Y	N	Y	N	Y	N	Y	N	–
Actions													
Discount rate is 0%	X												
Discount rate is 2%			X		X								
Discount rate is 3%		X											
Discount rate is 4%							X		X				
Discount rate is 5%				X		X							
Discount rate is 6%										X	X		
Discount rate is 7%								X					
Discount rate is 8%												X	
Impossible number of orders													X

Table 7.4 Extended-entry decision table – first step

Conditions	R1	R2	R3	R4	R5	R6	R7	R8	R9	R10	R11	R12	R13
Fewer than Limit1 units ordered	Y	Y	Y	Y	N	N	N	N	N	N	N	N	Y
Fewer than Limit2 units ordered	Y	Y	Y	Y	Y	Y	Y	Y	N	N	N	N	N
Paid by card	Y	Y	N	N	Y	Y	N	N	Y	Y	N	N	–
Retail outlet	Y	N	Y	N	Y	N	Y	N	Y	N	Y	N	–
Actions													
Discount rate (%)	0	3	2	5	2	5	4	7	3	6	5	8	
Impossible number of orders													X

Table 7.5 Extended-entry decision table – final version

Conditions	R1	R2	R3	R4	R5	R6	R7	R8	R9	R10	R11	R12	R13
Number of orders: No	$0 \leq No < Limit1$				$Limit1 \leq No < Limit2$				$Limit2 \leq No \leq MAX$				Otherwise
Paid by card	Y	Y	N	N	Y	Y	N	N	Y	Y	N	N	–
Retail outlet	Y	N	Y	N	Y	N	Y	N	Y	N	Y	N	–
Actions													
Discount rate (%)	0	3	2	5	2	5	4	7	3	6	5	8	
Impossible number of orders, error handling needed													X

that it would be possible to apply the decision tree technique to transform the rule combinations in a more visual way, to 'see' our test cases. Observe that in our case, equivalence partitioning and boundary value analysis can be used as supporting techniques during test design.

Before writing down the test cases, we should carefully analyse our final decision table. For example, we should elicit from the test basis the maximal number of orders, MAX. If such a value does not exist, then let MAX be the biggest integer that can be represented in the data structure containing the number of orders. Then, we should elicit/decide who will control the type matching of the different variables. Lastly, we should design the error handling mechanisms. Assuming that the number of orders is an integer, the resulting test suite can be the following:

TestSet = {([0, Y, Y]; 0), ([1, Y, N]; 3), ([a, N, Y]; 2); ([Limit1-1, N, N]; 5); ([Limit1, Y, Y]; 2); ([Limit1+1, Y, N]; 5); ([b, N, Y]; 4); ([Limit2-1, N, N]; 7); ([Limit2, Y, Y]; 3); ([Limit2+1, Y, N]; 6); ([c, N, Y]; 5); ([MAX, N, N]; 8); ([MAX+1, Y, Y]; ErrorMsg)},

where a = Limit1/2, b = (Limit2 - Limit1)/2 and c = (Max - Limit2)/2

Altogether we have 13 test cases. Note that with these test cases we satisfied BVA as well.

> We think that a practical test design book must answer the question of when decision tables and when EP and BVA should be used if both methods are applicable. The answer is obvious: it depends on many factors (risk, experience, complexity of rules, etc.).

We shall apply risk and complexity analysis as described in Chapter 3. The result will be a (near) optimal solution.

How to construct decision tables

To construct a decision table we suggest the following steps:

1. Understand the requirements: read the test basis thoroughly.
2. Make risk and complexity analyses and, based on them, decide to apply this method.
3. Create the first version of the table and analyse it carefully.
   a. Analyse the content and make sure you understand everything.
   b. Think of the exception cases.
   c. Count the possible values for each condition and determine how many unique combinations of conditions should present.
4. Simplify the table using 'don't cares'.
   a. Search for similar actions and look for the applicability of 'don't cares' in the conditions belonging to them.

5. Ensure that:

    a. The rules are complete.

        i. There are no missing rules.

    b. The rules are consistent.

        i. There does not exist more than one different action set for the same rule pattern.

        ii. Every combination of predicate truth values is explicit in the decision table.

        iii. Every combination of predicate truth values results in only one action or set of actions.

    c. The rules are not redundant, otherwise there are:

        i. More rules than needed (more than the possible condition combinations);

        ii. Similar columns.

6. Analyse and refactor the table; go to step 4 for checking.

7. Derive the test cases, at least one test case for each column. If there are too many test cases to derive (too many columns) then analyse, discuss and redesign your coverage criteria.

Ticket vending machine example

Let's model the ticket selection process, including the ticket prices of the TVM example, with decision tables. We know from the specification that there are three types of tickets, and only one type of a maximum of 10 tickets can be selected during a transaction. After analysis, the following questions can be raised:

1. What about the cases when more than one ticket type is selected? Is it possible?

2. What about the cases when more than 10 tickets are asked for? Is it possible?

3. What should be done when zero tickets are selected for a ticket type?

4. What about other exceptional cases?

Suppose we got the following answers from the customer:

1. The program should be written in a way that only one ticket type can be selected during a transaction. If no ticket type has been selected, then any ticket type can be selected.

2. Only fewer than or equal to 10 tickets of that type can be selected during a transaction.

3. In the case of zero EUR to be paid, payment is not possible, and if no ticket type is selected, then no logging is done.

4. A negative number of tickets is not possible. For all the above mentioned and other exceptional cases, the logging mechanism should report the situation without messaging anything to the user.

Then, the resulting decision table is shown in Table 7.6.

Table 7.6 Extended-entry decision table for the TVM example

Conditions	R1	R2	R3	R4	R5	R6	R7	R8	R9	R10	R11	R12	R13
Number of sel. tickets, No	1 ≤ No ≤ 10								No = 0				10 < No or No < 0
Standard ticket	Y	N	N	Y	Y	N	Y	N	Y	–	–	N	–
Short distance ticket	N	Y	N	Y	N	Y	Y	N	–	Y	–	N	–
24-hour ticket	N	N	Y	N	Y	Y	Y	N	–	–	Y	N	–
Actions													
Payment possible	X	X	X										
Total price (EUR)	No x 2.1	No x 1.4	No x 7.6										
Any ticket type is selectable												X	
Ticket selection error, logging				X	X	X	X	X	X	X	X		X

When the number of selected tickets is zero, then according to the specification, no ticket types are marked. Otherwise, there is an error.

Let's check the total number of columns without 'don't cares'. The rules R1–R8 constitute a full table for the case 1 ≤ Number of selected tickets ≤ 10. The four rules R9–R12 represent eight columns as well, which are reduced to four because of the 'don't care' symbols. R13 represents $2^3 = 8$ columns again. Hence, all the equivalence partitions 1 ≤ No ≤ 10, No = 0 and 0 > No or No > 10 are covered in eight columns, resulting altogether in 24 columns. The task for checking the completeness, consistency and non-redundancy we leave to the reader.

Regarding the test selection we use boundary values with non-defensive design. Then, the test suites can be the following: the test set

TS1 = {

1. ([StandardTicket, SelectedTickets = 1], [Any ticket type is selectable = No, Payment = Yes, Price = EUR 2.1]),

2. ([StandardTicket, SelectedTickets = 10], [Payment = Yes, Price = EUR 21]),

3. ([ShortDistanceTicket, SelectedTickets = 1], [Any ticket type is selectable = No, Payment = Yes, Price = EUR 1.4]),

4. ([ShortDistanceTicket, SelectedTickets = 10], [Payment = Yes, Price = EUR 14]),

5. ([24HourTicket, SelectedTickets = 1], [Any ticket type is selectable = No, Payment = Yes, Price = EUR 7.6]),

6. ([24HourTicket, SelectedTickets = 10], [Payment = Yes, Price = EUR 76]),

7. ([No ticket type selected, SelectedTickets = 0], [Payment = No, Any ticket type is selectable = Yes]) },

contains positive test cases from rules R1, R1, R2, R2, R3, R3 and R12, respectively, while the test set

TS2 = {

8. ([StandardTicket, SelectedTickets = -1], [Payment = No, err_msg('Negative number of tickets']),

9. ([ShortDistanceTicket, SelectedTickets = 11], [Payment = No, err_msg('More than 10 tickets are selected'])},

covers the rule R13. For the rules R4–R11, we do not design concrete tests. The total time used for this design was approximately 1 hour.

Suppose that for some reason we need to follow defensive test design, that is we have to write concrete tests for the rules R4–R11. Then, the test set

TS3 = {

10. ([StandardTicket and Short distance ticket, SelectedTickets = 2], [Payment = No, err_msg('At least two ticket types are selected at the same time']),

11. ([StandardTicket and 24HourTicket, SelectedTickets = 9], [Payment = No, err_ msg('At least two ticket types are selected at the same time']),

12. ([Short distance ticket and 24HourTicket, SelectedTickets = 5], [Payment = No, err_msg('At least two ticket types are selected at the same time']),

13. ([SelectedTickets = 1], [Payment = No, err_msg('Tickets are selected without type']),

14. ([StandardTicket, SelectedTickets = 0], [Payment = No, err_msg('Zero ticket is selected from StandardTicket']),

15. ([ShortDistanceTicket, SelectedTickets = 0], [Payment = No, err_msg('Zero ticket is selected from ShortDistanceTicket']),

16. ([24HourTicket, SelectedTickets = 0], [Payment = No, err_msg('Zero ticket is selected from 24HourTicket']) },

contains negative test cases from rules R4, R5, R6, R8, R9, R10, R11, respectively. You can see that we did not choose a test case from the rule set R7 since the rules R4, R5, and R6 cover this case.

The TVM example highlights the importance of designing the logging mechanisms together with the test design.

Hierarchically extended decision tables

In some cases, the condition values of an extended-entry decision table are not explicitly given. In these cases, further decisions are needed to determine the values. The following simple example shows how the decision tables can be extended hierarchically.

EXAMPLE: REDSHOE ORDER HANDLING

The order handling mechanism of company RedShoe in its brand store is the following:

- There are two types of clients: normal clients and VIP clients.

- VIP clients must have RedShoe company cards and their average past orders have to be above or equal to EUR 1000.

- The payment can be made by cash or card, but only VIP clients are allowed to pay by card.

- Orders can be initialised for standard products; discontinued and non-existent products are not orderable.

- If the ordered quantity is greater than the available quantity in stock, follow-up orders are possible but only for standard products. In this case the order handler adds the order to the waiting list.

Firstly, a so-called **dependence diagram** helps us to make a decision table more easily (see Figure 7.1). The nodes are variables and labelled with the potential values of that variable. The edges represent dependences bottom-up.

Figure 7.1 Dependence diagram for 'RedShoe' order handling

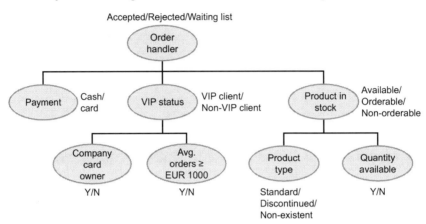

For example, Order handler depends on the Payment, on the VIP status, and on the Product in stock status. The values on that node can be Accepted, Rejected or Waiting list. Based on the condition diagram in Figure 7.1 we can deduce the hierarchically extended decision tables as follows. The first table (Table 7.7a) contains the highest-level decision table. The two others (Tables 7.7b and 7.7c) are lower-level tables, where VIP status and Product in stock are modelled respectively.

Table 7.7a Top level (Level 1) decision table for 'RedShoe'

Conditions	R1	R2	R3	R4	R5	R6	R7
Payment	Cash			Card			
VIP Status	–			VIP client			Non-VIP client
Product in stock	Available	Orderable	Non-orderable	Available	Orderable	Non-orderable	–
Actions							
Order handling	Accepted	Waiting list	Rejected	Accepted	Waiting list	Rejected	Rejected

Table 7.7b Level 2 decision table for 'RedShoe'

Conditions	R1'	R2'	R3'
Company card owner	Y		N
Avg. orders ≥ EUR 1000	Y	N	–
Actions			
VIP client	Y	N	N

Table 7.7c Level 2 decision table for 'RedShoe'

Conditions	R1"	R2"	R3"	R4"
Quantity available	Y	N		
Product type	–	Standard	Discontinued	Non-existent
Actions				
Product in stock	Available	Orderable	Non-orderable	Non-orderable

It is easy to observe that the top-level decision table can be further refactored (see Table 7.8).

Table 7.8 Reduced top-level decision table for 'RedShoe'

Conditions	R1	R2	R3	R4
VIP status and payment method	Non-VIP client with card	Otherwise		
Product in stock	–	Available	Orderable	Non-orderable
Actions				
Order handling	Rejected	Accepted	Waiting list	Rejected

Test case creation based on hierarchical decision tables do not result in less abstract test cases, but regarding the test design, the complexity of the original problem is reduced. The situation is a bit similar to reorganising (refactoring) code in programming languages: we can reduce the complexity and at the same time preserve the functionality.

Now it's time to design the concrete test cases:

TS = {

TC1 = ([Non-VIP client who wants to pay with card or product is not orderable], [Order rejected]).

TC2 = ([VIP client paying with a card or any client paying with cash, ordered product quantity is available], [Order is accepted]).

TC3 = ([VIP client paying with a card or any client paying with cash, ordered product quantity is unavailable but orderable], [Order put to waiting list]).

TC4 = ([Client has company card and the past average orders ≥ EUR 1000], [VIP client = yes]).

TC5 = ([Client does not have company card or the past average orders < EUR 1000], [VIP client = no]).

TC6 = ([Non-available standard product], [Orderable = yes]).

TC7 = ([Non-available discontinued or non-existent product], [Orderable = no])}.

You can see that during the test case creation process we optimised the coverage.

Method evaluation

This subsection deals with the evaluation of the decision table test design method.

Applicability
Decision tables are easy to understand and can be embedded within any kind of software systems and in any test levels (but are mainly used in integration, system and acceptance levels). They are used to control the flow (logic and/or data) of the program. Decision table testing is most appropriate when:

- There are well-defined decision-making requirements in the business flow.
- There are cause and effect relationships between input and output.
- There are different operations involving subsets of input variables.
- There is complex computation logic (high cyclomatic complexity).

Types of defects
Typical defects include a faulty process or data flow based on particular combinations of conditions resulting in unexpected behaviour. Sometimes, during the creation of the decision table, defects may be found in the test basis. There may be some omissions or contradictions found. The decision table analysis may also find issues with condition combinations that are improperly handled.

Adequacy
The minimum test coverage criterion for a decision table is to have one test case for each column (in the case of 'not too many' columns). When determining tests from a decision table, we have to combine the rules with the boundary conditions if it is reasonable to

do so. These boundary conditions may or may not increase the number of test cases. Note that boundary value analysis and equivalence partitioning are complementary to the decision table technique.

Advantages and shortcomings of the method
The advantages of decision tables are as follows:

- Allows developers to work on the same basis as the relevant stakeholders (policy experts, testers, customers, etc.), especially when formulated with a domain-specific language.

- Can be used to present different scenarios to management, hence **informed decisions** can be made.

- **Support in designing** test cases.

- Each column in a decision table should be converted into **at least one** test case providing **complete coverage** of test cases.

- Defines expected results **for all input combinations** in an easy-to-read format.

- Guarantee that every possible combination of condition values is considered (**completeness property**).

- Helpful for **reporting test results** as well.

- Decision tables can easily be checked for redundancy, the absence of contradictions and completeness.

Shortcomings are as follows:

- Decision tables are not easy to scale; they should be iteratively refined. In most cases, we use extended decision tables or algebraically simplified tables.

- Finding all the interacting conditions can be challenging, particularly when requirements are under-defined or do not exist.

- Connections between separate conditions can only be expressed implicitly (in contrast to the cause-and-effect graphs).

For valid decision tables, all the expected outcomes for all condition combinations must be designed, based on the specifications or test oracles. For large tables, this situation is close to combinatorial testing. The combinatorial explosion may prohibit applying decision tables for too many variables. Large tables should be refactored into smaller ones, if possible. If not, then risk-based techniques may help to reduce the full decision table to a collapsed one, where we can remove a subset of conditions that are not relevant. You have to investigate carefully the necessity and type of combinatorial method used during decision table test design.

Theoretical background

Decisions are part of our everyday life. The concept of decision tables goes back to 1957, where Johnston and Davis (1970) applied the technique successfully in data processing applications, more specifically in programming. The story is that General Electric, the Sutherland Corporation, and the US Air Force had unsuccessfully tried to clear up a complex file maintenance problem for more than six person-years, and then solved the problem with four people in four weeks (i.e. 16 person-weeks) using decision tables. Other interesting notes can be found in McDaniel (1968), Pollack et al. (1971), and Maes (1978). Much effort was taken in converting decision tables into program code (Shwayder 1971, 1974; Smillie and Shave, 1975; and Sethi and Chatterjee, 1980). A nice historical overview is available thanks to Garcia et al. (2000). Some general treatments are available in Martin and McClure (1985) and Curtis (1995).

CAUSE–EFFECT GRAPHS

Cause–effect graph testing is a rule-based dynamic testing strategy. The technique describes a semiformal way of expressing requirements that are based on Boolean expressions restating the requirements specification regarding the logical relationship between the input and output conditions. Not surprisingly, the logical relationship uses Boolean operators like AND, OR and NOT. The requirements can be originated from real-time systems, data-driven systems, object-oriented systems, state transition diagrams and so on or even from a complex logical condition in the code. In other words, the technique supports selecting test cases that are logically related. This relation can be considered as **causes** and **effects**. Here, causes represent input conditions while the effects constitute the output conditions, system transformations, or states. The causes/effects are represented as nodes of a directed acyclic graph (DAG), where the edges denote the logical transformations. The graph may include some intermediate nodes linking causes and effects together. Using conjunctive or disjunctive normal forms, the graph can always be rearranged in such a way that there is only one intermediate node between any causes and any effects. The cause–effect graphing technique was invented by Bill Elmendorf of IBM in 1973 (Elmendorf, 1973).

Why are cause–effect graphs important?

Requirements in practice are commonly specified informally. The cause–effect graph testing technique **visualises the logic relations** between causes and their effects in specifications using Boolean algebra-based operations and symbols.

The cause–effect graph testing technique determines the minimum possible test cases for maximum test coverage, which helps to reduce test execution time and cost, hence, it supports avoiding combinatorial explosion. The graphical notation may make the design process more understandable. As a side-effect, the technique supports unfolding incompleteness and ambiguities in the specifications.

Using cause–effect graphs in test design

The logical operators used most commonly in cause–effect diagramming are the following:

- **Identity**, which defines a situation in which effect E is true if cause C is true. The truth table is shown in Table 7.9.

Table 7.9 Cause–effect truth table for Identity

Cause C	Effect E
True	True
False	False

- **NOT**, which defines the instance where effect E is true only if cause C is false (see Table 7.10).

Table 7.10 Cause–effect truth table for NOT

Cause C	Effect E
True	False
False	True

- **AND**, which defines a circumstance where causes C1 and C2 must be true for effect E to be true (Table 7.11).

Table 7.11 Cause–effect truth table for AND

Cause C1	Cause C2	Effect E
True	True	True
True	False	False
False	True	False
False	False	False

- **OR**, which defines a condition in which either cause C1 or cause C2 must be true for effect E to be true (Table 7.12).

Table 7.12 Cause–effect truth table for OR

Cause C1	Cause C2	Effect E
True	True	True
True	False	True
False	True	True
False	False	False

- **NAND**, which defines the circumstance where both C1 and C2 must be true for effect E to be false (Table 7.13).

Table 7.13 Cause–effect truth table for NAND

Cause C1	Cause C2	Effect E
True	True	False
True	False	True
False	True	True
False	False	True

- **NOR**, which defines the condition where if neither C1 nor C2 is true then effect E is true (Table 7.14).

Table 7.14 Cause–effect truth table for NOR

Cause C1	Cause C2	Effect E
True	True	False
True	False	False
False	True	False
False	False	True

Figure 7.2 shows standard notations for describing the logical operators for the first four items described.

Figure 7.2 Some standard operators used in cause–effect graphs

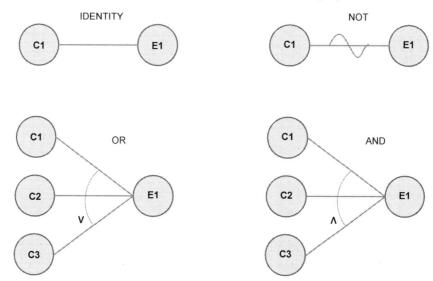

Of course, different notations are possible, or other operators can be introduced, by which the complexity of the representation can be reduced. One of the authors of this book has his own (non-commercial) tool that uses the notation shown in Figure 7.3.

Figure 7.3 Representations used in cause–effect graphs. INP and OUT stand for input and output, respectively

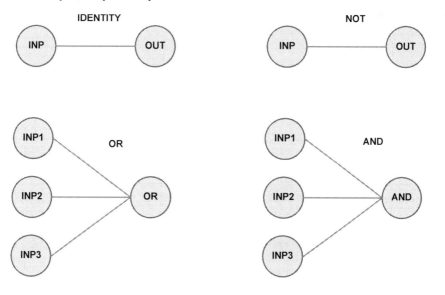

In real projects, there are always constraints (syntactic or semantic), which make some combinations of causes impossible. Also, certain causes or effects may mask others, and when this occurs, it must be indicated on the graph. The following notations are usually used for the constraint.

- **Exclusive** constraints describe situations where cause C1 and cause C2 cannot simultaneously be true. Maybe neither of them is true (see Figure 7.4).

Figure 7.4 'Exclusive' constraint for cause–effect graphs

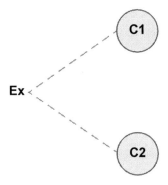

- **Inclusive** constraints define situations where causes C1 or C2 (at least one node) must always be true (see Figure 7.5).

Figure 7.5 'Inclusive' constraint for cause–effect graphs

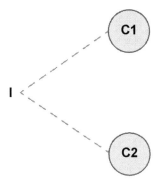

- **Require** constraints define circumstances where cause C2 must be true if cause C1 is true (see Figure 7.6).

Figure 7.6 'Require' constraint for cause–effect graphs

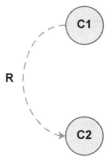

- The **Only** constraint defines the instance when one and only one of causes C1 and C2 has to be true (see Figure 7.7).

Figure 7.7 The 'Only' constraint for cause–effect graphs

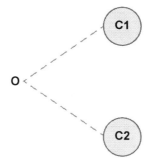

- The **Mask** constraint states that if effect E1 is true then effect E2 is forced to be false (see Figure 7.8).

Figure 7.8 'Mask' constraint for cause–effect graphs

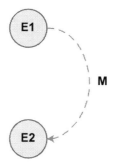

Myers (1979) defined the following six steps that cause–effect graph software testing includes when generating test cases from software specifications.

1. Divide the specification into small, workable parts (units) that contain a full description of the logic of some business.

2. For each such unit identify causes and effects in the specification. Recall that a cause is an input condition or equivalence class of input conditions, and an effect is an output condition or a result of a transformation.

3. Analyse the semantic content of the specification, and transform it into a Boolean DAG by linking the causes and effects. You can use intermediate nodes, which may help during the transformation.

4. Annotate the graph with constraints, for example describe combinations of causes and effects that are impossible for some reason.

5. Convert the graph into a limited-entry decision table:

   a. Select an effect to be the present state.

   b. Based on the graph, find all combinations of causes (subject to constraints) that will set this effect to true.

   c. Create columns in the decision table for each combination of such causes.

   d. For each combination determine the states of all other effects and place these truth values in each column.

6. Derive test cases from the table by converting each column to a separate test case, as we have seen in the decision table technique.

In practice, it is desirable to keep the number of test cases minimal while achieving higher fault coverage. The number of the tests depends on the test case design/generation method while the fault coverage depends on the fault assumption applied.

EXAMPLE: REDSHOE SPECIAL ORDERING

There is a special offer in company RedShoe. Three colour types of loaf shoes (black, brown and – of course – red), with two types (female, male) and two sizes (large and small) are reduced. Large female loaf shoes are reduced by 10% if they are not black, small black ones by 20%, red male shoes again by 20%, small brown shoes by 10%, small red shoes by 15% and brown male shoes by 15%. There is no reduction for the remaining loaf shoes. Note that small male loaf shoes are not sold in the store.

After careful investigation of the specification, the cause–effect graph can be drawn (Figure 7.9).

The cause–effect graph in Figure 7.9 can be converted into a decision table representing the logical relationships between the causes and the effects. The basic conversion process is again attributable to Myers (1979):

1. Choose an effect node and assume that it has true value. The inner nodes are traversed in the graph backward (towards the cause nodes).

2. All the combinations leading to this true valued node are taken by considering the following:

   a. Suppose that the node is an 'OR' node.

      i. When it takes true value then at most one of the nodes leading to this node must get true value as well. Hence, we should examine the influence of only one variable's effect at a time.

      ii. When it takes false value, then all the other nodes leading to this node get false values.

   b. Suppose that the node is an 'AND' node.

      i. When it takes true value, then all the nodes leading to this node must have true values.

      ii. When it takes false value, then only one case is chosen for each node getting false value. In those cases, where at least one node gets false value, only one combination should be selected; all the other nodes get true values.

The reduced decision table belonging to the graph is shown in Table 7.15.

Figure 7.9 Cause–effect graph for 'RedShoe' special. INP and OUT stand for input and output, respectively

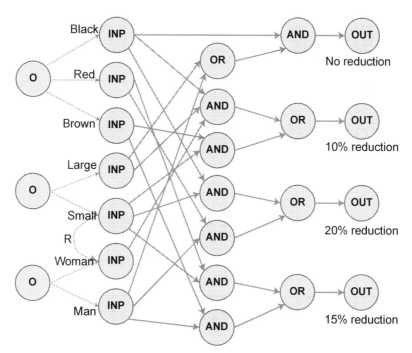

Table 7.15 Reduced, extended-entry decision table for 'RedShoe' special

Conditions	R1	R2	R3	R4	R5	R6	R7	R8
Size and type	Large female shoes		Small female shoes			Male shoes		
Colour	Black	Non-black	Black	Red	Brown	Black	Red	Brown
Actions								
Reduction	0%	10%	20%	15%	10%	0%	20%	15%

The concrete test cases can easily be constructed:

TS = {

1. ([Large, Female, Black], [Reduction = 0%]);

2. ([Large, Female, Non-Black], [Reduction = 10%]);

3. ([Small, Female, Black], [Reduction = 20%]);

4. ([Small, Female, Red], [Reduction = 15%]);

5. ([Small, Female, Brown], [Reduction = 10%]);

6. ([Male, Black], [Reduction = 0%]);

7. ([Male, Red], [Reduction = 20%]);

8. ([Male, Brown], [Reduction = 15%]) }.

METHOD EVALUATION

This subsection contains the evaluation of the cause–effect test design technique.

Applicability

Cause–effect graphs help in selecting test cases in a systematic way, out of a huge set of input combinations. Appropriate tools can support the design process.

Types of defects

The technique is able to reveal logical faults in the test basis, mainly erroneous logical relationships between the input and output conditions.

Advantages and shortcomings of the method

Advantages are as follows:

- A beneficial side-effect of the combination analysis performed during cause–effect test design is that it may also reveal incompleteness and ambiguities in the specifications.

- The maintenance of a graph is much easier than the maintenance of a large decision table.
- The table or graph format can easily be followed by others.

Shortcomings are:

- Cause–effect graphs cannot be used in all scenarios; they can only be used in cases where the test output depends on a logical combination of test inputs.
- It takes time to model the requirements and build the graph.
- Cause–effect graphs need considerable effort and practical experience.

The method helps to understand the requirements better, and is able to unfold faults in the specifications. For this reason, the method is best used complementarily with other testing methods.

THEORETICAL BACKGROUND

The cause–effect graph model was developed by Elmendorf (1973) to describe system specifications together with the relationships and dependencies of their components. Myers defined a systematic technique to generate the test cases from cause–effect graphs (Myers, 1979), by which a refined decision table can be obtained that guarantees to cover all decisions in the model. With this technique, the number of combinations in the decision table is reduced. Later, Mathur (2008) and Srivastava (2009) discussed how cause–effect graphs could be converted into decision tables. To generate test cases from Boolean expressions many different techniques are defined and studied.

KEY TAKEAWAYS

Decision tables and cause–effect graphs can be used in test design as they help testers explore the effects of combinations of different inputs and other software states that should implement business rules. The table or graph format can easily be followed by others. Some of the main benefits are:

1. easy to draw;
2. results in solid documentation;
3. simple;
4. analysable;
5. modularisable.

153

EXERCISES

E7.1 Assignment

Consider the following specification.

A university course registration software assigns labs for the informatics faculty courses based on the number of registered students and the required software toolchain. There are three common toolchains used in teaching: GNU toolchain, Apache-Maven toolchain, and SharePoint Framework toolchain. There are four labs of different sizes (with a different number of computers) in the faculty.

1. If the number of registered students for a course is fewer than 10 and Apache-Maven is needed, then the course will be in lab A.

2. If the number of registered students for a course is between 10 and 30 and Apache-Maven toolchain is needed, then the course will be in lab B.

3. If the number of registered students for a course is fewer than 10 and GNU or SharePoint is needed, then the course will be in lab B.

4. If the number of registered students for a course is between 10 and 30 and GNU is needed, then the course will be in lab C.

5. If the number of registered students for a course is above 30, or between 10 and 30 with SharePoint requirement, then the course will be in lab D.

Model and design tests for the software.

E7.2 Police control rules

A police department has specific rules that should apply in on-road control. Measuring speeds of all the passing cars, the police officer stops a car to check the driver's licence, the vehicle registration and the driver's alcohol level. If there are licence problems (it is non-existent or expired), a penalty of EUR 350 should be given and the car is confiscated. In cases where the alcohol level is not zero, the penalty is EUR 300, the driver's licence is withdrawn and the car is confiscated. If the vehicle is unregistered or the registration is expired, the penalty is EUR 200. If the driver has exceeded the speed limit by less than or equal to 10 per cent, the penalty is EUR 50. If the speed limit was exceeded by more than 10 per cent, but less than or equal to 20 per cent, the penalty is EUR 100; above 20 per cent the penalty is EUR 200. Note that the penalties are added together. If the car is not confiscated, then the police officer returns all the documents, and the driver can leave in the car.

Design tests for this specification based on the decision table technique.

8 SCENARIO-BASED TESTING

WHY IS THIS CHAPTER WORTH READING?

In this chapter, you will learn the notion and importance of use case testing and user story testing. Moreover, you will learn how to apply these techniques together with state transition testing and equivalence partitioning. We apply use case testing and user story testing for the ticket vending machine example.

A **general scenario** is a scene that illustrates some interaction with a proposed system. It may refer to the full interaction or parts of it, describing why the interaction occurs. To be more precise, general scenarios

1. Define **who** the user is,
2. Explain **why** the user uses the service (system, equipment),
3. Explain **what the main goals** the user wants to achieve are,
4. Define the **assumptions** about the service (software, equipment),
5. Outline what the **steps** are.

Cem Kaner, the director of Florida Tech's Center for Software Testing Education & Research, describes the scenario on his website[1] as a 'hypothetical story, used to help a person think through a complex problem or system'. Scenarios are examples of real-world experience, expressed in natural language, or in other media. Scenarios are generalised during requirements analysis to produce models that are familiar to practitioners in requirements or software engineering.

There are different types of **specific scenarios** used in software development (Alexander and Maiden, 2004). A scenario can either outline the steps that a **specific user plans to take**, or it specifies the steps **you plan to set up for users**. In both cases, interactions are defined between a role and the system to achieve a specific goal. However, in the first case, the steps are detailed from the user's point of view, while in the second case they explain how the system supports the goals.

Scenario-based testing focuses on the **interactions between an 'actor' and the system,** with different roles and environments, hence, it is used for writing tests for individual

---

[1] www.kaner.com

scenarios. Actors can be humans or external systems. Scenario-based tests are performed to verify that the actor can execute the desired actions completely from the beginning to the end. A test scenario can be an independent test case or a series of test cases that follow each other. It supports the tester in unfolding interaction defects that cannot be found with other types of testing.

In this chapter, we analyse the two most important scenario-based test strategies: **use case testing** and **user story testing**.

> Please remember the difference between use cases/user stories and test scenarios: the former are **business artefacts** defining some software requirements, while the latter are **test artefacts** defining the steps to validate and verify the requirements.

USE CASES

A use case is a document that describes actions or steps of events. Actions are interactions between an actor and a system obtaining a goal. A use case may have 'user actions', which define the actions performed by the user, and 'system actions', which describe the actions done by the system. **A use case is always user-oriented,** that is it specifies the interactions the user can do. A use case document outlines these interactions. The document can be written in different abstraction (formality) levels, for example applying UML diagrams, flow or sequence charts, Petri nets or simple texts. Since use cases have to be understandable for all the stakeholders, the simplest solution is the textual form. Accordingly, in the following sections, we omit the UML representation of use cases. We refer the interested reader to Cockburn (2001) for those.

There are two main types of use cases:

1. business use cases, which define a sequence of actions that the business needs to perform, achieving some observable result; and

2. system use cases, which refer to specific processes performed by different parts of the system.

Use case testing is a technique of deriving test cases from the document/model containing use cases. It tests interactions from the user's point of view and **not** on the basis of input and output. In use case testing the testers put themselves in the user's shoes and with assistance from clients and other stakeholders they figure out real-world scenarios that can be performed.

Use cases in test design

There are many ways to write a use case. Different formats can be applied to different cases (Cockburn, 2001; Fowler, 2004). The usual fields in a use case template, which is also the test design template, are the following (based on Cockburn (2001), with some reasonable modifications):

1. Use case name – such as Enter/Leave Building.

2. ID – such as SYS-UC-6.1.1.

3. Description – such as 'The user can enter to and exit from a building and its security zones assuming s/he has a valid security card'.

4. Use case level – for example very high-level summary, summary, user goal, sub-function.

5. Primary actor – who initiates an interaction with the system to realise some goal.

6. Supporting actors – an external actor providing a service to the system under design.

7. Stakeholders – primary actor, company shareholders, customers, vendors and so on.

8. Preconditions – such as 'User has a card with valid rights, the card reader is on, and the gate is closed'.

9. Postconditions – such as 'User can enter/leave the zone'.

10. Failure end condition – what happens when the goal of the primary actor has not been achieved.

11. Trigger – the event that starts the use case.

12. Main (success) scenario (or happy path or basic flow) – which contain a numbered list of steps describing the interaction between the actor and the system.

13. Extensions – conditions that result in different interactions. There are two kinds of extensions: (1) normal extension (alternative flow), where the actor's goal is achieved following different steps from those described in the main success scenario, (2) exception, that leads to **not** achieving the use case's goal. Exception flow always finishes the use case. Note that CANCEL is not an alternative, it is an exception.

14. Special requirements, constraints – such as performance, security, user interface (UI) and so on.

In practice, some of them can be ignored. There are five main steps in deriving test cases from requirements:

1. Identify the use cases from the requirements.

2. For each use case, identify the various scenarios/flow of events (main and extensions).

3. For each scenario/flow, identify test conditions that will cause it to execute.

4. For each test condition, design a test case by adding data values. Combine options, if necessary, by applying other techniques (EP, BVA, combinatorial testing, etc.).

5. Review.

EXAMPLE: ENTER/LEAVE BUILDING ZONES

A system monitors and controls entries and exits of a building and its security zones. Personal security cards are used to enter and exit the building and particular zones within the building. The system controls the locks and requires the card to be swiped through the security card reader at the doors. The gate opens only if the card is valid and the user has rights to enter/leave. The door is open for a predefined time period, then closed by the system. When the door is closed the system locks it. The card reader has an LED to show the result of the action to the user. It will light green when the user successfully unlocks the door, and it will light red when the user's card isn't valid or the user doesn't have the rights to open it. When the system unsuccessfully tries to close the door (after a predefined time period), the system tries to close it once again. If it fails, then it sends an alarm message and logs the event. When the system unsuccessfully tries to lock the door, the system waits for timeout and then tries to lock again. If it fails, then it sends an alarm message and logs the event.

Suppose that we have the use case specification document as the test basis (describing the requirements above), as shown in Tables 8.1–8.4.

Table 8.1 Use case 'Enter/Leave Building Zone'

Use case: *Enter/Leave Building Zones*			
Use case ID:	SYS-UC-6.1.1		
Use case name:	Enter/Leave Building	**Version no:**	1.0
Purpose:	The user can enter and exit from a building and its security zones assuming s/he has a valid security card		
Created by:	Attila Kovács	**Date:**	18-01-2019
Last update by:		**Date:**	
User/actor:	Card owner		
Stakeholder:		**Contact:**	
Trigger:	User		
Frequency of use:	Often		
Safety:	Critical		
Other special reqs:			
Preconditions:	The user has a card with valid rights, the card reader is on (its light is red) and the gate is closed.		

(Continued)

Table 8.1 (Continued)

Use case: *Enter/Leave Building Zones*	
Postconditions:	The user enters/leaves the zone.
Includes or extension points:	
Other notes (assumptions, issues):	

Table 8.2 Basic flow for 'Enter/Leave Building Zone' use case

Basic flow		
Step	User actions	System actions
1	The user slides her/his card through the card reader	
2		The card reader scans the user's ID from the card
3		The system validates the user access and then the reader's red light turns to green
4		The system unlocks the door for a predefined time period
5	The user opens the door and enters/leaves	
6	The user closes the door	
7		The system locks the door a. The system waits for a timeout b. The system attempts to relock c. The system notices that the door is locked d. The card reader's light turns to red

Table 8.3 Alternative flow for 'Enter/Leave Building Zone' use case

Step	User actions	System actions
Alternative flow		
6A		The system successfully closes the door (after the predefined period)
		a. The system waits for a timeout
		b. The system tries to close the door
		c. The system notices that the door is closed
6B		The system unsuccessfully tries to close the door (after the predefined period)
		a. The system waits for a timeout
		b. The system tries to close the door
		c. The system notices that the door is open
		d. Sets alarm parameters
		e. Logs the event
7A		Door fails to lock
		a. The system waits for a timeout
		b. The system attempts to relock
		c. The system notices that the door is not locked
		d. Sets alarm parameters
		e. Logs the event

Table 8.4 Exception flow for 'Enter/Leave Building Zone' use case

Step	
Exception flow	
2E	Card is unable to be read, the card reader's LED does not light
	a. Log the event
3E	User ID is invalid or no rights to open, the reader's LED light remains red
	a. Log the event
4E	The system is unable to unlock the door
	a. Log the event
	b. The reader's LED light switches to red

(Continued)

Table 8.4 (Continued)

Exception flow
Step

5E   User does not open the door

      a. The system waits for a timeout

      b. The system relocks the door

      c. The reader's LED light switches to red

You may ask why 6B and 7A are alternatives and not exceptions. The answer is simple: the user has achieved their goal. 5E is especially interesting. The user does not open the unlocked door, and after some predefined time limit, the system relocks the door. Why is it an exception? Because from the user perspective their goal is not achieved. However, from the system perspective, the door is ready for opening. A similar phenomenon can be seen in 6B and 7A. The user achieved their goal, but the door is not properly closing, or the system fails to lock the door.

Now we turn our attention to the test cases based on the use case. The test cases traverse paths through the use case. The test selection criterion for this test design technique requires simply picking all possible paths. In our case, the paths traversing the use case graph can be seen in Figure 8.1.

Figure 8.1. Use case graph for 'Enter/Leave Building Zone'

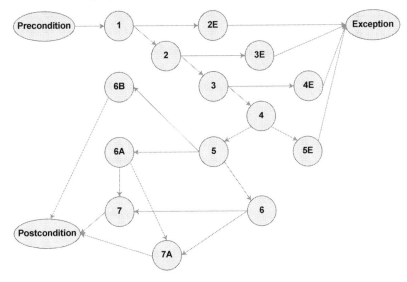

Now we specify the abstract test cases. The first one is always the happy path test,

T1 = 1-2-3-4-5-6-7

which means that (1) user swipes the card, (2) card reader scans user valid ID, (3) system validates the user's existing rights, (4) system unlocks door, (5) user opens the door and enters/leaves, (6) user closes the door, (7) system locks the door. The expected result is that the user successfully entered/left and the door is closed.

The other abstract test cases relate to the alternative and exception flows:

T2 = 1-2-3-4-5-6A-7   User swipes the card, the system verifies the (valid) ID, the system validates user's (existing) rights, the system unlocks the door for the predefined period, the user opens the door and enters/leaves, the system successfully closes the door, the system successfully locks the door. The expected result is that the user successfully entered/left and the door has been closed and locked.

T3 = 1-2-3-4-5-6A-7A   User swipes the card, the system verifies the (valid) ID, the system validates user's (existing) rights, the system unlocks the door for the predefined period, the user opens the door and enters/leaves, the system successfully closes the door, but the system is unable to lock the door. The expected result is that the user has successfully entered/left, the door has been closed but is unlocked (logged).

T4 = 1-2-3-4-5-6B   User swipes the card, the system verifies the (valid) ID, the system validates the user's (existing) rights, the system unlocks the door for the predefined period, the user opens the door and enters/leaves, the system is unable to close the door after a timeout. The expected result is that the user successfully entered/left and the door has not been closed (logged).

T5 = 1-2-3-4-5-6-7A   User swipes the card, the system verifies (valid) ID, the system validates user's (existing) rights, the system unlocks the door for the predefined period, the user opens the door and enters/leaves, the user closes the door, the system tries to lock the door, but the door fails to lock. The expected result is that the user successfully entered/left, the door has been closed but is unlocked (logged).

T6 = 1-2E   User swipes the card, the system tries to verify the ID but the card cannot be read. The expected result is that the user was unable to enter/leave since the card could not be read (logged).

T7 = 1-2-3E   User swipes the card, the system verifies ID, the system validates user rights, but user ID is invalid or does not have rights to open. The expected result is that the user was unable to enter/leave since ID was invalid or the user did not have the appropriate rights (logged).

T8 = 1-2-3-4E   User swipes the card, the system verifies ID, the system validates user (existing) rights, the system tries to unlock the door for the predefined time period, but the system is unable to unlock the door. The expected result is that the user was unable to enter/leave since the door remained locked (logged).

T9 = 1-2-3-4-5E   User swipes the card, the system verifies ID, the system validates user rights, the system unlocks the door for a pre-defined time period, but the user does not open the door. The expected result is that the user did not enter/leave, the door has been, however, closed and relocked.

The use case tester should know the following important rules regarding use case design:

- A common mistake in writing use cases is to confuse requirements with design specifications. Use case writers should avoid technical details in use cases.
- Of course, an alternative flow may start in another alternative flow.
- Use cases are usually time ordered, but sometimes there are temporal constraints in them ('action X can occur at any time before action Y').
- A use case cannot contain IF statements. They usually suggest either multiple requirements or they refer to the fact that the use case contains other models/techniques (state machines, decision tables, etc.). Let's consider the well-known ATM money withdrawal use case excerpt. An anonymous author in his blog describes the following:

  a. If an incorrect PIN is entered, the ATM displays the appropriate message.

  b. If there are still tries remaining, the flow rejoins to the Basic Flow at the Enter PIN step.

  c. If the entered PIN is incorrect on the final try, the card is retained, ATM returns to Ready State, and the use case terminates.

Such a description is avoidable; however, from the tester's point of view, it is testable. The test design technique that is applicable in this case is attributed to structure-based design techniques. A possible (better) use case description is the following:

1. The user inserts a card.

2. The system validates the card and asks for the PIN.

3. The user enters the PIN.

4. The system validates the PIN.

5. The system allows access to the account.

6. ...

Alternatives:

> 4A. The PIN is invalid; the system displays a message and asks for re-try (at most two times).

Exceptions:

> 2E. The card is invalid; the system displays a message and rejects card.
>
> 4E. The PIN is invalid three times; the system eats the card and exits.

You can see that 4, 4A and 4E can be modelled and tested together with a finite-state machine. The advantages of such layered solutions are: (1) business logic is represented in atomic forms; (2) this type of grooming supports iterative development; (3) separating the different model layers eases the maintenance.

Test selection criterion for use case testing

A use case model (graph) cannot be large; it has to be split. Clearly, use cases can call other use cases and may contain other models, which reduces the complexity. Hence, the following test selection criterion is reasonable: **cover all the executable paths in the use case graph, including the happy path, the alternative and the exception paths.**

A use case may result in many test cases to cover the happy path and the alternatives. The coverage level is determined by the coverage of the various defined paths. When the suggested test selection criterion results in too many test cases, other structure-based criteria can be used. However, we suggest splitting the use case in those cases (if possible) and applying the suggested criterion.

Ticket vending machine example

Let's examine the following use case for our ticket vending machine example. For demonstrating preconditions we consider the machine itself and not the just the software of the machine (see Tables 8.5–8.7).

Table 8.5 'Buy Tickets' use case

Use case: *Buy Tickets*			
Use case ID:	TVM-UC-6.1.2		
Use case name:	Buying Tickets	**Version No:**	1.0
Purpose:	A passenger buys tickets from TVM		
Created by:	Attila Kovács	**Date:**	18-01-2019
Last update by:		**Date:**	
User/actor:	Passenger		

(Continued)

Table 8.5 (Continued)

Use case: *Buy Tickets*	
Stakeholder:	Contact:
Trigger:	Passenger
Frequency of use:	Often
Safety:	
Other special reqs:	
Preconditions:	TVM must be functioning, it is idle (showing the initial screen), the Reduced Mode is OFF (enough paper for printing tickets, enough coins and notes for change). A passenger has sufficient money to buy tickets.
Postcondition:	The passenger has the selected tickets.
Includes or extension points:	
Other notes (assumptions, issues):	

Table 8.6 Basic flow for the 'Buy Tickets' use case

Basic flow		
Step	User actions	System actions
1	The passenger finishes selecting one of the ticket types and sets the number of tickets. Types can be: standard, short distance, 24-hour ticket. The amount is between 1 and 10	
2		The system computes and displays the allowed banknotes
		The system decides its state (normal or reduced)
		The system computes and shows the remaining amount to be paid, and shows the allowed banknotes

(Continued)

Table 8.6 (Continued)

Basic flow		
Step	User actions	System actions
3	The passenger inserts money as long as the amount to be paid is positive	
4		The system provides the tickets
		The system displays the amount to be returned. It can be zero
		The system prints ticket(s)
		The system returns the change (if any)
		The system shows a message about the successful transaction for a predefined time
		The system returns to the initial screen

Table 8.7 Exception flow for the 'Buy Tickets' use case

Exception flow	
Step	
1Ea	The passenger starts a transaction, and before finishing resets the selection process. The initial screen appears
1Eb	Timeout. The initial screen appears
3Ea	The passenger starts the payment then cancels. The system returns the money. The initial screen appears
3Eb	Timeout during the payment. The system returns the money. The initial screen appears

Let's describe the scenarios. The happy path is the following:

T1 = 1-2-3-4

with (1) the passenger selects ticket type and amount, (2) the system displays the total price and shows all the acceptable banknotes for payment, (3) the passenger inserts money, (4) the system provides the tickets and returns the change. The expected result is that the passenger has the chosen number and type of tickets for the appropriate price, and the system shows the initial screen.

The other abstract tests are the following:

T2 = 1Ea   The passenger starts a transaction, but before finishing, resets the selection process. The initial screen appears.

T3 = 1Eb   The passenger starts the selection process but becomes inactive. After a timeout, the initial screen appears.

T4 = 1-2-3Ea   The passenger selects ticket type and amount, the system displays the total price and shows all the acceptable banknotes for payment, the passenger starts the payment by inserting money, then cancels. The system returns the money, the initial screen appears.

T5 = 1-2-3Eb   The passenger selects the ticket type and amount, the system displays the total price and shows all the acceptable banknotes for payment, the passenger becomes inactive after inserting some money, the system returns the money after a timeout, the initial screen appears.

Use case testing extended by EP and BVA

Use case and state transition testing are significantly different techniques. However, we can and sometimes should perform use case and EP and BVA testing together. TVM is a good example of this. We have the abstract test cases based on the use cases and now we consider the EPs. Then T1, the only happy path, will be extended by BVA test cases.

Actually, we have the following EPs with regards to ticket types and number of tickets:

- EPs for positive tests with regard to ticket types and number of tickets:
  - EP1: standard ticket, $1 \leq$ number of tickets ≤ 10.
  - EP2: 24-hour ticket, $1 \leq$ number of tickets ≤ 10.
  - EP3: short distance ticket, $1 \leq$ number of tickets ≤ 10.
  - EP4: no ticket type, number of tickets $= 0$.
- EPs for negative tests with regard to ticket types and number of tickets:
  - EP5: standard ticket, number of tickets >10.
  - EP6: standard ticket, number of tickets <1.
  - EP7: 24-hour ticket, number of tickets >10.
  - EP8: 24-hour ticket, number of tickets < 1.
  - EP9: short distance ticket, number of tickets >10.
  - EP10: short distance ticket, number of tickets < 1.

Finally, considering the acceptable banknotes, we have four EPs (see Chapter 5), shown in Table 8.8.

Table 8.8 Equivalence partitions for the 'Buy Tickets' use case of the TVM, for the happy path

EP	Remaining amount to be paid	Acceptable banknotes
11	<=5	€5
12	> 5 and <= 10	€5, €10
13	> 10 and <= 20	€5, €10, €20
14	> 20	€5, €10, €20, €50

For EPs 1, 2, 3 we have two test cases for each based on the BVA (ticket numbers 1 and 10). For all other EPs (from 4 to 10), we have only one test case. Considering EP11–14, we have seven test cases. Summarising, we have 5 test cases based on use case testing, 13 test cases with regard to the types and number of tickets, and 7 test cases for acceptable banknotes. It takes 25 test cases together.

The next step in test design is to harmonise these test cases into one reliable test set. To do this, we should merge the test cases.

Let's start with the acceptable banknotes. Instead of executing seven different test cases, we can start with the total ticket price and we can insert coins and banknotes in a way that all the boundary values are tested. In Chapter 5 the boundary values and test cases for testing acceptable banknotes were given. Here, the test steps are shown in Table 8.9 and then the extended table with sub-steps are in Table 8.10.

Table 8.9 Use case tests for TVM

Number of 24-hour tickets	10			
Total price of the tickets	76			
Test step	EP	Inserted amount	Remaining amount to be paid	Acceptable banknotes
S0	4	0	76	€5, €10, €20, €50
S1	4	55.9	20.1	€5, €10, €20, €50
S2	3	0.1	20	€5, €10, €20

(Continued)

Table 8.9 (Continued)

Test step	EP	Inserted amount	Remaining amount to be paid	Acceptable banknotes
S3	3	9.9	10.1	€5, €10, €20
S4	2	0.1	10	€5, €10
S5	2	4.9	5.1	€5, €10
S6	1	0.1	5	€5
S7	1	5	0	–

Table 8.10 Extended use case test tests for TVM

Refinement for steps into sub-steps

Test step	Sub-step	Inserted coin/ banknote	Remaining amount to be paid	Acceptable banknotes
S1	S1_1	50	26	€5, €10, €20, €50
S1	S1_2	5	21	€5, €10, €20, €50
S1	S1_3	0.5	20.5	€5, €10, €20, €50
S1	S1_4	0.2	20.3	€5, €10, €20, €50
S1	S1_5	0.2	20.1	€5, €10, €20, €50
S3	S3_1	5	15	€5, €10, €20
S3	S3_2	2	13	€5, €10, €20
S3	S3_3	2	11	€5, €10, €20
S3	S3_4	0.5	10.5	€5, €10, €20
S3	S3_5	0.2	10.3	€5, €10, €20
S3	S3_6	0.2	10.1	€5, €10, €20
S5	S3_1	2	8	€5, €10
S5	S3_2	2	6	€5, €10
S5	S3_3	0.5	5.5	€5, €10
S5	S3_4	0.2	5.3	€5, €10
S5	S3_5	0.2	5.1	€5, €10

These test steps can be involved in the happy path T1.

Now let's try to harmonise use case tests and EP and BVA tests for various ticket types and number of tickets to buy. We have to test all the ticket types separately. However, based on our risk analysis, we can assume that if the TVM is able to print 10 tickets of any type, then it is able to print only one ticket as well. Therefore, we design three test cases for each ticket type and 10 tickets to buy, which are then printed. For the 24-hour ticket, we include the test steps S0–S7 (Table 8.9).

Based on the competent programmer's hypothesis we can assume that the acceptable banknotes are implemented once and not for all different ticket types. Of course, for a safety-critical system, we would not assume this. In this way, the other two test cases will be much simpler.

If the number of tickets to buy is one, it is enough to test that after selecting a ticket type, we can buy the ticket, that is we do not need to select two, three or more tickets. Those test cases can be merged with use case test cases T4 and T5, where we cancel buying or remain inactive for the predefined time, respectively.

Considering the negative tests, when selecting 10 tickets of any type, we shall try to increase the number of tickets, and if we are able to increase them, then the test fails. Similarly, when the number of tickets to buy is 0, we have to try to decrease it.

With this consideration we have the following test cases:

T1:

- (Step 1) The passenger selects ticket type '24 hour' and increases the number of tickets to 10, then tries to increase the number of tickets.
- (Step 2) The system displays the total price 76 and shows that banknotes €5, €10, €20, €50 are acceptable for payment.
- (Step 3) The passenger executes steps S1–S7 of Table 8.9.
- (Step 4) The system prints the 10 24-hour tickets, no returns remain, the system returns to the initial screen.

T2:

- (Step 1) The passenger selects ticket type 'standard' and increases the number of tickets to 5.
- (Step 1Ea) The passenger resets the selection process, the initial screen appears.
- (Step 1) The passenger selects the ticket type 'standard' and increases the number of tickets to 10, then tries to increase the number of tickets.
- (Step 2) The system displays the total price 21 and shows banknotes €5, €10, €20, €50 are acceptable for payment.
- (Step 3) The passenger inserts €50.
- (Step 4) The system prints the 10 standard tickets, gives back EUR 29, the system returns to the initial screen.

T3:

- (Step 1) The passenger selects ticket type 'short distance' and increases the number of tickets to 3.
- (Step 1Eb) The passenger waits for a timeout, the initial screen appears.
- (Step 1) The passenger selects ticket type 'short distance' and increases the number of tickets to 10, then tries to increase the number of tickets.
- (Step 2) The system displays the total price 14 and shows banknotes €5, €10, €20 are acceptable for payment.
- (Step 3) The passenger inserts €20.
- (Step 4) The system prints the 10 short distance tickets, gives back EUR 6, the system returns to the initial screen.

T4:

- (Step 1) The passenger selects ticket type 'short distance' and tries to decrease it, then increases the number of tickets to 1.
- (Step 2) The system displays the total price 1.4 and shows banknote €5 is acceptable for payment.
- (Step 3Ea) The passenger inserts €1 then cancels, the system returns 1 EUR, the initial screen appears.
- (Step 1) The passenger selects ticket type 'standard' and tries to decrease it, then increases the number of tickets to 1.
- (Step 2) The system displays the total price 2.1 and shows banknote €5 is acceptable for payment.
- (Step 3Eb) The passenger inserts €2 then waits for a timeout, the system returns 2 EUR, the initial screen appears.
- (Step 1) The passenger selects ticket type '24-hour' and tries to decrease it, then increases the number of tickets to 1.
- (Step 2) The system displays the total price 7.6 and shows banknotes €5 and €10 are allowed for payment.
- (Step 3) The passenger inserts €10.
- (Step 4) The system prints one 24-hour ticket, gives back EUR 2.4, the system returns to the initial screen.

USER STORIES

While a use case is a **heavyweight** document, a **user story** is a **lightweight** document that can be written on a card. A user story does not capture all the requirement's details, but is a more or less informal, short, simple description of a feature described from the perspective of the user or customer. The descriptive part of a user story typically follows a simple template:

As a < type of user, role>

I want < some goal>

so that < some reason, benefit>.

User stories are written and maintained by the project stakeholders throughout the project. They describe the system's functionality and place the stories into the product backlog. Stories are used to capture various kinds of requirements, including non-functional ones.

User stories are incomplete at the beginning, and they are discussed and refined continuously. **Epics** (sometimes called **features**) are large user stories, typically ones that are too big to be implemented in a single iteration and therefore need to be refined into smaller stories. A **theme** is a collection of related user stories, used to organise the stories into releases. A **spike** is a special type of user story for investigation or research activity.

There are four common occurrences when user stories must be discussed: (1) during the model brainstorming with stakeholders (brief description of the need, screen sketches, confirmations, etc.), (2) during release planning (epics are broken down into smaller chunks), (3) during iteration planning (the Agile team agrees on a set of stories for the upcoming iteration, taking into consideration the complexities, sizes, dependencies of the stories, capabilities of the team, etc.) and (4) during the implementation. Note that user stories may be different sizes, but they are still user stories.

User stories contain not only a description but should include other important information as well: the estimated complexity, the effort required to complete the story, the priority, a unique identifier, and from the test design perspective the most important one, the **acceptance criteria**. Acceptance criteria are the set of requirements that must be met for a user story to be completed. The **definition of done** is a set of criteria that are common across related user stories that must be met to close the stories. The acceptance criteria help in deciding which functionality must be delivered at each project milestone. In other words, the testing process must validate that the acceptance criteria meet the requirements established in the user story. Well-formed stories meet the criteria of Bill Wake's INVEST acronym (Wake, 2003):

- I: Independent (the stories are self-contained, there is no inherent dependency on another story, can be developed in any order).
- N: Negotiable (avoids too much detail, keeps the stories flexible, leaves space for implementation details).
- V: Valuable (stories deliver value to the stakeholders).
- E: Estimable (the team can use the stories for planning).
- S: Small (stories should be small, they should be able to be designed, coded and tested within the iteration).
- T: Testable (the acceptance criteria must be documented for each story; they lead to test cases).

In addition to testing the required functionality, other test cases may be required around the user story, where all the previously known test design techniques may be used. We highlight the details in the following subsection.

User stories and test design

When we want to test a user story-related requirement (or some of them) the first task is to determine the test object. There are four types:

1. an individual user story;
2. a set of user stories inside an epic;
3. a flow of stories that can be tested within a sprint;
4. a flow of stories across sprints.

The test conditions for the non-functional requirements can be derived by the FURPS+ model (Functionality, Usability, Reliability, Performance, Security and so on. (Grady and Caswell, 1987)), or by other models (ISO 25010, 2011). When we move from the individual scenario testing to the flow of stories across sprints, we get closer and closer to the end-user scenario testing (use case testing). It is important to note that by determining the complexity of the user story and the effort that is needed to complete the user story, it is possible to evaluate the risks of the story. It is advisable to share the risk database with the customer/product owner so that they know what to concentrate on during (acceptance and other) testing.

The individual user story can be tested by checking or determining the following:

- Specification related:
  - Functionality: business logic, behaviour, data specification, FURPS+ (e.g. access control) and so on.
  - Input: syntax, data type, EP, BVA and so on.
  - User interface: layout, properties of the UI elements and so on.
  - Application programming interface (API) interface signatures, dependencies, data types, conformance to protocols and so on.
- Structure related:
  - Architecture.
  - Internal dependencies.
  - Resource usage.
  - Concurrency.
  - Error handling and so on.

A set of user stories inside an epic can be tested by the usual functional tests. The flow of stories can be tested by end-to-end testing, FURPS+ related testing (load, stress, capacity, performance, endurance, data volume, resource consumption, security, compatibility, etc.), environment testing, and by deployment-related tests (installation, etc.). Note that none of the test types mentioned previously are limited to the functional behaviour.

Before we turn our attention to the acceptance tests, we clarify first the difference between the acceptance criteria and the acceptance tests. Acceptance criteria are a set of test conditions that a given requirement must meet. If the test object (system, epic, story) fulfils all the acceptance criteria, then it should behave correctly. Acceptance tests for a system, epic or story are designed based on the acceptance criteria for that system, epic or story.

The acceptance tests are often derived as a result of a conversation with various stakeholders. Hence, conventions have been proposed connecting the business-level concept to the application-level concept. One of the most popular such conventions is the application of Gherkin syntax (details in Chapter 12), which plays a central role in behaviour-driven development (BDD). Gherkin connects the business causes and effects with application input/process/output:

Scenario: <short description of the test/example of how the system behaves in a given situation>

>*Given* <input | preconditions>

>*When* <actions | triggers>

>*Then* <output | consequences

Gherkin syntax outlines how a test condition is going to be confirmed. Gherkin is a business readable, domain-specific language created especially for behaviour descriptions. It is a useful tool for business analysts and product owners as well as for developers. Note, however, that it does not tell you how it will be implemented.

Ticket vending machine example

Let's consider our TVM example.

Story (epic):	As a passenger, I want to buy tickets from the ticket vending machine, so that I can travel on public transport vehicles for which the ticket is valid.

Story (individual):	As a passenger, I want to select a ticket type and amount, so that I can travel within a selected time-frame, distance and number of trips.

...

Behaviour-driven test design:

Scenario: I can select only one type of ticket

>Given the TVM is working,

>When I select the short distance ticket type,

>And I set number of tickets to 1,

>Then I am unable to select other types of tickets.

Scenario: I buy 5 short distance tickets

> Given the TVM is working,
>
> When I select the short distance ticket type,
>
> And I set the number of tickets to 5,
>
> Then I can continue with buying the tickets,
>
> And the acceptable banknotes are €5 and €10
>
> And the total price of the tickets will be EUR 7.

Scenario: reset short distance tickets

> Given the TVM is working,
>
> When I select the short distance ticket type,
>
> And I set the number of tickets to 8,
>
> And reset the process,
>
> Then the number of short distance tickets will be 0,
>
> And I cannot proceed to buy.

Scenario: successful buying of short distance tickets

> Given the TVM is working,
>
> When I select the short distance ticket type,
>
> And I set number of tickets to 10,
>
> Then I can proceed to the payment process,
>
> And the acceptable banknotes are €5, €10 and €20
>
> And the total price of tickets will be EUR 14.

Here are only some examples regarding applying Gherkin syntax. The scenarios are selected according to EP, BVA and STT. Gherkin code makes test cases understandable for every stakeholder, but it is not a test design technique in itself.

METHODS EVALUATION

This section evaluates the test design techniques of use cases and user stories.

> Note that use cases and state transition diagrams are different views of the same specification. It is usually not the testers' task to design use cases. Testers start their work on the given, existing specifications.

Applicability

Use cases are useful in exercising business rules or process flows. They provide a holistic view of the system. Use cases support:

- Identifying test cases that exercise the whole system on a step-by-step basis.
- Designing acceptance tests with user participation.

Use case tests:

- Are related to 'user scenarios'.
- Are generally used for system and acceptance tests.
- Are able to uncover integration defects.
- Can be used even for component testing if interactions occur inside a component.
- May serve for specifying performance tests because they demonstrate real usage.

User stories are useful in exercising and documenting application needs (e.g. interactions on a website) since they describe what the user/customer will do on the application. User stories:

- Are related to 'user scenarios'.
- Facilitate collaboration among stakeholders and team members.
- Encapsulate business needs (while acceptance tests encapsulate business understanding).
- Help to prevent feature creep and infinite design loops.
- When completed, serve as living documentation.

Types of defects

Use cases are defined in terms of interactions between the actors and the system that accomplish some goal. Use case tests are designed to exercise the defined behaviour of a specific system (basic, alternative and exceptional). Use case testing includes possible variations of behaviour including system response, application and communication errors and so on. Defects include mishandling of defined scenarios, missed alternative/exceptional path handling and incorrect processing of the conditions presented or incorrect error reporting.

User stories describe small functional units that can be designed, developed, tested and demonstrated in a single Agile iteration. Defects are usually functional in that the software fails to provide the specified functionality. Note, however, that defects are also seen with integration issues of the functionality (already existing or overlapping functionality). Since stories are in most cases developed independently, performance, interface and error handling issues may be checked as well.

Advantages and shortcomings of the method

Advantages

Scenarios are critical both for designing interfaces and for usability tests. Use case testing is advantageous for investigating end-to-end situations, transaction by transaction, from start to end, covering various user scenarios. Use case testing focuses on realistic events/data during the interactions. We can use all the dynamic testing techniques to test the correct flows, the alternate flows and the exceptions. On the other hand, use case testing can be used as a guideline for generating more detailed testing.

Negative tests can be included easily. That's a significant advantage over STT.

User stories facilitate the team in determining the acceptance criteria during design. This helps in understanding user needs, and how the story should be tested. One of the main benefits of Agile user stories is that they can be written at varying levels of detail.

BDD, as its name says, is not a test design technique. This is a method by which test cases become understandable for every stakeholder and compilable for test execution tools as well. In this way, the tests can be easily validated by business analysts, product owners and so on. BDD tests can also be considered as live specification.

Shortcomings

In simple cases, test cases can be created from a textual description of use cases. However, in more complex cases, it is advisable to use a graph. This can be time-consuming. Maintaining use case graphs is also time-consuming.

The textual description is sometimes less understandable than graph representation. When the graph representation includes backward edges (hence cycles), state transition diagrams are probably behind the scenes.

Scenario-based strategies are great when there are scenarios. Scenarios, however, need users. In some cases, there are no users present. In these situations, the feature-driven development (FDD) approach is preferable. It is straightforward to use in object-oriented programming, API programming and so on. FDD has the syntax

<Result> <by | of | for | on | to> <Object>

For example 'Generate a unique identifier for all transactions', 'Change the colour of the text in the main menu' (see Palmer and Felsing, 2002).

When the product is unstable, scenario testing becomes complicated. Use case testing is not suitable for testing any kind of non-functional requirements such as platform, timings, performance, security and so on.

User stories written on physical cards are hard to maintain, difficult to scale and may be annoying for geographically distributed teams (this is not the case with digital cards). Being informal, they can be interpreted differently. This may badly influence their testing as well. When multiple stories should be built together, there may be gaps in the functionality. Another weakness with stories is that the testing tasks may become unnecessarily large (this is called 'iterative/incremental over-testing'). However, this phenomenon may force the team into automation.

THEORETICAL BACKGROUND

Use cases were formulated first by Jacobson for textual, structural and visual modelling. The most comprehensive book about use cases was written by Cockburn (2001). He suggested two alternative descriptions of use cases: one is the 'fully dressed', the other is the 'casual' description. In this chapter, we used a slightly modified version of the former.

User stories were part of the planning game in the Extreme Programming methodology (based on Cockburn, 2001). Jeffries proposed the 3Cs (Card-Conversation-Confirmation) formula in 2001.

Scenarios have numerous possible applications in system development; Carroll (1995) distinguished 10 different scenario roles in the SDLC.

Use case testing can be automated in a probabilistic way when the system under test can be depicted as a relatively simple finite-state machine. The key point here is to minimise the effort taken in finding realisable paths in the abstract state machine covering the main and alternative paths.

KEY TAKEAWAYS

- Both use cases and user stories keep products user-focused.
- User stories are formal requirements with context and structure.
- User stories can be more easily written by a user or customer; use cases are mainly written by user proxies (business analysts, etc.).
- A user story does not model the interaction between the actor and the system, which the use case does.
- User stories are used for planning (via story points and velocity), use cases are not.
- User stories are implemented and tested inside an iteration; use cases can be implemented in several iterations.

- To design test cases for more complex specifications:

  1. Carefully select the test design techniques for the specification.

  2. Work out the test cases separately based on the related test design technique.

  3. Harmonise the test cases by creating more complex tests based on the original ones while paying attention to their independence.

  4. Validate the test cases.

EXERCISES

E8.1 Consider the specification of E7.2. Design tests by applying use case testing.

E8.2 Consider the specification of E7.2. Design five important user stories based on it.

9 COMBINATIVE AND COMBINATORIAL TESTING

WHY IS THIS CHAPTER WORTH READING?

In this chapter, you will learn why combinative and combinatorial testing are important and what the main techniques are regarding test design. We introduce a new testing technique and analyse its reliability. We compare the usability of the described techniques from two aspects: when the code has either computational or control-flow faults. Finally, as well as the TVM, we give another complex example.

Combinatorial testing aims to determine **data combinations** to be tested. In a complex testing environment, this testing technique has practically two main application areas: (1) testing **combinations of configuration parameter** values and (2) testing **combinations of input parameter** values. Multidimensional EP and BVA testing is a special case in the latter.

In combinative testing, the number of reliable tests can be described by a linear function of the maximal number of parameter values or by the number of parameters. This is especially useful when a large number of parameter combinations is given.

Let's look at an example. Given n parameters, when each of them can have m_i different values ($i \in \{1, 2,...,n\}$), the question is how to choose a reliable test set among the parameter values. Unfortunately, testing all of the possible combinations $m_1 \times m_2 \times ... \times m_n$ may result in a large number of test cases that is infeasible and inefficient – exhaustive testing of complex computer software is still impossible.

Fortunately, thorough investigations show that a considerable percentage of software faults are triggered by a single parameter, while most of the faults arise from the interaction of two or just a few parameters (see Kuhn et al., 2008). Concentrating on those combinations, testing may become more effective in practice. Kuhn determined that up to 97 per cent of software failures can be detected by only two variables interacting and practically 100 per cent of software failures are detected by at most six variables in combination. This means that testing every combination up to six variables can be considered practically as good as exhaustive testing.

Figure 9.1 Fault detection at interaction strength according to Kuhn et al. (2008). The region shows the most probable fault detection rate in various interaction levels

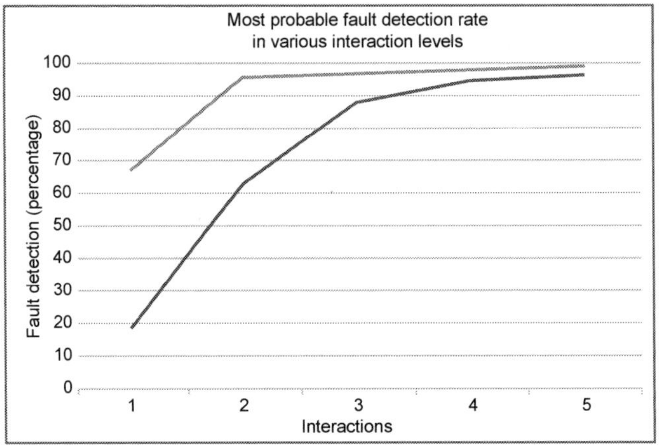

To deal with the combination set, the main problems are:

- More tests need more maintenance and more resources to be run.

- More tests raise the oracle problem, that is for each input combination, the expected output must be determined. This is the main reason for researching methods of sub-quadratic test set size.

EXAMPLE: CONFIGURATION TESTING

Consider a system under test with four parameters, A, B, C, D. These parameters have the following values:

- Parameter A: a1, a2, a3, a4,
- Parameter B: b1, b2, b3,
- Parameter C: c1, c2,
- Parameter D: d1, d2, d3, d4.

Analyse the possible combinatorial testing techniques.

Before we discuss the various selection techniques let's consider the extreme cases. When the test suite is created randomly, the sampling is based on some input distribution (often uniform distribution). Not underestimating the power of random choice, do you really want to design your test cases randomly?

On the other hand, when every combination of each parameter value is used, the number of test cases can be large; in our example above it is 4 × 3 × 2 × 4 = 96. Of course, in general, this is not feasible.

Real combinatorial testing is expensive as it requires an over-linear number of test cases. However, for non-safety critical programs, this is usually not necessary. Let's assume a large program with 5000 test cases. Let's also assume that we would like to extend the test by combinatorial testing, but only for four per cent of the tests. This means that 5000 × 0.04 = 200 test cases should be extended. Combining all test data pairs results in 200 × 200 = 40,000 test cases (all pairwise combinations), that is, the total number of test cases will be 40,000 + 5000 × 0.96 = 44,800 at worst case. This means that the number of test cases has increased by 796 per cent.

For normal projects this growth is impossible. Let's assume that we have a technique by which the number of reliable tests is just doubled. Considering the same example, the total number of test cases will be 5200 at worst case, where the growth is only four per cent. This is usually manageable, especially if we also detect tricky bugs, the fixing of which would be more expensive than the additional testing cost. Therefore, linear and yet reliable techniques are preferable.

COMBINATIVE TECHNIQUES

Combinative test design techniques are easy to generate, with the number of test cases depending linearly on the maximal number of parameter values.

Diff-pair testing

The rationale behind the combinative technique introduced in this book is to ensure that for a single variable each computation is calculated in more than one context. The basic variant of the presented combinative testing is called **diff-pair testing**. Informally, it requires that each value p of any parameter P be tested with at least two different values q and r for any other parameters. For example, if the parameter P has two possible values, let us say x and y, and there are two more parameters Q and R with values: Q: (1, 2) and R: (Y, N), then we have to test the value pairs (x, 1), (x, 2), (x, Y), (x, N). Thus, the test suite required for testing parameter P contains the data combinations {(x, 1, Y), (x, 2, N)} or {(x, 1, N), (x, 2, Y)}. Similarly, for y, we test {(y, 1, Y), (y, 2, N)} or {(y, 1, N), (y, 2, Y)}.

We test the values of the other parameters R and Q similarly. More formally, diff-pair testing requires the testing of each parameter pair (P, Q) in such a way that there should be at least two test data pairs (pi, qj) and (pi, qk) present in the test suite for each pi ∈ P, qi, qk ∈ Q, where qj ≠ qk.

Example diff-pair
Suppose that we have five parameters (A, B, C, D, E) and all of them have two possible values, 1 and 2. Then the test sequences shown in Table 9.1 satisfy the criteria of diff-pair.

For example, let's see the third parameter C:

- In cases (C, A), 1 ∈ C, the tests T1 and T6, while for 2 ∈ C the tests T3 and T5 are appropriate.
- In cases (C, B), 1 ∈ C, the tests T1 and T2, while for 2 ∈ C the tests T3 and T4 are appropriate.
- In cases (C, D), 1 ∈ C, the tests T1 and T6, while for 2 ∈ C the tests T3 and T4 are appropriate.
- In cases (C, E), 1 ∈ C, the tests T1 and T2, while for 2 ∈ C the tests T3 and T5 are appropriate.

Consider now the last parameter E:

- In cases (E, A), 1 ∈ E, the tests T1 and T6, while for 2 ∈ E the tests T2 and T3 are appropriate.
- In cases (E, B), 1 ∈ E, the tests T1 and T6, while for 2 ∈ E the tests T2 and T3 are appropriate.
- In cases (E, C), 1 ∈ E, the tests T1 and T5, while for 2 ∈ E the tests T2 and T3 are appropriate.
- In cases (E, D), 1 ∈ E, the tests T1 and T6, while for 2 ∈ E the tests T2 and T4 are appropriate.

We leave the remaining three parameters to the reader.

Diff-pair-N testing

We can extend diff-pair testing in such a way that for a pair of test data not only one but N parameter values are different.

Table 9.1 Diff-pair example for five parameters having two values each

Test	diff-pair				
	A	B	C	D	E
T1	1	1	1	1	1
T2	1	2	1	1	2
T3	2	1	2	1	2
T4	2	2	2	2	2
T5	1	1	2	2	1
T6	2	2	1	2	1

The technique requires the testing of each parameter value $p \in P$ at least twice in the following way: there must always be at least two tests such that whenever both tests contain data p, then for all other arbitrary N parameters their data values differ, that is if

$$T1 = (p, q1, q2,...,qN,...) \text{ and}$$

$$T2 = (p, q1', q2',...,qN',...)$$

then $q1 \neq q1'$, $q2 \neq q2'$,...,$qN \neq qN'$.

Diff-pair testing is actually diff-pair-1 testing. Experience shows that in most of the cases the value N = 1 is strong enough.

Example diff-pair-4
Let the five parameters (A, B, C, D, E) with values 1 and 2 be given again. Then the test sequences in Table 9.2 satisfy the criteria of diff-pair-4.

- Considering the first parameter A, $1 \in A$, the tests T1 and T2, while for $2 \in A$ the tests T3 and T4 are appropriate.

- Considering the second parameter B, $1 \in B$, the tests T1 and T3, while for $2 \in B$ the tests T2 and T4 are appropriate.

- Considering the third parameter C, $1 \in C$, the tests T4 and T5, while for $2 \in C$ the tests T3 and T6 are appropriate.

- Considering the parameter D, $1 \in D$, the tests T1 and T7, while for $2 \in D$ the tests T5 and T8 are appropriate.

- Considering the parameter E, $1 \in E$, the tests T1 and T8, while for $2 \in E$ the tests T5 and T7 are appropriate.

Example diff-pair-3
The diff-pair-3 test set for the 'Configuration Testing' example can be seen in Table 9.3.

Then, the parameter value

- a1 is tested by tests T1, T2;
- a2 is tested by tests T3, T4;
- a3 is tested by tests T5, T6;
- a4 is tested by tests T7, T8;
- b1 is tested by tests T1, T3;
- b2 is tested by tests T2, T4;
- b3 is tested by tests T6, T7;
- c1 is tested by tests T1, T4;
- c2 is tested by tests T2, T3;

- d1 is tested by tests T1, T6;
- d2 is tested by tests T2, T5;
- d3 is tested by tests T3, T7;
- d4 is tested by tests T4, T8.

Table 9.2 Diff-pair-4 example for five parameters having two values each

Test	diff-pair-4				
	A	B	C	D	E
T1	1	1	1	1	1
T2	1	2	2	2	2
T3	2	1	2	2	2
T4	2	2	1	1	1
T5	1	1	1	2	2
T6	1	2	2	1	1
T7	2	2	2	1	2
T8	2	2	2	2	1
T9	1	1	2	2	1

Table 9.3 Diff-pair-3 tests for the 'Configuration Testing' example

Test	A	B	C	D
T1	a1	b1	c1	d1
T2	a1	b2	c2	d2
T3	a2	b1	c2	d3
T4	a2	b2	c1	d4
T5	a3	b1	c1	d2
T6	a3	b3	c2	d1
T7	a4	b3	c1	d3
T8	a4	b1	c2	d4

Note that for this example the same number of test cases are required for diff-pair-1 (diff-pair) testing.

Consider the diff-pair technique. We prove that the number of test cases remains linear. Assume that we have the parameters A, B, C,...,Z with values a1, a2,...,an, b1, b2,...,bn, ...z1, z2,...,zn. Let's generate 2n test cases in the following way.

$$T(1) = (a1, b1,..., z1) \qquad\qquad T(n+1) = (a1, b2,..., zn)$$

$$T(2) = (a2, b2,..., z2) \qquad\qquad T(n+2) = (a2, b3,..., z1)$$

and

$$... \qquad\qquad ...$$

$$T(n) = (an, bn,..., zn) \qquad\qquad T(2n) = (an, b1,..., z(n-1)).$$

It is easy to see that each data aj appears in two test cases for all j $\in$ {1,...,n}. For example, a1 appears in T1 and T(n+1) but all the other parameter values are different in those tests. Similar reasoning can be given for other parameter values, since in the first n tests the values have the same indices in a test, while in the second n test cases the indices are permutations.

We can see that in this case, assuming that n is not less than the number of parameters, these test cases also satisfy diff-pair-n. If the number of test cases can be the same for diff-pair-k and diff-pair-n technique, we have to satisfy the stronger technique. This was the case in our 'Configuration Testing' example. In general, if diff-pair-k testing requires a minimum of K test cases and with K test cases we can cover diff-pair-m as well (m > k), then diff-pair-k testing satisfies diff-pair-m testing.

COMBINATORIAL TECHNIQUES

The aim of combinatorial testing is to produce high-quality tests at a relatively low cost even if the number of the possible data combinations are over linear.

Base choice

This technique starts with identifying the base test case. The choice depends on any test object-related criterion: most risky, most likely values and so on. Then, the other test cases are created by varying the base test case by **one** parameter value at a time in all possible ways, while keeping the other values fixed (see Table 9.4).

Clearly, the technique satisfies the 1-way coverage. The number of test cases in our example is 1 + (4 − 1) + (3 − 1) + (2 − 1) + (4 − 1) = 10. In general, considering n different parameters having m different values, the number of test cases is 1 + n x (m − 1).

Table 9.4 'Configuration Testing' example: base choice

Test	A	B	C	D
T1 (base)	a1	b2	c2	d3
T2	a2	b2	c2	d3
T3	a3	b2	c2	d3
T4	a4	b2	c2	d3
T5	a1	b1	c2	d3
T6	a1	b3	c2	d3
T7	a1	b2	c1	d3
T8	a1	b2	c2	d1
T9	a1	b2	c2	d2
T10	a1	b2	c2	d4

N-way testing

This technique takes N-way combinations of all the parameter values, eliminates the combinations that are unlikely or impossible, and uses the realistic combinations for testing. Though the method can be automated, only 2-way (pairwise) or 3-way testing is realistic in practice. At most those cases are computationally tractable and effective. In our 'Configuration Testing' example the all-pairs table is shown in Table 9.5.

In the table '-' denotes the 'don't care' symbol. Please check that all data value pairs can be found in a test case, for example a2–d4 pair is in T10.

The convention for describing the variables and values (called configurations or signatures) in combinatorial testing is $v_1^{k1}v_2^{k2}...$, where v_i are the size of the variable sets and k_i are the number of their occurrences. Our 'Configuration Testing' example has the signature $2\times3\times4^2$. To get an insight into the reduction rate of N-wise combinatorial techniques, the examples in Table 9.6 show the number of tests for various configurations.

The number of test cases including all N-way combinations depends on:

- the number of parameters;
- the maximum parameter cardinality;
- the variability of parameter cardinality.

Table 9.5 All-pairs tests for the 'Configuration Testing' example

Test	A	B	C	D
T1	a1	b1	c1	d1
T2	a1	b2	c2	d2
T3	a2	b2	c1	d1
T4	a2	b1	c2	d2
T5	a3	b3	c2	d1
T6	a3	b3	c1	d2
T7	a4	b1	c1	d3
T8	a4	b2	c2	d4
T9	a1	b3	c2	d3
T10	a2	b3	c1	d4
T11	a3	b2	–	d3
T12	a3	b1	–	d4
T13	a4	b3	–	d1
T14	a1	–	–	d4
T15	a2	–	–	d3
T16	a4	–	–	d2

To be more precise, the number of N-way tests is **proportional** to $v^N \times \log(n)$ for n parameters with v values each. Hence, the method is reasonable even for larger parameter spaces (i.e. $v \leq 10$ and N = 2,3). For example, if there are 20 variables with 10 different values each, then using pairwise testing, 180 test cases are sufficient. Exhaustive testing would need 10^{20} tests. This logarithmic growth means that if a project uses combinatorial testing for a system having (let's say) 30 parameters and applies a few hundred tests, then the larger system with 40 parameters (after 5 years in the project life cycle) may only require a few dozen more tests. Hence, it is scalable.

Note that although pure random choice covers a high percentage of N-way combinations, increasing the coverage level requires significantly more and more tests. For example, the configuration 4^{10} (10 parameters with four values each) can be covered with 151 tests by applying 3-way testing. However, pure random generation needs over 900 tests to provide full coverage.

There are supporting tools for N-way test generation. Moreover, these tools allow the inclusion of certain important configurations, relevant interactions, and take into account constraints, or impossible combinations.

Table 9.6 Comparison of some combinatorial methods

Configuration	N-wise	Number of tests	% of Exhaustive testing
$2^3 \times 3^2$	N = 2	10	14
	3	18	25
	4	36	50
	5	72	100
$2^3 \times 7 \times 8$	2	56	12.5
	3	112	25
	4	224	50
$3^3 \times 4^4 \times 5^2$	2	29	0.02
	3	137	0.08
	4	625	0.4
	5	2532	1.5
	6	9168	5.3

Orthogonal arrays

Orthogonal array (OA) testing is a systematic, statistical method for constructing parameter value combinations. It is used when the parameter space is large, but the number of possible values per parameter is small. It is especially effective in finding logic errors in complex software systems (e.g. in telecommunications).

An **orthogonal array** OA(N, t, k, v, λ) is an N x k array with the following property: in every N x t subarray, each t-tuple occurs **exactly λ times**. We refer to t as the **strength** of the coverage of interactions, k as the number of **parameters** or **components** (degree), and v as the number of possible **values** (levels) for each parameter or component (see Kuhn et al., 2008). The property for the t-tuples shows a kind of 'orthogonality', where the method name comes from.

A test suite based on an orthogonal array of strength t = 2 satisfies the criterion of pairwise testing, that is, for every pair of factors all possible pairs of the test values are exercised. The clear advantage of the test suites based on OAs is the size of the test set. For example, in the case of t = 2, v = 2, k = 11 the array has N = 12 columns (λ = 3); in the case of v = 2, k = 15 the array has N = 16 columns (λ = 4); in the case of v = 3, k = 13 the array has N = 27 columns (λ = 3) and so on.

Practical considerations
For mixed OAs, where there are various factors and levels, the test generation is still useful. The system $2^9 \times 4^2$ (nine factors with level = 2 and two factors with level 4) has 16 runs (λ = 4). For the pairwise cases (t = 2) some descriptions use the notation $L_{Runs}(Levels^{Factors})$ for OAs. Here

- **runs** mean the number of rows in the array, which can be translated into the number of test cases that will be generated;
- **factors** (parameters) denote the number of columns in the array, which is equal to the number of independent parameters;
- **levels** mean the number of values taken on by any single factor.

EXAMPLE

Suppose that we have a system with seven ON/OFF switches controlled by an embedded processor. v = 2 and k = 7. Suppose that we want to have a test set with t = 2. Then the following orthogonal array satisfies the desired property (four factors, two levels each):

Parameters/Factors/k

Runs/N	1	2	3	4	5	6	7
1	OFF	OFF	OFF	OFF	OFF	OFF	OFF
2	OFF	OFF	OFF	ON	ON	ON	ON
3	OFF	ON	ON	OFF	OFF	ON	ON
4	OFF	ON	ON	ON	ON	OFF	OFF
5	ON	OFF	ON	OFF	ON	OFF	ON
6	ON	OFF	ON	ON	OFF	ON	OFF
7	ON	ON	OFF	OFF	ON	ON	OFF
8	ON	ON	OFF	ON	OFF	OFF	ON

As an example, let's examine columns 1 and 7. All possible pairs (ON, OFF), (ON, ON), (OFF, ON), (OFF, OFF) occur exactly λ = 2 times. This property holds for any two columns. Each run can be a test case. All combinations would need 2^7 = 128 tests.

The basic process of using OA to select balanced pairwise subsets is:

1. Identify the parameters (variables).
2. Determine the number of possible values (options, choices) for each parameter.
3. Locate (e.g. find on the web) an appropriate orthogonal array according to the parameters and values.
4. Map the array to the requirements and review the designed test cases.

Regarding the last two steps, note that you do not have to create the OA. You have to figure out the proper size of the array (various websites[1] maintain comprehensive OA catalogs of orthogonal arrays) then harmonise the test problem with the array.

OA does not guarantee 100 per cent (pairwise) test coverage; it can only ensure a balanced one. Scripts generated through OA have to be manually validated, and additional test cases have to be added to ensure better test coverage.

However, there are limitations for orthogonal test design: (1) such OA may not exist, (2) for a given OA the test cases (designed based on the requirements basis) may contain invalid pairs of tests. For example, an orthogonal array with strength = 2 and structure $2^4 \times 3^1$ does not exist. In such cases, a suitable OA is modified to fit the need.

Covering arrays

Fortunately, there is a generalisation for OAs in the sense that the test suite should cover all valid pairs of test values with as-few-as-possible test cases (Sloane, 1993) (supposing that no fault involves more than two factors jointly). A fixed-value **covering array** CA(N, v^k, t) is an N x k matrix of entries from the set {0, 1,..., (v-1)} such that each set of t-columns contains every possible t-tuple of entries **at least once**. Similarly, a mixed-value covering array CA(N, v_1^{k1} v_2^{k2} ... v_n^{kn}, t) extends the fixed value, where k = k1 + k2 + ... + kn. In other words, k_i columns have v_i distinct values. All orthogonal arrays are covering arrays but not vice versa.

Table 9.7 Covering array for $2^1 \times 3^1 \times 4^2$

Test	A	B	C	D
T1	a1	b1	c1	d1
T2	a1	b2	c2	d2
T3	a2	b2	c1	d1
T4	a2	b1	c2	d2
T5	a3	b3	c2	d1
T6	a3	b3	c1	d2
T7	a4	b1	c1	d3
T8	a4	b2	c2	d4
T9	a1	b3	c2	d3
T10	a2	b3	c1	d4
T11	a3	b2	c1	d3
T12	a3	b1	c2	d4
T13	a4	b3	c2	d1
T14	a1	b1	c1	d4
T15	a2	b1	c2	d3
T16	a4	b2	c1	d2

---

1   https://www.york.ac.uk/depts/maths/tables/orthogonal.htm
    http://neilsloane.com/doc/cent4.html

In our 'Configuration Testing' example, we have two factors (parameters) with four options, the others have just three and two. The covering array for $2^1 \times 3^1 \times 4^2$ is shown in Table 9.7.

In the table, in any two columns, the pairs appear a maximum of two times. Observe that the (a_i, d_j) pairs appear exactly once.

Note that orthogonal arrays are likely to produce more test cases than covering arrays.

COMPARISON OF THE TECHNIQUES

There are different types of faults, such as logic, computational, interface, data handling and so on (see IEEE 1044, 2009). Basically, there are two main types of programming errors (Howden, 1976): (1) computation error and (2) control-flow error. A program is said to cause a **computation error** if a specific input follows a correct path, but the output is incorrect due to faults in some computations along the path. A control-flow error occurs when a specific input traverses a wrong path because of faults in the control flows of the program. For simplicity, it is assumed that the control-flow error involves the missing case errors as well (when some control in the code is missing). In this section, we compare the previously defined combinatorial techniques and investigate their reliability. We provide two examples, one related to computation, the other one to control-flow errors.

Example: testing computation errors

EXAMPLE: PACKAGING AND DELIVERY SERVICE

Company RedShoe offers 10% discount for VIP customers from the original price of a product. Moreover, there is a new service for packaging and delivery. The prices are:

Packaging

    a.   Basic packaging: EUR 1;

    b.   Safety packaging: EUR 4;

    c.   Exclusive packaging: EUR 5;

    d.   Safety exclusive packaging: EUR 9.

Delivery price with regard to the VIP reduced price (or with regard to the original price for non-VIP customers):

    1.   Local (surroundings): 2%;

    2.   City: 5%;

    3.   Town: 8%.

Assume that we have one of the following code excerpts (we neglect function and variable declarations):

// Correct implementation (excerpt)

```
1. if price == 0 then return(0);
2. if VIP == true then
3.       price = price * 0.9;
4. if delivery == local then
5.       price = price * 1.02;
6. else if delivery == city then
7.       price = price * 1.05;
8. else price = price * 1.08;
9. if packaging == basic then
10.      price = price + 1;
11. else if packaging == safety then
12.      price = price + 4;
13. else if packaging == exclusive then
14.      price = price + 5;
15. else price = price + 9;
```

// Implementation with three bugs

```
1. if price == 0 then return(0);
2. if VIP then
3.       price = price * 0.9;
4. if delivery == local then
5.       price = price * 1.02;
6. else if delivery == city then
7.       price = price * 1.08; //BUG HERE
8. else price = price * 1.08;
9. if packaging == basic then
10.      price = price + 1;
11. else if packaging == safety then
12.      price = price + 1;//BUG HERE
13. else if packaging == exclusive then
14.      price = price + 5;
15. else price = price + 8;//BUG HERE
```

Of course, the tester knows nothing about the implementation. After analysing the specification, the clever tester asks for the average purchase amount (needed for the tests). The sales department answers that it is around EUR 70–100. Since the project is 'extremely agile', the tester does not want to write more than 10 tests. You may ask, how many test cases would result in the all-pairs technique? Table 9.8 shows a possible set of tests for the correct implementation (rounding is to one euro cent).

We have only 12 test cases, while exhaustive testing would require 24. Note that product price is not a parameter here as it is not mentioned explicitly in the specification. Hence, we could have selected the same price for each test.

Let's consider the base choice method with the basis parameter set (VIP, Basic, Town) (Table 9.9).

Based on Tables 9.8 and 9.9 you can observe that Test2 = T3, Test3 = T1, Test4 = T2, Test5 = T6, Test6 = T8, Test7 = T12. Now the test suite reveals two out of the three bugs. Let's suppose that the developer corrects line 7 and line 12 in the buggy code and reruns the

Table 9.8 Tests for the 'Packaging and delivery service' example

Test	Product price (EUR)	VIP	Packaging type/price (EUR)		Delivery type/price (%)		Total price
T1	500	Y	Basic	1	Local	2	460
T2	232	Y	Basic	1	City	5	220.24
T3	120.5	N	Basic	1	Town	8	131.14
T4	110.5	N	Safety	4	Local	2	116.71
T5	100	N	Safety	4	City	5	109
T6	85	Y	Safety	4	Town	8	86.62
T7	60.4	Y	Exclusive	5	Local	2	60.45
T8	50	Y	Exclusive	5	Town	8	53.6
T9	40	N	Exclusive	5	City	5	47
T10	30.1	N	Safety exclusive	9	Local	2	39.7
T11	20	N	Safety exclusive	9	City	5	30
T12	0	Y	Safety exclusive	9	Town	8	0

Table 9.9 Base choice tests for the 'Packaging and delivery service' example

Test	Product price (EUR)	VIP	Packaging type/price (EUR)		Delivery type/price (%)		Total price	Expected outcome
Test1	90	Y	Basic	1	Town	8	88.48	88.48
Test2	120.5	N	Basic	1	Town	8	131.14	131.14
Test3	500	Y	Basic	1	Local	2	460	460
Test4	232	Y	Basic	1	City	5	226.5	220.24
Test5	85	Y	Safety	4	Town	8	83.62	86.62
Test6	50	Y	Exclusive	5	Town	8	53.6	53.6
Test7	0	Y	Safety exclusive	9	Town	8	0	0

previous test suite against the corrected code. Then all of the tests pass. To summarise, this method has a shortcoming: the fault in line 15 has not been revealed.

Finally, let's consider the diff-pair technique (see Table 9.10).

First, we check the fulfilment of the diff-pair criteria.

- VIP: Y has Packaging pair (Test1: Basic, Test3: Safety), Delivery pair (Test1: City, Test3: Local).
- VIP: N has Packaging pair (Test2: Basic, Test4: Safety), Delivery pair (Test2: Town, Test4: City).
- Packaging: Basic has VIP pair (Test1: Y, Test2: N), Delivery pair (Test1: City, Test2: Town).
- Packaging: Safety has VIP pair (Test3: Y, Test4: N), Delivery pair (Test3: Local, Test4: City).
- Packaging: Exclusive has VIP pair (Test5: Y, Test6: N), Delivery pair (Test5: Local, Test6: Town).
- Packaging: Safety exclusive has VIP pair (Test7: Y, Test8: N), Delivery pair (Test7: Local, Test8: Town).
- Delivery: City has VIP pair (Test1: Y, Test4: N), Packaging pair (Test1: Basic, Test4: Safety).
- Delivery: Town has VIP pair (Test6: Y, Test2: N), Packaging pair (Test2: Basic, Test6: Exclusive).
- Delivery: Local has VIP pair (Test3: Y, Test7: N), Packaging pair (Test3: Safety, Test7: Safety exclusive).

Table 9.10 Diff-pair tests for the 'Packaging and delivery service' example

Test	Product price (EUR)	VIP	Packaging type/price (EUR)		Delivery type/price (%)		Total price	Expected outcome
Test1	232	Y	Basic	1	City	5	226.5	220.24
Test2	120.5	N	Basic	1	Town	8	131.14	131.14
Test3	110.5	Y	Safety	4	Local	2	102.44	105.44
Test4	100	N	Safety	4	City	5	109	109
Test5	60.4	N	Exclusive	5	Local	2	66.61	66.61
Test6	50	Y	Exclusive	5	Town	8	53.6	53.6
Test7	30.1	N	Safety exclusive	9	Local	2	38.7	39.7
Test8	0	Y	Safety exclusive	9	Town	8	0	0

After running the test set against the faulty code three bugs can be found.

- Correcting only line 7 the tests Test3, Test4 and Test7 will fail.
- Correcting only line 12 the tests Test1, Test4 and Test7 will fail.
- Correcting only line 15 the tests Test1 and Test3 will fail.
- Correcting line 7 and line 12 the test Test7 will fail.
- Correcting line 7 and line 15 the tests Test3 and Test4 will fail.
- Correcting line 12 and line 15 the tests Test1 and Test4 will fail.

Hence, this eight-test set is reliable. This shows the power of the method. If the tester chooses another diff-pair test set, similar results can be obtained.

Observe that the erroneous code contains only the typos 5 to 8 (line 7) and 4 to 1 (line 12) and 9 to 8 (line 15), therefore the competent programmer hypothesis is not violated. Clearly, the pairwise test set gives a similar result with 12 tests.

Example: Testing control-flow errors

This next example demonstrates the usage of combinatorial test design techniques together with other traditional design techniques. We concentrate on control-flow errors.

EXAMPLE: ONLINE SHOP

Company RedShoe is selling shoes in its online shop. If the total ordering price is below EUR 100, then no price reduction is given. The customer gets 4% reduction when reaching or exceeding a total price of EUR 100. Over a value of EUR 200 the customer gets 8% reduction. If the customer is a premium VIP they get an extra 3% reduction. If the customer is a normal VIP, they get a 1% extra reduction. Normal VIPs must be registered and the customer is a premium VIP if the amount of their purchases has reached a certain limit in the past year. The system automatically calculates the VIP status. If the customer pays immediately at the end of the order they get 3% more reduction in price. The output is the reduced price to be paid. The lowest price difference is 10 euro cents.

We have three equivalence partitions concerning the price reduction: 0-99.9, 100-199.9, 200 and above. According to the test selection criterion discussed in Chapter 5, we can apply the following boundary values for testing: 0, 99.9, 100, 199.9, 200, 10,000. We have three possible customer statuses: non-VIP, normal VIP and premium VIP customer (exclusively). The prepaid status can be YES or NO. Altogether we have 6 × 3 × 2 = 36 possible data combinations.

We do not consider any unstructured, un-refactored code (however, it exists in practice).

Suppose that we have the following Python code:

```
# Correct implementation
def webshop(price, vip, prepay):
  reduction = 0
  if price >= 200:
    reduction = 8
  if price >= 100 and price < 200:
    reduction = 4
  if vip == 'normal':
    reduction = reduction + 1
  if vip == 'premium':
    reduction = reduction + 3
  if prepay == True:
    reduction = reduction + 3
  return(price*(100-reduction)/100)

# Buggy implementation
def webshop(price, vip, prepay):
  reduction = 0
  if price >= 200:
    reduction = 8
  if price >= 100 and price <= 200:#BUG HERE
    reduction = 4
  if vip == 'normal':
    reduction = reduction + 1
  if vip == 'premium':
    reduction = reduction + 3
  if prepay == True: #BUG HERE
    reduction = reduction + 3
  return(price*(100-reduction)/100)
```

The number of test cases for pairwise testing is 18, and the possible test cases against the faulty implementation are in Table 9.11.

When the tester chooses some EP and BVA tests, for example T1, T3, T5, T7, T11, and, for the price EUR 200, any one of T9, T10 or T17, then they will find the bug.

Suppose that the bug is corrected (shaded line in the faulty code) and the tests changed (see Table 9.12).

Now, the EP and BVA test suite TS = {T1, T3, T5, T7, T10, T11} does not reveal the remaining control-flow bug.

Let's construct a test suite satisfying the diff-pair criterion. Consider the test suite in Table 9.13.

Table 9.11 Pairwise tests for the 'Online Shop' example

Test	Price	VIP	Prepay	Total price expected/real	
T1	0	non	Y	0	0
T2	0	normal	N	0	0
T3	99.9	non	N	99.9	99.9
T4	99.9	normal	Y	95.9	98.9
T5	100	premium	Y	90	90
T6	100	non	N	96	96
T7	199.9	premium	N	185.9	185.9
T8	199.9	non	Y	185.9	191.9
T9	200	normal	Y	176	190
T10	200	premium	N	178	186
T11	10000	normal	N	9100	9100
T12	10000	premium	Y	8600	8600
T13	0	premium	- (Y)	0	0
T14	99.9	premium	- (N)	96.9	96.9
T15	100	normal	- (Y)	92	95
T16	199.9	normal	- (N)	189.9	189.9
T17	200	non	- (Y)	178	192
T18	10000	non	- (N)	9200	9200

Table 9.12 Changed tests for the 'Online Shop' example

Test	Price	VIP	Prepay	Total price Expected/Real	
T9	200	normal	Y	176	182
T10	200	premium	N	178	178
T17	200	non	- (Y)	178	184

We check the fulfilment of the diff-pair criterion:

- Price: every pairwise consecutive line contains different values for both VIP and Prepay.
- VIP = non: the tests Test1 and Test3.
- VIP = normal: Test2 and Test9.

197

- VIP = premium: Test10 and Test12.
- Prepay = Y: Test1 and Test4.
- Prepay = N: Test2 and Test3 are appropriate.

Observe that the test cases Test9 and Test10 detect the bug, hence, our method is reliable.

Table 9.13 Diff-pair tests for the 'Online shop' example

Test	Price	VIP	Prepay	Total price expected/real	
Test1	0	non	Y	0	0
Test2	0	normal	N	0	0
Test3	99.9	non	N	99.9	99.9
Test4	99.9	premium	Y	93.9	93.9
Test5	100	premium	Y	90	90
Test6	100	non	N	96	96
Test7	199.9	normal	N	189.9	189.9
Test8	199.9	premium	Y	179.9	179.9
Test9	200	normal	Y	176	190
Test10	200	premium	N	178	186
Test11	10000	normal	N	9100	9100
Test12	10000	premium	Y	8600	8600

Clearly, there are bugs for which neither the diff-pair-N nor even the pairwise methods are reliable. However, even in these cases, in applying the diff-pair technique, the probability of revealing the bug is considerable.

CLASSIFICATION TREES

A classification tree (CT) is a graphical technique by which various combinations of conditions can be tested. The technique allows combining EP and BVA with combinatorial methods. The process of constructing CTs consists of the following steps:

1. Identify the test object and determine its input domain.
2. Classify the test object-related aspects together with their corresponding values (apply it recursively, if needed).
3. Combine the different values from all classes into test cases by forming a combination table.

Each test object can be typified by a set of classifications (input parameters, environment states, preconditions, etc.). Each classification can then have any number of disjoint classes. These classes describe the parameter space. The class selection mechanism is basically an equivalence partitioning (forming abstract test cases). Then, BVA is applied to the classes producing the concrete test cases. This structuring results in the classification tree.

If the classification tree has been created, the next task is to specify suitable test cases. A test case specification comes from the combination of classes. The minimum number of test cases is usually (but not necessarily) the maximal number of classes in the classification. The maximal number of test cases is the Cartesian product of all classes of all classifications.

Figure 9.2 Classification tree for the ticket selection process. We used BVA for the Amount class data. The highlighted tests are the negative tests

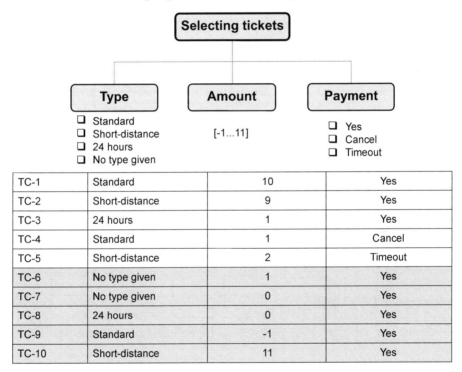

TC-1	Standard	10	Yes
TC-2	Short-distance	9	Yes
TC-3	24 hours	1	Yes
TC-4	Standard	1	Cancel
TC-5	Short-distance	2	Timeout
TC-6	No type given	1	Yes
TC-7	No type given	0	Yes
TC-8	24 hours	0	Yes
TC-9	Standard	-1	Yes
TC-10	Short-distance	11	Yes

There are commercial tools[2] for supporting CT drawings with various test case selection mechanisms incorporated.

A ticket selection process (similar to our TVM) can be modelled with the classification tree shown in Figure 9.2.

---

2   https://www.razorcat.com/en/product-cte.html
    https://www.assystem-germany.com/en/products/testona/classification-tree-method/

199

This technique can be used at any level of testing. We suggest you start with small tables (at a high level). If your tree becomes too large, break it down, referring to a higher-level tree.

Probably the greatest benefit of CTs is when there is a continuous need for maintenance. In these cases its graphical approach provides an easy-to-follow overview.

TVM EXAMPLE

BUYING PROCESS

Payment is possible if the customer has selected at least one ticket. Payment is made by inserting coins or banknotes. The ticket machine always shows the remaining amount necessary for the transaction. For the remaining amount to be paid, the machine only accepts banknotes for which the selection of the smaller banknote does not reach the required amount. EUR 5 is always accepted. For example, if the necessary amount is EUR 21, then the machine accepts EUR 50 since EUR 20 will not exceed EUR 21. If the user inserts EUR 10 and then EUR 2, then even EUR 20 is not accepted since the remaining amount is EUR 9; EUR 10 would exceed the necessary amount. The remaining amount and current acceptable banknotes are visible on the screen. If the user inserts a non-acceptable banknote then it will be given back to them and an error message will appear notifying the user of the error.

Too long selection time. In a case where neither coins nor banknotes are inserted 20 seconds after the last modification of any value of the necessary ticket, then the initial screen appears again and the previous ticket selection is deleted.

Delete selection. The transaction can be deleted any time prior to the successful transaction. In this case, all the inserted money is given back.

Here we design test cases for the following part of the TVM.

As the risks are not very high, we apply diff-pair testing. Let's consider item 6 in Chapter 3, Table 3.2:

Risk item	Probability	Impact		Aggregate risk
		On customer W = 0.7	On supplier W = 0.3	
Neither the timeout nor the reset feature is working.	3	4	4	12

Though these features (timeout, delete) are different, they can be used interchangeably. If reset does not work, we can wait for timeout. If timeout does not work when a guest leaves the TVM, the next guest can use the reset function. Therefore, we consider an aggregate parameter Delete with three values: No, Reset, Timeout.

We start from the test cases of TVM in Chapter 5. We had seven test cases. We extend the test cases by the values of Delete. During the (later) actual test execution, we first insert the coins, then press reset or wait for the timeout. The test cases are shown in Table 9.14.

Table 9.14 Test design for the TVM example

Test	EP	Ticket price	Inserted amount	Delete	RAP in EUR	Acceptable banknotes	Screen
T1	1	1.4	1, 0.2, 0.1	No	0.1	€5	Payment
T2	1	1.4	1, 0.2, 0.1	Reset	~~0.1~~	~~€5~~	Initial
T3	1	7 (5 x 1.4)	2	No	5	€5	Payment
T4	1	7 (5 x 1.4)	2	Timeout	~~5~~	~~€5~~	Initial
T5	2	6.2 (3 x 2.1)	1, 0.1	No	5.1	€5, €10	Payment
T6	2	6.2 (3 x 2.1)	1, 0.1	Reset	~~5.1~~	~~€5, €10~~	Initial
T7	2	10.5 (5 x 2.1)	0.5	No	10	€5, €10	Payment
T8	2	10.5 (5 x 2.1)	0.5	Timeout	~~10~~	~~€5, €10~~	Initial
T9	3	10.5	0.2, 0.2	No	10.1	€5, €10, €20	Payment
T10	3	10.5	0.2, 0.2	Reset	~~10.1~~	~~€5, €10, €20~~	Initial
T11	3	21	1	No	20	€5, €10, €20	Payment
T12	3	21	1	Timeout	~~20~~	~~€5, €10, €20~~	Initial
T13	4	21	0.5, 0.2, 0.2	No	20.1	€5, €10, €20, €50	Payment
T14	4	21	0.5, 0.2, 0.2	Reset	~~20.1~~	~~€5, €10, €20, €50~~	Initial

We can see that the number of test cases has doubled, and we design inputs Reset and Timeout for each EP, maximising the diversity as much as possible. For the test cases with Reset or Delete, we only validate whether we can go to the initial screen in all circumstances. Therefore, in these test cases, it is unnecessary to check RAP and acceptable banknotes. That's why we used strikethrough characters.

When one of the authors lectured on an ISTQB course for experienced testers in a large telecommunication company, the feedback forms showed an interesting result. The attendees marked the most useful and practical parts of the course to be the N-way testing and the orthogonal/covering arrays.

METHOD EVALUATION

Combinatorial testing provides a means to identify an appropriate subset of data combinations, where the data combinations come from combinatorial combinations. The aim is to achieve a predetermined level of coverage.

Regarding combinative and combinatorial test design, we suggest using:

- On-the-fly test design for very low or low risks.

- Non-combinatorial test design for low and medium risks.

- Diff-pair test design in the case of medium or high risks. The number of test cases is linear, and therefore the test suite is manageable even when the previous methods are not sufficient. It is especially suitable for computational faults, but is also reliable for control-flow bugs.

- N-wise testing in the case of high or very high risks.

- Orthogonal/covering/sequence covering arrays for very large parameter spaces.

Applicability

Combinatorial testing is used extensively in:

- crash testing (running the test set against the SUT, checking whether unusual input combinations cause a crash or other failures);

- testing embedded assertions (ensuring proper relationships between data, e.g. preconditions and postconditions); and

- model-checker-based test generations.

Configuration testing is probably the most commonly used application of combinatorial methods in software testing.

We suggest using combinative testing with a trade-off for higher risks and manageable test effort. The optimum costs described in Chapter 3 can be often reached by applying diff-pair testing, as we can unfold bugs undetectable by other non-combinatorial techniques at low additional testing effort.

Types of defects

The most common type of defects related to combinatorial testing arises from the combined values of several parameters.

Advantages and shortcomings of the method

Combinatorial testing reduces the overall number of test cases compared to exhaustive testing. Combinative testing further reduces the number of combinatorial test cases. They detect:

- All faults due to single parameters via base choice.
- All faults due to the interaction of two parameters via pairwise testing (with quadratic time).
- Most of the faults due to the interaction of two parameters via diff-pair testing (with linear time).
- All faults due to the interaction of N parameters via N-way testing.

Combinative and combinatorial testing can be automated in part, that is the input combinations can be generated. The technique can be applied at any level of testing. Classification trees raise the visibility of test cases and improve maintainability.

The key limitation of combinatorial test design is the testing cost, due to its non-linearity. For high risk software generating N-way tests, the oracle problem is challenging. Moreover, efficient N-way testing requires that:

- Parameters should be independent.
- Parameter space should be unordered.
- The order of the parameter choice should be irrelevant.

In most cases, fixed-level orthogonal arrays (same number of values for each parameter) do not exactly match to the current test problem. For mixed level orthogonal arrays there are many options to choose, hence, finding the optimal one can be difficult.

THEORETICAL BACKGROUND

Combinatorial testing is an application of the mathematical theory called combinatorial design. It concerns the arrangements of a finite set of elements into various patterns (subsets, words, arrays, etc.) according to specified rules. Generating the optimised list of such combinations for specific input is an NP-hard problem (they are at least as hard as the hardest problems in NP). With the increase of the input parameters, there is an exponential increase in the computational time as well as in the degree of the problem complexity. Hence, there is a need for efficient and intelligent strategies for generation.

There exist three different types of methods for constructing combinatorial test suites:

1. algebraic methods;
2. greedy algorithms; and
3. heuristic search.

The first group of methods do not result in accurate results on general inputs; however, they are very quick. The second group has been found to be relatively efficient regarding running time and accuracy. The heuristic search provides even more accuracy at the expense of execution time. The first and widely cited heuristic approach was implemented in the Automatic Efficient Test Generator (AETG) System (Cohen et al., 1997).

For software testing, Mandl was the first to propose pairwise combinatorial coverage to test the Ada compiler in 1985 (Mandl, 1985). He generated appropriate test sets as well. There is a comprehensive survey of this topic by Nie and Leung (2011). Another good review article has been written by Czerwonka (2008).

The classification tree method was developed by Grochtmann and Grimm (1993) partly using and improving ideas from the category-partition method defined by Ostrand and Balcer (1988).

In many systems, the input is a permutation of some event set. One can define a **sequence covering array** in such a way that the test suite ensures testing of all N-way sequences of events. Normal covering arrays are unusable for generating N-way sequences since they are designed to cover combinations **in any order**. However, in a sequence covering array, every N-way arrangement of variables, v_1, v_2,...,v_N, the regular expression $.^*v_1.^*v_2...^*v_N.^*$ should match at least one row in the array.

Sequence covering arrays are developed to solve interoperability testing problems. For more details see Kuhn et al. (2012).

EXAMPLE

In an automation system, certain devices interact with a control program. The events are: a, b, c, d and e, and one interaction is a permutation of the events. Altogether, there are 5! = 120 possible input sequences. The control software should respond correctly, independently of the sequence order. We want to design a sequence covering array that covers all 3-way event sequences. The number of all 3-way sequences is 5 x 4 x 3 = 60. All of them should be covered by a minimal number of permutation sequences. A possible solution is the following (showing that eight tests are enough):

e c a d b	covers: adb cab cad cdb eab ead eca ecb ecd edb
b e d a c	covers: bac bda bdc bea bec bed dac eac eda edc
d b c a e	covers: bae bca bce cae dae dba dbc dbe dca dce
a c e b d	covers: abd acb acd ace aeb aed cbd ceb ced ebd
c b d e a	covers: bde cba cbe cda cde cea dea
a d e b c	covers: abc adc aec ade deb dec ebc
d a c b e	covers: abe dab dcb
e b c a d	covers: bad bcd eba

KEY TAKEAWAYS

- Combinatorial methods can be applied in safety critical systems (e.g. to configurations or input parameter testing, etc.).

- Empirical analyses show that software failures are caused by the interaction of relatively few parameters. Fortunately, in these cases, we can reach a high level of assurance by testing all N-way combinations for N = 2, 3, 4 or 5. For other, smaller risky software the diff-pair method is preferable.

- Diff-pair testing can be useful for many specifications as it is linear and reliable for many types of defects.

- No statistical methods can be 100 per cent safe. To minimise the risk, we should always review the selected combinations.

- A classification tree is a graphical way of showing and organising test cases.

EXERCISES

E9.1 Consider the specification of E5.1 (Payment). Design test cases by applying the diff-pair testing technique.

E9.2 You want to test your favourite word processor. You are interested in the following attributes in combination:

- fonts: Arial, Calibri, Cambria, Comic, Courier, Times New Roman, Verdana (7 types);
- style: regular, italic, bold, bold italic (4 types);
- size: 8, 9, 10, 12, 14, 16, 18, 20, 24, 28 (10 types);
- effect: strikethrough, double strikethrough, superscript, subscript, small caps, all caps, hidden (7 types).

Construct test cases for pairwise testing.

10 ON-THE-FLY TEST DESIGN

WHY IS THIS CHAPTER WORTH READING?

In this chapter, you will learn the main benefits of using on-the-fly test design techniques. We apply one of them, exploratory testing, for the ticket vending machine example and show that in one hour a considerable ratio of the bugs can be detected.

All of the previous chapters are about script-oriented test design. This means that the output of the test design is some script, which can be executed either manually or automatically. In addition, these techniques are implementation independent, and therefore can be used as a test-first approach. However, there is another possibility, when there are no pre-designed test cases but the testers design them gradually when executing the program. We refer to this as on-the-fly test design.

The script-oriented approach is similar to an old-fashioned university lecture. It is based on a prescribed syllabus; usually, there are only a limited number of questions raised during the lecture. Questions are more often stated during exercise practice. Lecturing helps in cognition, exercises help in understanding. One of the largest surveys on knowledge and mindset in software development (Kovács and Szabados, 2018) shows that IT professionals (and students) learn mainly from forums and colleagues. How? On the fly.

Test design cannot be just script based. One of the most successful approaches is the experience-based one, which substitutes scripting with exploring. Cem Kaner defines **exploratory testing** (ET) as

> a style of software testing that emphasises the personal freedom and responsibility of the individual tester to continually optimise the quality of his/her work by treating test-related learning, test design, test execution, and test result interpretation as mutually supportive activities that run in parallel throughout the project. (Kaner, 2008)

Exploratory testing gives the developers the opportunity to see the product quality features on the fly in a real environment, can help project owners see their work through a different perspective, and help testers to examine their own scripted tests' thoroughness.

Printed by Amazon POD

EXPLORATORY TESTING

Exploratory testing is a simultaneous process of thinking and executing. It is similar to the 20-question game, in which one person in a group thinks of an object or substance and the others ask them questions about it that can only be answered by 'Yes' or 'No' until they determine what is. The players do not have a prescribed list of 20 questions in advance; they ask, get the answer, then think, design a new question, and ask again. Similarly, in exploratory testing, the tester analyses the result of an execution, thinks, designs new questions, runs the test and examines the behaviour in the new execution.

In exploratory testing, test design is ad hoc. This means that the designed tests do not follow a given rule set, but depend on the specification, the actual code and the former test results. In this way, there is no exact test selection criterion for exploratory testing. On the contrary, there may be a time constraint. The test design is dependent on the entire testing process. If other techniques are also used, then we should design tests to find tricky bugs, which would remain undetected otherwise.

We use on-the-fly testing techniques as they are very simple, easy to apply and entirely different from the other techniques, making it possible to find other types of bugs. The design is based on the tester's knowledge and intuition.

Test execution happens in parallel with the test design. The tester may have a clear plan for the test case; however, they may change the plan during the test execution. In this way, test execution explores the software for the tester. If the test fails, the bug has to be reported as usual.

Let's summarise the advantages of exploratory testing.

- **Learning and understanding**. The exploratory tester is able to learn, understand, design, execute and improve the existing tests related to the system's behaviour. The tester is able to analyse the system from different perspectives along with defect logs.

- **Rapid feedback**. ET provides fast feedback on quality, helps in lowering the product risks, and accelerates the necessary reforms in development and testing. ET is especially helpful when the product is unstable.

- **Less preparation time**. The testers need to know only the specification of the code and the purpose of testing.

- **Effectiveness**. Under a controlled environment, ET is very effective in finding faults since testers may exploit their creativity. ET brings freedom and fun to testers' daily work and increases their sense of accomplishment.

However, it does not mean that exploratory testing is perfect and all the other test techniques can be discarded. Exploratory testing is an ad hoc method: if the same application is tested twice, the executed test cases will be different. It is not as thorough as the other test design techniques described in this book. In addition, simple problems could remain hidden, since the on-the-fly test design concentrates mainly on **some** cornerstone issues. Another drawback is that exploratory testing lacks documentation.

Some concerns with respect to exploratory testing are:

- Exploratory testing cannot be automated. An automaton executes, but cannot collaborate, refine and synthesise. Only a human can.

- It is not random; it is ad hoc with the purpose of finding bugs.

- It is not unstructured. The structuring in ET is rather cognitive than procedural. The latter is related to charters and time boxing.

- It is not a technique, rather it is an approach. The next steps are governed by the actual results.

Some good advice regarding exploratory testing:

- The mixture of scripted and exploratory tests should be well-balanced to find different types of bugs.

- The test manager should schedule the exploratory testing process according to the project needs and progressions.

- Make exploratory testing measurable, so that testers' work and the method itself is comparable.

To summarise this section, we know that in the Agile environment there is little or no time to develop formal test design and scripts. Exploratory testing can be performed on the fly, which saves a lot of time. However, appropriate coverage, repeatability and automation of the test cases can only be reached by scripted techniques.

Session-based testing is a method designed to make exploratory testing measurable, repeatable and auditable on a wider scale. Since test managers focus on numerical progress reporting that clearly shows the status of testing, measurability can be a key expectation.

SESSION-BASED TESTING

Session-based testing is a variant of exploratory testing that adds some management to the basic 'freestyle' version (Bach, 2000). It aims to extend ET with some control in such a way as not to deteriorate the flexibility of the method. According to Bach (p. 2) 'a session is an uninterrupted block of reviewable, chartered test effort'. By 'chartered', he means that each session is associated with a mission – what we are testing or what problems we are looking for. By 'uninterrupted', he means no significant interruptions, such as email, meetings, chats or telephone calls. By 'reviewable', he means a report, called a session sheet, is produced that can be examined by a third party, such as the test manager, that provides information about what happened.

The goal of the session-based extension is that testers can organise their work and make reports of what they tested. This method may include pairs of testers working together. The session-based test management (SBTM) protocol may consist of the following steps:

1. Create or reuse a bug taxonomy (classification).

   a. Categorise common types of faults found earlier in the project. Alternatively, you can use historical data on similar projects.

   b. Analyse the causes of the problems or faults.

   c. Find the risks and develop ideas to test the application.

2. Create the Test Charter.

   a. This should suggest (1) what conditions to test and (2) how these can be tested,

   b. It should contain ideas for testing. These ideas come from the:

      i. specification (if it exists) or product knowledge;

      ii. tester's domain experience;

      iii. results and experiences of earlier tests.

   c. It should help in determining how the end user could use the system.

3. Determine the time box for the test.

   a. The basic protocol suggests a 30-120 minute session without interruption.

4. Perform the session.

   a. The precondition is a clear understanding of the mission, clear knowledge about the system specification (to be able to judge the correct/incorrect outcome of the tests) and knowledge about the test design techniques (EP, BVA, etc.).

   b. During the session, the testers should react to the response from the system and should be able to prepare for the next test.

   c. Testers should note what is tested and why it needs to be tested.

   d. Testers should track the issues raised during the session.

5. Review the results.

   a. Evaluate the defects.

   b. Analyse the coverage areas.

   c. Assess the product quality.

6. Debrief.

   a. Summarise the output results.

      i. test coverage;
      ii. risks (covered risks, residual risks);
      iii. issues/queries.

   b. Compare the results with the charter.

   c. Check whether any additional testing is needed.

For a debrief, Bach (2000) suggested the PROOF method:

- **P**ast. What happened during the session?
- **R**esults. What was achieved during the session?

- **O**bstacles. What got in the way of good testing?
- **O**utlook. What still needs to be done?
- **F**eelings. How does the tester feel about all this?

There are several forms of charters. The content of the charter document is more or less similar to the following:

- Session charter – the name of the charter, which is a sentence describing what will be explored.
- Areas to be tested – for example inventory system. It should contain the test harness used to test the SUT. Each entry in this section should begin on its own line.
- Tester name(s).
- Start date and time.
- Task breakdown:
  - Duration: Short (30–60 mins)/Normal (60–90 mins)/Long (90–120 mins).
  - Test design and execution: the percentage of time spent on this phase, for example 57 minutes.
  - Bug investigation and reporting: the percentage of time spent on this phase, for example 23 minutes.
  - Session setup: the percentage of time spent on this phase, for example 10 minutes.
- Data files – any data that was gathered during the test, such as screenshots and so on.
- Test notes – a step by step 'journal' of the test, for example 'I tried to traverse each menu item, but because of a critical error some menus were unreachable', or 'I successfully added a new item to the database' and so on.
- Bugs – inserted to the bug tracking system, add the bug ID here.

One of the authors, with a colleague, executed exploratory tests for testing a Gherkin-based MBT tool – see Chapter 12. They used a freestyle alternative. An interesting bug found during the test was as follows:

In order to find the affected test cases (which have to be re-executed) after model modification, the tool starts from the original test cases exported to an Excel file and the modified model. Unfortunately, the tool selected the wrong test cases, which had not been modified at all. Executing the process again, it worked properly. We realised that the reason for the bug is that the Excel file had been modified after selection, then re-selected in the tool again. However, this re-selection had not been effective, causing the bug. Based on this bug description the developers were easily able to fix the fault.

This bug would probably not have been detected easily with other test design techniques.

For small projects, we suggest using the freestyle version of ET (it is simpler and faster), but when process measurability is important, the session-based protocol is advantageous.

TVM EXAMPLE

Now let's consider on-the-fly testing in practice.

In this example we applied the freestyle version of ET. We did not determine a time limit in advance, but we tested the whole application instead, and measured the total time. You will be familiar with the specification by now.

- Happy path: buy 10 standard tickets – **Passed.**

- Select 10 standard tickets; decrease to 0; select ten 24-hour tickets; decrease to 0; select 5 short distance tickets and buy – **Failed**. Only standard tickets were possible to select.

- Select 10 24-hour tickets; test all acceptable banknotes by inserting different banknotes and coins – **Failed**: when the remaining amount goes below EUR 1, €5 banknote is not acceptable.

- Buy one short distance ticket and insert 10 cents, investigating whether some positive amount of money will not activate the printing of the tickets – **Passed**.

- Cancel operation during the ticket selection period – **Passed.**

- Timeout when incrementing tickets – **Failed**. Timeout happened after about 30 seconds, instead of 20 seconds.

- Cancel during the ticket buying process – **Passed**.

- Reduced mode test, selecting one 24-hour ticket and pay – **Passed.**

- Reduced mode test 2, start by selecting 10 24-hour tickets and insert banknotes in the reduced mode – **Failed.** Starting from remaining amount EUR 76, inserting €20, then €10, the remaining amount is EUR 46; however, banknote €50 remained acceptable, a bug.

- Testing changing OFF–ON for reduced mode – **Failed**. Changing OFF–ON works only before the buying process, but not on the fly; this is not a bug in the planned system, only it makes testing a little bit more difficult.

- Reset during ticket selection, select 10 24-hour tickets, reduce to 2, then reset – **Passed.**

- Reset during payment period, select eight normal tickets, go to pay, insert some banknotes/coins, then reset – **Passed.**

- Timeout after pushing pay – **Passed.**

Most of the bugs have been found in just one hour. Altogether 13 test cases were executed. Almost the entire code has been covered.

A young colleague of ours did the same ET. She executed 26 simpler test cases and found the same bugs, except the bug regarding the timeout.

METHOD EVALUATION

On-the-fly testing is becoming more popular especially in Agile, as testers can find tricky bugs immediately. In some cases, testers are pushed to execute testing in a short time, so that the software can be released as soon as possible. In this case on-the-fly testing may be the only option.

Applicability

On-the-fly testing can be applied to any software when it is ready to execute. It is reasonable to apply it if the application is stable enough for testing. For non-risky code, it can be used together with unit testing. For risky code, that is in critical applications, it can be applied together with script-based test design techniques. It is appropriate for any SDLC.

Types of defects

Typical defects found with exploratory testing are scenario-based or workflow-related issues that were not uncovered during scripted functional testing. Exploratory testing can also be useful for finding other non-functional weaknesses such as security or performance.

Advantages and shortcomings of the method

The most important advantage of ET is that it is basically different from all other techniques. Hence, they can be used together. Remember that applying different techniques together is more efficient than applying only one. ET is able to find different bugs compared to other script-based methods, hence its usage is advantageous.

Another important advantage is that ET does not require a comprehensive specification. However, the tester needs to know the product, the domain, and the user stories and acceptance criteria, otherwise they are unable to decide the correctness of the execution.

ET can also be applied by itself (with of course unit testing, which is compulsory and a part of coding), if both the project risk, the complexity and the budget is moderate. Using ET is fun, and testers (including the authors) like it, especially the freestyle version of it.

A case study (Itkonen and Rautiainen, 2005) reported some advantages in practice. Five out of the seven exploratory testers mentioned that they tend to test things that they might not have included in traditional test design. Examples of such tests include testing the dependencies of new and existing features based on expertise and knowledge of the system. Another advantage is retesting a corrected defect. Testers mentioned that they do not just re-execute the formerly failed test in the same way as before, but also explore for possible new defects.

In some cases, the person who found and reported the defect was not the one who tested the correction. In this way, the other tester explored the software from a different perspective and could detect other bugs. The result of this case study stated that applying ET was really useful and efficient.

Session-based testing may offer benefits when formal requirements are not present, are incomplete or are changing rapidly.

Nowadays everything is automated. Test design is not an exception. However, exploratory testing cannot be automated. It is a non-modelling technique as its key feature is exploring the software and inventing new tests based on the former tests and the bugs that have been found.

Automated test design supports feature modifications (see Chapter 12 on Gherkin-based MBT). This means that only modification-affected test cases have to be re-executed. This makes the maintenance cheaper. For ET we need to repeat the whole testing process or concentrate only on the modification. The former solution is too expensive; the latter is not reliable. Consequently, the advantage of cheap test selection after the first implementation may be lost during the later phases of the life cycle.

We tested an application containing a Gherkin compiler. We modified the colour of some language elements. Then, only the change was retested by considering all the language elements with the new colours. The ET process did not find any faults. However, a colleague of ours later found faulty colours at a special keyword using scripted techniques. The reason for not detecting the bug is that we did not test the entire tool, only the modifications, and this is usually not enough.

THEORETICAL BACKGROUND

Exploratory testing is a loosely defined method that was introduced by Kaner et al. in their book *Testing Computer Software* in 1987 (Kaner et al., 1987). The authors describe ET as a method to avoid investing effort in designing and documenting tests carefully when the software is unstable. Nowadays there are various definitions of ET. The Software Engineering Body of Knowledge (SWEBOK) defines ET as:

> simultaneous learning, test design, and test execution; that is, the tests are not defined in advance in an established test plan, but are dynamically designed, executed, and modified. The effectiveness of exploratory testing relies on the software engineer's knowledge, which can be derived from various sources. (SWEBOK, 2015)

Exploratory testing was extended by Bach (2000). The session-based variant extends exploratory testing with some basic documentation. The goal is to keep the advantage of fast testing by extending it with reporting, such as noting the tested areas, time spent and so on.

A session is a continuous period spent testing, usually lasting 30 minutes to two hours. Each session is focused on a charter, which describes the testing tasks, the goal and the target for a test session. However, testers can also change the test target, especially when they find some bugs, and want to explore more. Session-based testing can offer benefits when the specification is not present, is incomplete or changes frequently.

KEY TAKEAWAYS

- On-the-fly test design overcomes the limitations of scripted testing by extending it, emphasising learning and adaptability.

- On-the-fly test design helps in improving the test suite.

- Use freestyle exploratory testing if the risk and complexity are low, the time for testing is limited and no documentation except a bug description is needed. Use session-based testing if the risk is higher or measurability is important for management.

EXERCISE

E10 Let's extend our exploratory test cases with those related to the hardware of TVM including the testing of correct coins, banknotes and so on. Write the test cases in a similar way to how we have for the TVM example in this chapter.

PART III
AUTOMATED TEST DESIGN

11 MODEL-BASED TESTING

WHY IS THIS CHAPTER WORTH READING?

In this chapter, you will learn the basic idea of model-based testing (MBT). This is essential for the subsequent two chapters describing free and efficient MBT tools. We explain the whole MBT process and describe how to handle more complex specifications in multi-level models. Test selection criteria for multi-level models are also explained.

Model-based testing (MBT) has become more and more popular in the last couple of years. There are several goals of MBT, such as shared understanding, validating specifications, that is defect prevention, generating test cases from models or even creating executable tests. As our book is about practical (functional) test design, we restrict our description mainly to automated (functional) test design. Therefore, we use MBT and automated test design interchangeably, as we do not consider other automated test design techniques than MBT.

Nowadays we are living in an Agile and DevOps world where automation is necessary for all phases of the software life cycle. Test design cannot be an exception. The result of test design automation is automatedly generated test cases. Whenever the specification changes so does the model. You do not need to look for the modified/obsolete test cases since the MBT tool regenerates the test cases for you. What's more, it can regenerate only the modified test cases, that is, the test cases influenced by model modification, by which test case maintenance becomes easier.

Figure 11.1 shows the general process of MBT.

WHAT IS A MODEL?

A model is usually believed to be an abstract representation of reality. Abstraction is a process that involves recognising and focusing on the important characteristics of a selected segment of the real world, ignoring all of the unessential details.

Models represent abstraction in a formal or a semiformal way. We use models even if we know that they are not perfect. For example, a map is a good model. When you try

Figure 11.1 Iterative process of MBT

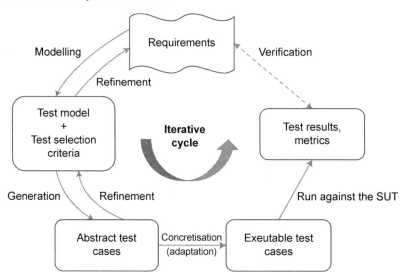

to get from one town to another, you really need a big picture, that is the entire route from start to finish. However, when you are on the way you are only interested in where to turn left, right and so on. Therefore, you need the map in different scales. This is true for MBT as well.

Models have been used to support coding for many years. The most widely known format is a UML diagram, based on the unified modelling language that is intended to provide a standard way to visualise system design for developers and architects. Some such models can be used in model-based testing as well.

Test design models are a formal or structured representation of the SUT from which reliable test cases can be generated.

Modelling, in general, involves the construction and testing of a representation that is analogous to a system. A test model should be an abstraction based on reliable test cases that can be generated.

WHAT IS MODEL-BASED TESTING?

ISTQB defines model-based testing as 'Testing based on or involving models'. Thus, instead of creating test cases one by one manually, we create an appropriate test model from which an MBT tool is able to generate test cases. However, a model itself is not enough. Traditional test design necessitates the application of test selection criteria, which make it possible for testers to know when to stop creating test cases. Therefore, an MBT tool generates test cases from the model and based on the appropriate test selection criteria.

Testing is complex. Modelling is a divide-and-conquer activity. We can make relatively simple models in a hierarchical way, and from these models, a tool is able to generate complex test cases. Though the key part of MBT is test case generation, lots of MBT tools do more: they make test execution possible. Thus, automation of test design and test execution coincides.

TEST DESIGN AND MBT

MBT is not a different paradigm regarding test design. On the contrary, MBT extends test design techniques by providing a higher-level abstraction. Moreover MBT offers the possibility of automated test case generation. Therefore, MBT should use special test models, which are based on existing test design techniques. If somebody is a good modeller but does not know the 'traditional' techniques in depth they are not able to make appropriate models.

Some traditional test design techniques are closely related to test models. An obvious example is a state transition diagram (STD). STDs are actually models, where the test cases can be created by walking along the graph based on a test selection criterion.

Another example is a cause–effect graph; here we can also generate test cases from the graph. The decision table is a non-graphical model.

> During the first MBT hands-on training of one author of this book, the participants were not able to make models. The problem was inability to produce good test design. Therefore, the author had to develop a test design hands-on training session preceding the MBT one. After taking part in the test design training, the participants were able to create good models.

THE PROCESS OF MBT

The process of model-based testing contains the following steps, where some of them are optional:

1. **Requirements understanding**

   In the MBT process, the starting point is the requirements/specification. The requirements drive the modelling and serve as the basis for determining risks and the test selection criterion.

2. **Modelling**

   Modelling is usually done by the test analyst. The necessary inputs of modelling are the test design techniques to be used, the requirements and the testing strategy of the project. The specification may be divided into sub-specifications, prohibiting too complex models. Models can be created hierarchically so that each model remains manageable.

Modelling is supported by (sometimes graphical) MBT tools. Modelling is an iterative process, which means that during the creation of the model we can validate and improve it. Textual models can also be created iteratively (see the next chapter). However, models may contain bugs, similar to code or test cases. A modeller has to verify and validate the model and iteratively improve it.

3. Choosing a test selection criterion

The test analyst selects the appropriate test selection criterion. The input is the model itself, the testing strategy, the result of the risk analysis and the quality of the MBT tool. This selection is crucial, since if we select too simple a criterion such as covering every transition in a state transition diagram, then the generated test set will not be reliable. On the other hand, if we select too complex a criterion, then the number of test cases will be very high, and the testing costs exceed the optimum.

The families of the test selection criteria of MBT can be categorised (Utting et al., 2012; Kramer and Legeard, 2016) as:

- structural model coverage;
- requirement coverage;
- data coverage;
- random coverage;
- scenario-based coverage;
- fault-based coverage;
- project-related coverage (priorities, constraints on costs, etc.).

We detailed the structural criteria in Chapter 6, and compared them. For other types of criteria see Kramer and Legeard (2016).

The problem is that when choosing a test criterion, we do not know the number of test cases in advance, except in some very simple cases. For example, applying the all-transition–transition criterion, only a very rough assumption can be made. We also do not know the elapsed time that test generation takes. Therefore, this is also an iterative process, where the test analyst selects the best criterion related to the existent model and other conditions. As a general rule, the test selection criterion is based on the risk to optimise the cost and quality as described in Chapter 3.

Test selection criteria extended to layered abstraction levels will be considered below in the section 'Test selection criteria'.

4. Test case generation

When both the model is ready and the test selection criterion is selected, the test cases are generated. Test case generation will be described in detail later in the section 'Test case generation'. We will see in the next chapter that in some cases the test selection criterion has been done and the tests can be generated on the fly during model development. However, the test analyst has to control the test cases.

In the case of too many test cases, the criterion has to be simplified, or in the case of too few test cases, a more complex criterion can be chosen. The tester should also validate the test case documentation. Based on this, the test analyst may improve the model and the criteria.

5. Test adaptation

The generated abstract test cases are not executable. Even manual testing needs readable scripts and the ability to record the test result. In the case of automated test execution, the test adaptation is the process of converting abstract test cases generated from a model into the test execution framework. In the case of manual test execution, the test adaptation converts abstract test cases into manually executable test scripts. As case studies justify, test cases created during test-driven development (TDD) (Nagappan et al., 2008) make implementation easier and less error-prone. MBT-generated test cases offer a similar advantage, especially when the tests are very clear.

6. Test execution

The generated test cases can be executed manually or automatically, based on the applied MBT tool. However, this is only possible if the application under test is ready and executable. In this case, test design and automation are interwoven and controlled by the MBT tool. Note that executable test cases need manual work from the test automation engineer. The best solution is that we first generate the implementation-independent test cases as keywords, then we generate/write the executable test frames based on the running engine.

If the tool generates manually executable test cases, then the model should contain implementation-independent test cases, which is much better for validating, extending and re-executing.

Executable tests can be executed offline and on the fly. The former is more widely used nowadays. This means that generating the test cases and executing them are two different steps. The advantage is that different test execution tools may be used. During on-the-fly execution, generation and execution happen in one single step. Of course, even this type of MBT tool permits the validation of the generated test cases prior to execution.

An advanced MBT tool has to manage model modification. The best way of doing this is to generate and execute only those test cases that are affected by the model modification. For manual test execution, test case maintenance is more problematic. However, marking affected test cases for re-execution makes continuous manual testing possible. Observe that traceability is a very important issue here.

7. Verification

The generated manual test cases are also good documents for different stakeholders and should be used for verification purposes. The business analyst can validate the specification with respect to the test cases. The developer can use it as a starting point for the implementation, since good test cases are good examples as well.

MODELLING LANGUAGES

A model tries to describe the target of the model with some simplification and idealisation. Models have to be understandable for all model users. However, the models need to be understandable for MBT tools as well, since test cases are generated from these models.

This is very similar to programming languages. During application maintenance, programming languages must be understandable not only by the developer implementing the code but by the compiler/interpreter as well. Therefore, test modelling languages have syntax and semantics. The syntax determines the signs, symbols or keywords of the language, and how to use them together. The semantics determine the meaning of these elements.

Modelling languages differ depending on what their purposes are. The main categories of models are as follows:

- **Structural models**, which describe the system architecture, in particular, the system components and the interfaces among them.

- **Behavioural models**, which describe the internal aspects of information systems supporting the business processes. During analysis, behavioural models describe the internal logic of the processes. For example, STT is a behavioural model. Most of the MBT models are behaviour models.

- **Data models**, which describe the objects under test. For example, classification trees described in Chapter 9.

When we speak about modelling languages, one of the most important aspects is the degree of the language formalisation. A modelling language with a low degree of formalisation is easy to understand and use by all the stakeholders. The disadvantage is the weaker expressive power. On the other hand, languages with high degrees of formalisation are harder to understand.

There exist both **graphical and textual** modelling notations.

1. Probably the most used are **graphical** notations.

   The simplest is the FSM. Unfortunately for complex cases, it requires too many states and transitions. EFSM extends FSM by adding variables to store more detailed state information and transition guards. By applying EFSMs the size of the model can be significantly reduced. EFSM is used for several MBT tools and for modelling communication systems. We used EFSM for the 'RoboDog' example in Chapter 6. Another extension is hierarchical FSM (statecharts), which handle hierarchy, concurrency and communication. UML state machines are modified Harel's statecharts (Harel, 1987) with some complex features added. We used statecharts for the 'Two lifts in a 10-storey building' example in Chapter 6. But the state machine is just one of the 14 different diagram types of UML (OMG, 2017).

   Another popular graphical modelling notation is the Business Process Modelling Notation (BPMN). While UML focuses on software design, BPMN focuses on business processes.

Other graphical modelling languages exist, for example:

- Markov chains (transitions are extended with probabilities meaning that a transition happens with the labelled probability).

- Petri nets are usable for modelling distributed/reactive systems.

- Event-flow graphs (modelling graphical user interfaces (GUIs).

- Cause–effect graphs (see Chapter 7) and so on.

Except the last one, these graphical models have been introduced to support developers rather than testers.

2. The other type of modelling language is **text-based.** These languages are actually adaptations of existing formal languages, such as:

- Formal specification language: B, Z;

- Modelling language: Object Constraint Language (OCL);

- Programming languages: Java, C#, C++;

- Test specification language: Test and Test Control Notation Version 3 (TTCN-3);

- Business readable domain specific language: Gherkin++ (Harmony's extension of Gherkin).

The last two were especially made for testing.

How models can be used for test design

The main question is how these models can be used for test design. Obviously, state diagrams are perfectly suited for STT (see Chapter 6). By generating tests from these diagrams tremendous work and time can be saved. Similar is the case with decision table testing, where tables and cause–effect graphs are also models. Use case diagrams, however, do not contain sufficient information for test design. Therefore, additional information or models are necessary.

Finally, let's consider EP and BVA. Activity or state diagrams do not support this type of test design. However, we can extend the model with the necessary text containing the required values. Another method is to unite graphical and text-based models. This is a very common approach in practice.

OCL is just a UML extension, where constraints are defined formally. The goal of OCL was to address the limitations of UML, and in general, any graphical modelling language, by precisely specifying system design. In origin, OCL is a constraint language, which is very useful for test modelling. Constraints are input–output dependencies, describing the heart of test cases.

Example

The age for someone to view a horror movie is at least 18. We have to test age 18 and age less than 18. A constraint in the OCL language is the following.

context Spectator inv: self.age >=18

From this, an MBT tool may generate two test cases: **self.age = 18** and **self.age = 17.99.**

The problem with producing models with the help of these languages is that testers need to become developers and modellers at the same time. Fortunately, some test modelling languages mitigate this problem (see the next chapter).

Some tools make it possible to extract models from existing code. The result is the same: the bugs remain undetected. However, if the application works well for a longer period, and it can be considered bug free (which is not necessarily the case) then it is an appropriate approach.

An important requirement for modelling languages is to support creating models using multiple test design techniques. Since more complex specifications imply the application of multiple test design techniques in combination, the modelling should be able to handle this. In the next chapter, we apply combined test design techniques for the TVM example.

Some practical recommendations on modelling:

- You should know the specification/user story and so on perfectly. It is not enough to just understand them.
- Design abstraction layers – never try to squeeze everything into a single model.
- In designing your tests, you should know which test design techniques are the most appropriate for modelling.
- Make a mental model first. Then, you will have a clear, big picture on how to prepare the model.
- Prepare your model iteratively, step-by-step; make a first draft, then extend it.
- Validate your model by applying review techniques.
- Use clear, self-explanatory naming conventions for the model elements.

ABSTRACTION LEVELS IN MBT

We described models as a representation of abstractions. In simple cases, one abstraction layer is a good description of the entity we want to model. However, in more complex cases it is not enough. One of the biggest advantages of MBT is the possibility of using several abstraction layers, which can then be arranged in a hierarchical order.

On the lower level, there are basic functionalities such as Login, Enter PIN and so on Then we can use these models to build higher-level models, where the model elements are sub-models. By continuing this process, more and more models can be built up with increasing complexity. In this way, end-to-end testing becomes easy since we do not need to design complex test scripts that contain a huge number of manual steps. Instead, we consider relatively simple models one by one, and the MBT tool makes efficient test cases from them.

It is much easier to validate a higher-level model with few aggregated components than a very complex model with dozens of states and transitions. This is similar to program development, where one method is simple and can be used many times. Basic models such as 'Login' can also be used many times in higher-level models. This also fits test automation where keyword-driven testing can be applied.

KEYWORD-DRIVEN TESTING

Keyword-driven testing (KDT) is a software testing methodology that separates the test design from the implementation of the automated test execution. Any test case can be described in an implementation-independent way by applying keywords and input/output values. The keyword is then implemented according to the actual code. The same keyword can be used in multiple places.

> By applying KDT, test cases can be created without any implementation issues independently from the test code development.

In this way, functional tests can be developed before any implementation work.

Keywords represent functional operations such as 'Open browser' or 'Select Window'. These keywords with appropriate parameters can also specify a direct call to the related test code. Keywords covering simple operations can be organised into larger keywords. In this way, keywords can be structured and applied to different projects. Usable keyword libraries already exist,[1] so there is no need to reinvent the wheel.

Besides separating test design and test automation, the main advantage of keyword-driven testing is that test suites are understandable for everybody. Hence, the tests can be considered an executable specification as they are both human-readable and executable. Because of the structural properties of KDT, you will only need to modify a few test cases when the code is modified. Therefore, tests are stable and maintainable.

MBT and KDT are strongly connected. From appropriate models, test code can easily be generated containing keywords with parameters supporting the implementation-independent part of the test execution code. This can be extended by implementation-dependent code resulting in executable test cases. Implementation-dependent code can

---

1   See https://github.com/Hrabovszki1023/OKW/wiki/List-of-OKW-Keywords

also be generated. This is also a good divide-and-conquer solution by fully separating test design and test automation.

TEST SELECTION CRITERIA

When the models are ready, we have to set an appropriate test selection criterion, so that the number of test cases remains manageable, yet efficient enough to find a high percentage of the bugs. Test selection criteria also depend on the risks of the feature under test and the budget. However, there is always an optimum of testing, concerning the total life cycle costs (see Chapter 3).

There are a lot of different test selection criteria according to the different modelling languages. Some of them are very specific and relate to a unique modelling language. Some criteria are weak in themselves, for example the requirement coverage, where each requirement in the specification has to be covered by at least one test case. In Chapter 6 we described several test selection criteria for (E)FSM and statecharts. Other test selection criteria for model-based testing can be found in Kramer and Legeard (2016).

On the other hand, model-based test selection criteria often inherit the criteria of the test design technique related to the model. When we model a specification based on EP and BVA, then the test selection criterion is related to EP and BVA. The case is similar for STT, where we can use lots of criteria (see Chapter 6).

We have considered test selection criteria for one abstraction layer so far. The real challenge is, however, when we have several layers, and we have to select an appropriate test selection criterion for each. If we do not select the criteria efficiently, then we either get too many test cases, or some necessary test cases will be missing. In cases of more abstraction layers, we have two basic possibilities:

1. **Reduced solution** – in this case all the (sub)models are considered separately with respect to the test selection criteria. This means that we have to fulfil the criteria for all the models as if they were independent. In this case, the test selection criteria for the models can be different. We can fulfil the criteria in parallel. Therefore the number of test cases may not exceed the maximum number of the required test cases of any of the models.

2. **Enhanced solution** – in this case, we consider a model and its sub-models as one large model containing all the models in one. In this case, the number of generated test cases may be too large. This may happen for non-linear test selection criteria.

Demonstrating these two options we consider a simple example with only one sub-model **Sub** (Figures 11.2 and 11.3).

We apply the **all-transition-state** criterion and design test paths for both the simple and the multi-layered case. When we consider the sub-model as a simple state in the higher-level state transition graph, we have **three simple tests** ignoring all the transitions we can. We have **3 × 3 test cases** for covering pairs (t4, S), (t5, S) and (t6, S), where S involves all the states. However, when we cover (t4, Sub), (t5, Sub) and (t6, Sub), we can cover the three different paths starting with t11, t12 and t13, respectively. Altogether,

Figure 11.2 Multi-layered state transition graph

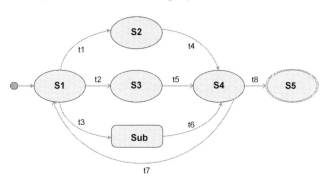

Figure 11.3 State transition graph for Sub

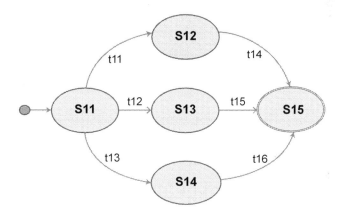

these 3 + 9 = 12 test cases are enough for the reduced approach as they also cover the necessary test cases for Sub. Note that we make the 3 × 3 test cases as short as possible. The reason for this is to be comparable with the enhanced case. Traversing transition t7 more times, we can create fewer test cases involving more steps. You can solve the exercise at the end of this chapter, and create these 12 test cases yourself.

Now let's consider the test paths for the enhanced case. We can also calculate the number of test paths for comparison. It is easy to see that instead of 3 × 3, now we have 5 × 5 test cases. In addition, we have five simple test cases. All together we have 5 + 5 × 5 = 30 test cases.

Since there is a large gap between 12 and 30, even this relatively simple case was able to stress the importance of the test selection. Obviously, the answer for the question of which test selection criterion should we select is: it depends. Here we do not consider the budget restrictions or any other non-technical aspects of testing.

We consider two different cases.

1. If in the sub-model the states and transitions relate to different functionality, then enhanced testing is reasonable. This is the case for the TVM example for the functionalities of normal and reduced modes; they are functionally different.

2. On the other hand, if the states or transitions are somehow similar, then reduced testing is reasonable. For example, if one state involves buying sparkling water, the other is buying still water, then enhanced testing is not necessary. The case is similar for the TVM, where we can reset ticket selection for any ticket types. However, we can also use reduced criterion if the model contains more test design methods such as STT and EP and BVA. In this case, all the necessary IN/OUT/ON/OFF points are tested at least once, but no multiple executions of them are needed.

Based on the arguments above we suggest the following:

1. If the states in a sub-model relate to different features, then enhanced test selection criteria have to be selected.

2. If the states/transitions in a sub-model relate to similar features, then reduced test selection criteria have to be selected.

3. If the budget does not permit enhanced criteria for the whole system, then apply them to the riskiest sub-systems.

TEST CASE GENERATION

When the models are ready, and the test selection criterion is also selected, then the test cases are ready to be generated. In practice, sometimes the test cases are generated based on some initial criterion and, depending on the number of test cases, the test selection criterion is fine-tuned according to feature risks and budget.

Basically, different types of test cases can be generated:

- Test cases for manual execution.
- Test cases for model validation.
- Test cases by which a test automation engineer can make automated tests (e.g. keyword-driven).
- Test cases from which another tool is able to make executable test cases.
- Test cases for automated execution.

All but the last one enable using implementation-independent models, which we believe are obligatory in test design. Based on a survey on model-based testing (Kramer et al., 2017) more than 30 per cent of MBT users apply model-based testing for manual test execution and more than 50 per cent of the generated artefacts are manual test cases.

Manually executable test cases have to be clear and understandable for testers. If the models contain sub-models, then detailed test cases have to be generated. Compact test cases should contain only higher-level test steps. In detailed test cases, test steps with regard to sub-models are detailed as well.

There are several algorithms for test case generation starting from a given model. The interested reader can study Németh (2015), where there is an overview of several algorithms.

SOME MBT TOOLS

In the next two chapters, we consider two free tools in detail. Here we briefly describe three key market players in MBT.

Conformiq Creator is a test generation tool that automatically creates test cases based on a model of the system under test, represented by either structure or activity diagrams. A **structure diagram** defines the interfaces available for testing the system. For **activity diagrams**, the tester can model the necessary elements such as variables, data flow, decision nodes, action properties, pop-ups, and requirements. The diagrams may be created manually in a simple drag and drop editor.

Models can also be imported from existing assets such as flowcharts, business process modelling, manual tests, Gherkin-user stories and so on. Then, selecting a test selection criterion, the test cases are generated. Besides test generation, Conformiq generates a coverage report on the parts of the model that have been covered. The tests generated by Conformiq Creator can be exported into various formats for manual or automated test execution such as Conformiq Transformer or some third-party test frameworks. The generated test suite can also be uploaded to an application life cycle management (test management) system.

Tricentis Tosca TestSuite is an end-to-end testing suite focused primarily on supporting automated testing. It is also a scriptless tool, that is test cases are generated instead of coding. Test cases can be efficiently created after scanning the running application, then data are selected for the generated fields with respect to GUI objects. Its key features are: (1) a comprehensive risk-based approach to test coverage (based on assessments of impact and probability) and (2) an easy-to-use solution for automating tests that can be applied by testers without programming knowledge. The tool allows automated, functional tests. The user can create requirements and test models involving test design techniques such as equivalence partitioning, boundary value analysis or pairwise testing.

Tosca is a non-graphical MBT tool, where the model is not displayed visually to the users. The tester can use Conformiq – a partner of Tricentis – if they prefer using visual models. Requirements can also be imported from third-party environments to generate test cases. The test cases and the requirements are mapped and one or more test cases belongs to each requirement.

CA Agile Requirements Designer is an automated testing solution for capturing, designing and modelling requirements in a flowchart, from which test cases and test scripts can be generated automatically. The product supports requirements model creation, offers possibilities for mapping requirements to visual flowchart models, and eliminates ambiguous requirements.

The product provides a simple, reusable approach for the creation of the test cases, which can then be executed. In addition, existing test cases can be inserted into the CA Agile

Requirements Designer environment. There are specific test case management capabilities built into the product. When generating test cases, the product supports several different types of test selection criteria and is able to optimise the number of test cases needed for the required coverage. Testers and business analysts can quickly model requirements, which then provide a reference for all subsequent test and development activities.

Traceability is preserved between test cases and requirements that drive those test cases, and similarly, any changes to the requirements will prompt an impact analysis that will create or repair test cases, maintaining the same level of coverage. Existing test cases can also be imported, optimised and executed as automated tests. The optimised test cases can be pushed out and allocated to testers in existing tools such as CA Agile Central, HP/MicroFocus ALM, Microsoft TFS and so on.

METHOD EVALUATION

Here we briefly evaluate MBT methods in general, as the related tools have common benefits and drawbacks.

Applicability

MBT is equally usable for manual and automated test design. The only difference is that for manual test design you can write less specific models using abstract values such as 'zero', 'ten per cent' instead of 0 and 10. For automated test design the model and the application should meet. Usually this is done by scanning the application.

MBT is mainly used for functional testing but it can also be used for performance, security and usability testing. It can be used for all test levels including unit, component, integration, system and acceptance testing. It is not surprising that most MBT users apply it for system testing.

MBT can be used for simple, medium and even very complex software. For complex applications MBT users should separate the specification into manageable levels.

MBT can also be used for several application domains such as web applications, embedded systems, gaming, enterprise IT, software infrastructure and so on.

Note that MBT can only be effective in industrial projects when the total efforts for applying an MBT approach are affordable. The modelling efforts can be crucial.

Types of defects

MBT approaches are typically applied to functional testing, but also support other types of testing such as performance, security and usability.

Advantages and shortcomings of model-based testing

There are several advantages of MBT. Lots of MBT experts and tool vendors believe that in the near future model-based testing will be dominant. We list the main advantages below.

- MBT reduces the time required in test design. Jones and Bonsignour (2011) investigated thousands of projects collecting lots of important metrics. According to their investigation, the design of one test case takes on average 15 minutes. Our experience shows that in applying a good MBT tool for generating manual test cases, this time can be reduced to below 10 minutes.

- Models are reusable. Models are similar to components and can be reused for other projects. However, be very careful: in reusing some existing components critical bugs may occur due to faults or inappropriate usage.

- MBT is able to manage complexity. Models can be arranged hierarchically. During test case generation test cases may contain several models at different levels. Complex test cases are difficult to create and can be error-prone. By the divide-and-conquer approach the complexity of the test design can be handled.

- MBT is a defect prevention method. Building models requires in-depth knowledge of the requirements/specifications/user stories, which usually lead to detecting issues in the available project documents.

- Models are considered living specifications. Since test cases are generated from the models, if a test fails, then either the code or the model is faulty. If this does not happen, then the code and the model correspond to each other and the model remains 'live'.

- Models are easier to maintain than test cases. With a large test set, it is very difficult to find those that are to be modified or deleted. In MBT the models are directly connected to the specification. If a specification is changed, the related model should be modified accordingly, and the test cases are regenerated. In addition, it is enough to generate the test cases affected by the modification (Németh, 2015). In the next chapter, we will consider an example for this situation.

- For engineers, models are more understandable than test cases. From relatively simple models quite complex test cases can be generated. This is valid for both graphical and text-based models.

- Different test design techniques can be used together with a single modelling language, resulting in a coherent and compact description for the whole test design.

- MBT is flexible. The testers can modify the test selection criterion a little bit, causing fewer or more test cases to be generated according to the actual needs. This is not possible for traditional test design.

Of course, there are some pitfalls to MBT too:

- Model-based testing requires a different mindset. MBT differs from traditional test design, and some testers do not like changes. Change management is not easy.

- Transition to MBT is costly. To become a proficient MBT user, the learning time takes almost 200 hours on average (Kramer et al., 2017).

- Models may also contain bugs. Sometimes it is easier to apply the same model for development and for testing, which is very dangerous and a clear sign of a misunderstanding of MBT. Some tools generate models from code, which is also to be avoided.

KEY TAKEAWAYS

- MBT involves automated test design, an efficient alternative to traditional test design.

- MBT is an important tool for defect prevention, supports implementation-independent test design, easy maintenance and quality improvement.

- MBT supports hierarchical modelling, by which complex test cases can be designed more easily and manageably.

- MBT and test execution automation can be connected via keyword-driven testing.

- MBT is an important step towards the automation of the development life cycle, which is necessary for today's DevOps philosophy and practices.

EXERCISE

E11 Consider the state transition graphs in Figures 11.2 and 11.3. Create test paths to satisfy the all-transition-state criterion by applying the reduced approach.

12 GHERKIN-BASED MBT

WHY IS THIS CHAPTER WORTH READING?

In this chapter you will learn the extended Gherkin modelling language of an MBT tool. You will also learn how to use it through creating a model by iteratively improving it. We will show you how to make models based on EP and BVA and STT test design. We model the specification of the TVM example.

Most MBT tools are commercial and rather expensive (Micskei, 2017). In this book, we only consider free tools. Fortunately, there are some free tools available. We selected one text-based and one graphical tool so that you can try and use them. In this chapter, we review a Gherkin-based modelling language and the related tool, Harmony (available at https://trial.harmony.ac). This tool is easy to learn and use and writing test code is not necessary (scriptless solution). Recall that independently of being graphical or textual, the main characteristics of test models to consider are as follows:

- Relation to the test design techniques – how closely is the model related to testing, that is, does it directly involve testing techniques such as EP, BVA, STT and so on or are there workarounds?

- The expressive power of the modelling language – how efficient is the model when applied to complex and different specifications?

- Understandability – how easy to understand is the model for the stakeholders? Models can be considered as an alternative specification.

- Usability – how easy is it to make models and generate complex test cases?

- Maintainability – how easy is it to modify the model and the test cases, so that unaffected test cases are not re-executed?

- Learning curve – how easy is it to learn the modelling language?

- Modularity – how easy is it to use a model, or especially a sub-model, contained in higher-level models?

Harmony has been developed to take into account these characteristics as much as possible. Also, Harmony supports the test-first method, which is very important since the generated test cases are implementation independent, similar to a good specification/ feature/user story. For example, if only the code changes are improving the GUI, then the designed test cases will not change, and only the automated executable test scripts will be modified. On the other hand, if the specification has been changed, then so is the model, and the affected test cases are regenerated. In this case, the tester knows the modified/new test cases and the maintenance will be easier, simpler and cheaper.

The tool's modelling language starts from and extends the **Gherkin syntax**, which was originally used in the BDD tool Cucumber (Wynne and Hellesøy, 2012) to define test cases. The Gherkin syntax defining a test case is the following:

```
Scenario: MyScenario
    Given precondition1
    And precondition2
    When action1
    And action2
    Then result1
    And result2
```

In this way, we can create test cases but not models. Harmony is based on the category-partition method (Ostrand and Balcer, 1988), which is a strategy for designing and specifying functional tests. By extending the Gherkin syntax and improving category-partitioning, the result is a modelling language.

Instead of scenarios, the basic element of the modelling language is the feature – a given part of the project's specification, represented by requirements or user stories. A Harmony model contains three basic elements: categories, choices and acceptance criteria (AC). A **category** is a precondition, an input or an output entity taken from the feature description. For example, 'logged in' is a precondition, 'PIN code' is input and 'total price of books' is an output category. Each category contains one or more **choices**, which are abstract or real values. For example, 'logged in' can be true or false, 'PIN code' can be correct or incorrect (abstract) or 7723 (real). Finally, 'total price of books' can be quite a few, very high (abstract) or 43.99 (real).

When the categories and the choices have been selected, the next step is to set the necessary **AC based on the requirements.** Acceptance criteria are dependences among input (including preconditions) and output choices. AC are described by an extended Gherkin syntax. For example, the constraint between a valid login name, password and the login status can be expressed in Harmony as:

WHEN login name IS Smith AND password IS 77abTH55 THEN login status IS logged

In Harmony the keywords are uppercase letters, and all three parts (WHEN, THEN) can be written on one line or can be structured in several lines. Now, let's consider a simple feature and discover how to create a simple model.

FIRST EXAMPLE

We describe here a feature by requirements, numbered R1, R2 and so on.

FEATURE: PRICE REDUCTION FOR ONLINE BOOK PURCHASING

> R1. For online new book purchasing, regular customers with cards obtain a 10% price reduction.
>
> R2. Similarly, any customer buying new books for at least EUR 50 gets a 10% price reduction.
>
> R3. If somebody has a card and buys new books for more than EUR 50, then the price reduction is 15%.
>
> R4. The price reduction holds only for new books even if the customer buys new and second-hand books together.
>
> R5. The total book price appears on the screen.

Firstly, read the requirements very carefully. You will never create a good model if you do not understand the requirements. Then try to extract the categories and the choices. They are in the text, but finding them needs some experience. After some modelling exercises, we can extract them easily. For example, read R1: *'For online new book purchasing'.* Here *online* is not important, because there is no alternative way of purchasing. However, we will recognise this when we learn the whole feature.

On the other hand, *new book* is relevant, since there are *second-hand books* on sale as well. Therefore, we can introduce a category **book type** with choices *new book* and *second-hand book*. Note that in this case, the book type is indirectly involved in the feature, and we can create it by recognising the two choices. Finally, *purchasing* is an action; however, the feature is only for price reduction, where actual buying does not happen. Thus, we can ignore it.

Reading R1 further, *'regular customers with cards'* is a choice but we rename it. The category can be **'card owner'** and the related choices are *'yes'* and *'no'*. **Price reduction** is an obvious category with choices: *10%, 15%* and *no reduction*. Since we know the whole specification, we can see that besides 10% the price reduction can be 15% and no reduction.

Considering R2 we can see that the new books have prices. Therefore, we have a new category, **new book price**. Determining its choices here BVA can help, since we have to test the ON point of the boundary, which is *EUR 50*; an OFF point, which is *EUR 49.99*; and an IN point, for example, *EUR 1000*.

Considering R3 we can find a new rule for a price reduction. Here is an open boundary, that is EUR 50 is an OFF point. This seems to be a little bit strange if the price boundaries for card owners and for the others are different. Here defect prevention works since the correct sentence is: *If somebody has a card and buys new books for at least EUR 50, then the price reduction is 15 per cent.*

In R4 we have 'second-hand book', and we have to validate that for second-hand books no price reduction happens. Therefore, we set prices for second-hand books as well. In this way, we have a category **second-hand book price,** with choices *0* and *100*. We select a value significantly larger than 50 in case a developer forgets the distinction between new and second-hand books.

Finally, in R5, we have to validate the book's price, which is calculated based on the original prices and reductions. This is an output category, and thus, the choices are the functions of the input values. However, it is not necessary to determine these choices in this phase. In some cases, it is better to postpone it until the creation of AC.

So, we have the following categories and choices (we modified the names when needed):

> *book type (I): new book; second-hand book*
>
> *card owner (I): yes (S); no*
>
> *new book price (I): 49.99 (D); 50; 1000*
>
> *second-hand book price (I): 0; 1(S); 100 (S)*
>
> *price reduction for new books (O): 10%; 15%; no reduction (D)*
>
> *total price (O).*

We extended the categories with (I) means input and (O) means output. A very important extension of choices is (D) means default, (S) means single. We explain the last two extensions below.

Now let's create the AC. This is relatively simple. The first is a condition: when the card owner is 'yes', then the price reduction for new books is 10 per cent. Also, the new book price has to be less than EUR 50. Otherwise, the reduction would be 15 per cent. And that's why (D) and (S) have been introduced. During test case generation, the generator selects a choice for each input category. However, choices with (D) will always be selected, while choices with (S) are selected only once for the categories missing in some AC. The only exception is that each choice has to be selected at least once. Thus, the acceptance criterion is as follows.

> *Card owner:*
> *WHEN card owner IS yes*
> *THEN price reduction for new books IS 10%*
> *AND total price IS 44.99*

The total price is implicitly set as 44.99 as the new book price 49.99 has an extension (D), and the second-hand book price is 0 because the test case generator selects the choices without (S). You can observe that each acceptance criterion may have a name such as *Card owner*. This will be the related generated test case name as well. Now we can easily create the three missing AC:

Expensive:
WHEN new book price IS 50
THEN price reduction for new books IS 10%
AND total price IS 45

Both:
WHEN card owner IS yes
AND new book price IS 50
THEN price reduction for new books IS 15%
AND total price IS 42.5

No reduction:
WHEN new book price IS 49.99
AND second hand book price IS 1
THEN price reduction for new books IS no reduction
AND total price IS 50.99

Note that second-hand book price is 1 in order to test the possibility of a bug when price reduction for new books is enabled based on the total price instead of the new book price.

When we create an acceptance criterion to test the case when second-hand books have no price reduction, the other choices have to be selected, forcing price reduction for new books. Here we also test the IN point (EUR 1000):

No reduction for second-hand books:
WHEN second-hand book price IS 100
AND card owner IS yes
AND new book price IS 1000
THEN price reduction for new books IS 15%
AND total price IS 950

We can also see that a 15 per cent price reduction for the new book is covered twice. Therefore, we can delete acceptance criterion *Both*. You may observe that we apply multiple fault assumption. Yes, in this case, the failure detection capability of this test is significantly higher than a test case where the buyer has no card and buys no new books at all. If the test fails, we can add the deleted acceptance criterion *Both* to help the developer discover whether price reduction for new or used books is faulty.

We are almost ready, but we can observe that the first category and the related choices remain unused. They are superfluous and can be removed. Modelling is an iterative work; after creating AC we may modify or delete some categories and/or choices.

Finally, we shall fill the output choices for *total price*:

   total price (O): 44.99; 45; 50.99; 950

The tool generates the test cases just in time. In Figure 12.1 you can see the model of price reduction. The generated tests are on the bottom of the window. In the figure the AC are not formatted for space utilisation.

You can observe that the test cases have been generated without setting any test selection criteria. The test selection criteria in Harmony are as follows:

- Each choice has to be selected at least once.
- Each acceptance criterion has to be extended to a test case.

Here, the four AC have been converted to four test cases.

Finally, the manually executable test cases are generated (see Table 12.1), where the detailed test cases are shown. The input and the output are distinguished by different colours in the tool, here bold and roman. After executing the test case and filling the result with passed or failed as happened, the results are summarised (see Table 12.2). Note that we executed three test cases out of the four, two passed and one has failed.

Note that the new version of Harmony is capable of generating test code and executing it. This new functionality is outside the scope of our book, however, you can try it freely.

THE MODELLING LANGUAGE

We have seen the basic elements of the Gherkin-based modelling language, and we have made a simple model. However, complex systems are modelled in practice applying various important test design techniques. Therefore, we summarise the syntax of the modelling language and then show you how to use it for some of our previous examples.

GIVEN, WHEN, THEN, AND, IS

These are the basic keywords in the Gherkin and Gherkin++. GIVEN is used for preconditions where we would like to test a feature, and we have to cover an execution path for the feature to be tested. An example is: *GIVEN Login is successful THEN...* GIVEN is optional.

Figure 12.1 The model of price reduction

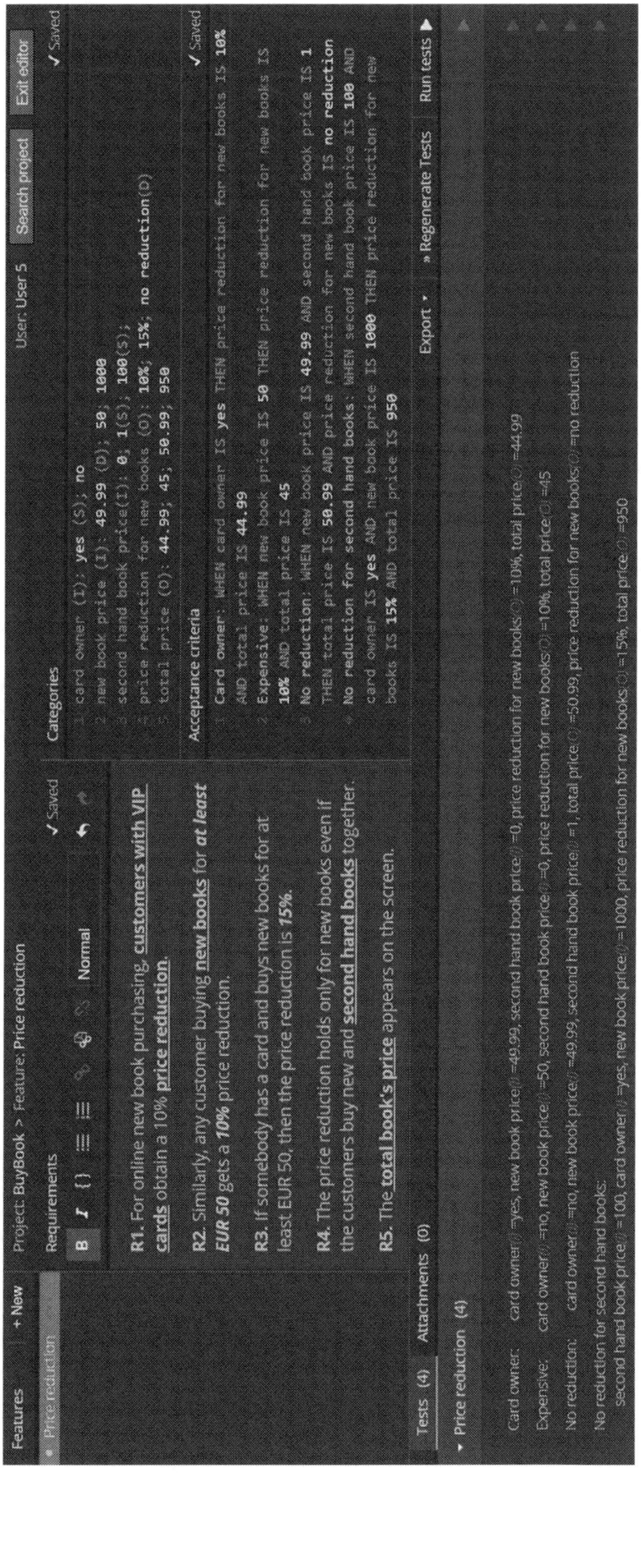

Features + New   Project: BuyBook > Feature: Price reduction   User: User 5   Search project   Exit editor

• Price reduction

Requirements ✓ Saved

B I {} ≡ ≡ ⚓ ◇   Normal

R1. For online new book purchasing, customers with VIP cards obtain a 10% price reduction.

R2. Similarly, any customer buying new books for at least *EUR 50* gets a *10%* price reduction.

R3. If somebody has a card and buys new books for at least EUR 50, then the price reduction is *15%*.

R4. The price reduction holds only for new books even if the customers buy new and second hand books together.

R5. The total book's price appears on the screen.

Categories ✓ Saved

1 card owner (I): yes (S), no
2 new book price (I): 49.99 (D); 50; 1000
3 second hand book price(I): 0; 1(S); 100(S);
4 price reduction for new books (O): 10%; 15%; no reduction(D)
5 total price (O): 44.99; 45; 50.99; 950

Acceptance criteria

1 Card owner: WHEN card owner IS yes THEN price reduction for new books IS 10% AND total price IS 44.99
2 Expensive: WHEN new book price IS 50 THEN price reduction for new books IS 10% AND total price IS 45
3 No reduction: WHEN new book price IS 49.99 AND second hand book price IS 1 THEN total price IS 50.99 AND price reduction for new books IS no reduction
4 No reduction for second hand books: WHEN second hand book price IS 100 AND card owner IS yes AND new book price IS 1000 THEN price reduction for new books IS 15% AND total price IS 950

Export ▾   » Regenerate Tests   Run tests

Tests (4) Attachments (0)
» Price reduction (4)

Card owner: card owner() =yes, new book price() =49.99, second hand book price() =0, price reduction for new books() =0, price reduction for new books() =10%, total price() =44.99
Expensive: card owner() =no, new book price() =50, second hand book price() =0, price reduction for new books() =10%, total price() =45
No reduction: card owner() =no, new book price() =49.99, second hand book price() =1, total price() =50.99, price reduction for new books() =no reduction
No reduction for second hand books: second hand book price() =100, card owner() =yes, new book price() =1000, price reduction for new books() =15%, total price() =950

Table 12.1 Manual test cases for 'Price reduction'

Test case	Card owner	
	card owner (I)	yes
	new book price (I)	**49.99**
	second-hand book price (I)	**0**
	price reduction for new books (O)	10%
	total price (O)	44.99
Test case	**Expensive**	
	card owner (I)	**no**
	new book price (I)	**50**
	second-hand book price (I)	**0**
	price reduction for new books (O)	10%
	total price (O)	45
Test case	**No reduction**	
	card owner (I)	**no**
	new book price (I)	**49.99**
	second-hand book price (I)	**1**
	total price (O)	50.99
	price reduction for new books (O)	no reduction
Test case	**No reduction for second-hand books**	
	second-hand book price (I)	**100**
	card owner (I)	**yes**
	new book price (I)	**1000**
	price reduction for new books (O)	15%
	total price (O)	950

The syntax requires using both WHEN and THEN in all the AC. In contrast to the original Gherkin syntax, any WHEN-THEN-WHEN-THEN sequence is possible. In the following model a faulty pin code is entered twice, but the correct one is entered the third time.

WHEN Pin IS wrong THEN Message IS 'wrong Pin code has been entered'
WHEN Pin IS wrong THEN Message IS 'wrong Pin code has been entered'
WHEN Pin IS good THEN Message IS 'Pin code is OK'

AND can be used to connect two (or more) GIVEN/WHEN/THEN statements.

IS/ARE connects a category and a choice of this category, such as *MyCat IS MyChoice*.

Table 12.2 Test results for 'Price reduction'

	A	B	C	D	E	F	G	H
1	All test cases	4	%					
2	passed	2	50%					
3	failed	1	25%					
4	passed+failed	3	75%					
5								
6		Test case	passed	failed	passed+failed	passed (%)	failed (%)	passed+failed (%)
7	Price reduction	4	2	1	3	50%	25%	75%

Multi-layer structure

In general, the structure of software systems is complex and can mostly be arranged in hierarchical ways. Models have to express this multi-level structure as well. Harmony supports a multi-layered structure. Test cases from lower-level models can be used in higher-level models. There are two possibilities to utilise available test cases from other features:

1. **(F)** is a category type where the category name is an existing (lower-level) feature. The choices of this category can be the test case/AC names. The number of the layers is not limited. In this way, very complex test cases can be generated based on relatively simple models.

EXAMPLE

There is feature *Login* with two test cases: successful, faulty. We can make a higher-level feature *Buy* as follows:

Feature Buy

CATEGORIES
Login (F): successful; faulty (S)

AC
MyTest: GIVEN login IS successful WHEN total price IS 0 THEN paying IS not possible

---

2. We can use available features and their test cases in another feature without any declaration. Therefore, we can delete *'Login (F): successful; faulty (S)'. from CATEGORIES.* Just type the feature name, and the selected test case name and Harmony will validate it.

Tables

Tables reduce the number of AC if they differ only with respect to the choices. For example, if there are two similar AC:

Twenty: WHEN original price IS 20 AND reduction is 10 THEN total price IS 18
One hundred: WHEN original price IS 100 AND reduction is 12 THEN total price IS 88

In this case, we substitute these two AC by one as follows.

MyTable: WHEN original price IS 20 | 100
*   AND reduction   IS 10 | 12*
*   THEN total price   IS 18 | 88*

The name of the generated test cases will be MyTable[20] and MyTable[100] and can be called from other models by applying this name.

If you are a test analyst, you will understand this acceptance criterion and your model will be shorter. The generated test cases will also remain understandable for everybody.

If some category is missing from the acceptance criterion, then the choices are selected according to the category declaration, and the generator will iterate them.

> *NewTable[100]: original price = 100, reduction = 10, payment method =*
> *money transfer, total price = 90*
> *NewTable[1000]: original price = 1000, reduction = 12, payment method =*
> *card, total price = 880*

You can see that the '*payment method*' is missing from the acceptance criterion in the example. In this case the choices are selected one-by-one repetitively.

Sub-AC

A sub-acceptance criterion is an acceptance criterion that can be used in other AC. This is similar to functions in programming. In this way, common parts of AC can be extracted and used to shorten the AC. An example is below.

EXAMPLE

Our former example contains the subparts:

> *WHEN PIN IS wrong THEN Message IS 'wrong PIN code has been entered'*
> *WHEN PIN IS wrong THEN Message IS 'wrong PIN code has been entered'*
> *WHEN PIN IS good THEN Message IS 'PIN code is OK'*

We can construct a sub-acceptance criteria:

> **Wrong PIN:** *WHEN PIN IS wrong THEN Message IS 'wrong PIN code has been entered'*

The original acceptance criterion can be shortened:

> *WHEN **Wrong PIN** WHEN **Wrong PIN** WHEN Pin IS good THEN Message IS 'Pin code is OK'*

Replication (GO/GOES)

GO/GOES makes it possible to model state transition diagrams. Let's assume a (transition, state) pair, for example, inserting an amount to be paid (a transition), and the remaining amount after this insertion (state). We can insert a series of amounts resulting in a series of remaining amounts. We can use WHEN-THEN-WHEN-THEN, but we simplify it by GO. Firstly consider the following acceptance criterion:

WHEN In IS 3 THEN Out IS yes
WHEN In IS 1 THEN Out IS no
WHEN In IS 2 THEN Out IS N/A

However, it is too verbose; fortunately, GO/GOES helps. The above acceptance crtierion can be transformed into:

WHEN In GOES 3; 1; 2 THEN Out GOES yes; no; N/A

Here for In = 3, Out = yes; for In = 1, Out = no; for In = 2, Out = N/A. It's pretty simple, isn't it?

TEST DESIGN MAINTENANCE

Until now we have not considered the question of maintaining test cases. As the specification and the code change, so do the test cases. Some of them become obsolete and some new test cases are required. We know that maintenance cost is the largest part of the project life cycle cost. Therefore test case maintenance is a critical issue. Fortunately, MBT can make test case maintenance cheaper. When the specification is changed the related model should also be modified. Based on the modified model, the test cases are generated again. Thus, no manual test case modification happens.

Also, maintaining the models instead of the test cases is a huge advantage. There is no need to generate all the test cases again; it is enough to generate only those affected by the modification. If the output is some new or modified executable test cases, then after the modification these test cases are automatically executed. More information about this can be found in Németh (2015).

For manual test execution, selecting the affected test cases is even more important. Assume that the tester has executed half of the test cases when a modification in the specification happens. They have to know what the new or the modified test cases are, otherwise very costly full re-execution is needed. By selecting and marking the affected test cases, the tester executes only some test cases. The result is not only a better code, but the team has continuous knowledge of the quality of the product.

Let's consider an example for test case maintenance. Consider our previous 'Price reduction' example. Let's modify the price reduction value from 15 per cent to 13 per cent. We select the original Microsoft Excel sheet as it contains the manual test results. Selecting 'EXPORT TEST FROM PREVIOUS RESULTS' we get the results shown in Table 12.3.

We can see that only one test case has been modified – 'No reduction for second-hand books' where the price reduction was modified to 13 per cent. The result of the test execution for all the other test cases remained 'passed', 'failed' and empty, as this test case is unexecuted. Only the empty and the modified test cases will be executed and re-executed, respectively. We have a test case 'no reduction' with no result as it has not been executed. There are several causes for a test case being unexecuted; for example, the related code was not ready, or the tester just ran out of time.

Table 12.3 Test results for 'Price reduction' after feature modification

Test cases	4	%
New or modified	1	25%
Passed	1	25%
Failed	1	25%
passed+failed	2	50%

Result (passed/ failed)	Test case	card owner (I)	new book price (I)	second-hand book price (I)	price reduction for new books (O)	total price (O)
passed	Card owner	yes	49.99	0	10%	44.99
failed	Expensive	no	50	0	10%	45
	No reduction	no	49.99	1	no reduction	50.99
modified	No reduction for second-hand books	yes	1000	100	13%	970

TICKET VENDING MACHINE EXAMPLE

We selected the user stories from Chapter 5 and Chapter 6 to show you how two test design techniques can be used in combination and how to model them. We extended these two with the successful transaction.

EXAMPLE: TVM TICKET SELECTION

There are three types of tickets:

a. Standard ticket valid for 75 minutes on any metro, tram or bus line.
b. Short distance ticket valid within five stations on a single line of any metro, tram or bus.
c. 24-hour ticket for unlimited metro, bus, and train travel for 24 hours from validation.

The price of the tickets can only be modified by the system administrator of the ticket vending machine company. The users cannot modify the prices. Currently (a) is EUR 2.10, (b) is EUR 1.40 and (c) is EUR 7.60.

The customer can buy tickets of one type only. If all the amounts of the tickets are zero, then any of them can be increased. The customer can increase the number of

---

tickets to be purchased to 10. The customer can also reduce the number of tickets to be purchased to zero. If the selected amount of tickets is greater than zero, the buying process can start.

Buying process. Payment is possible if the customer has selected **at least one ticket**. Payment is made by inserting coins or banknotes into the machine. The ticket machine always shows the remaining amount necessary for the transaction. For the remaining amount to be paid, the machine only accepts banknotes for which the selection of the smaller banknote does not reach the required amount. EUR 5 is always accepted. For example, if the necessary amount is EUR 21, then the machine accepts EUR 50 since EUR 20 will not exceed EUR 21. If the user inserts EUR 10 and then EUR 2, then even EUR 20 is not accepted since the remaining amount is EUR 9, EUR 10 would exceed the necessary amount. The remaining amount and current acceptable banknotes are visible on the screen. If the user inserts a non-acceptable banknote then it will be given back and an error message will appear notifying the user about the error.

Successful transaction. The ticket machine always shows the remaining amount necessary for the transaction, which is successful if the inserted money reaches or exceeds the required amount. In the latter case, the difference is given back to the user. After payment the tickets are printed.

Remember that we designed seven test cases for RAP (remaining amount to be paid) (see Chapter 5). We modified T1 and T3, see Table 12.4.

The state transition graph includes the payment process, and the successful transaction is shown in Figure 12.2.

The BVA tests are inserted into S5: Payment normal mode, as you insert banknotes and coins until payment is successful. We model these three (Ticket selection, Buying process – S5 and Transition OK – S6) with different features. The basic feature is ticket selection, which will call the other features.

Table 12.4 Modified test cases for RAP

Test	EP	Ticket price	Inserted amount	RAP in EUR	Maximum acceptable banknote
T1	1	2.1	2	0.1	€5
T2	1	7 (5 x 1.4)	2	5	€5
T3	2	5.6 (4 x 1.4)	0.5	5.1	€10
T4	2	10.5 (5 x 2.1)	0.5	10	€10
T5	3	15.2 (2 x 7.6)	5, 0.1	10.1	€20
T6	3	21	1	20	€20
T7	4	21	0.5, 0.2, 0.2	20.1	€50

Figure 12.2 State transition graph for the TVM

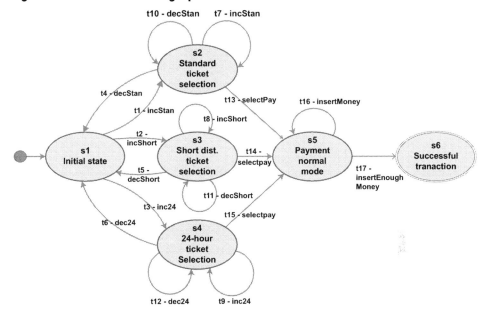

Feature: Buying process

Now let's consider the buying process. Tables are easily constructed in Harmony. The inputs are the inserted amounts; the outputs are the acceptable banknotes and the remaining amounts. Note that ticket prices are not inputs here. These are the output of the ticket selection process, and we will connect these two in the models. However, for clarity, we insert ticket prices as comments. The categories and the related choices are the following.

//Ticket price(I): 2.1; 7; 5.6; 10.5; 15.2; 21; 21

Inserted amount(I): 1; 5, 0.1; 2; 2.0; 0.5; 0.5, 0.2, 0.2; 0.50
Remaining amount(O): 0.1; 5; 5.1; 10; 10.1; 20; 20.1
Acceptable maximum banknote(O): 5; 10; 20; 50

Be careful with the colons and semicolons. If you press a colon instead of a semicolon, then two intended choices become one unintended choice.

If we insert more coins, we create a related choice such as *0.5, 0.2, 0.2;* meaning we insert these three coins one by one. Making identical choices such as 0.5 and 0.50 is intentional, making the test case more understandable (for example *BanknoteTest [0.50]* instead of *BanknoteTest [4]*).

247

We have only one acceptance criterion from which the tool generates the seven necessary test cases:

Feature: insertMoney

BanknoteTest:
WHEN Inserted amount IS 2 | 2.0 | 0.5 | 0.50 | 5, 0.1 | 1 | 0.5, 0.2, 0.2
THEN Remaining amount IS 0.1 | 5 | 5.1 | 10 | 10.1 | 20 | 20.1
AND Acceptable maximum banknote IS 5 | 5 | 10 | 10 | 20 | 20 | 50

We obtain eight test cases:

BanknoteTest [2]: Inserted amount(I) =2, Remaining amount(O) =0.1, Acceptable maximum banknote(O) =5

BanknoteTest [2.0]: Inserted amount(I) =2.0, Remaining amount(O) =5, Acceptable maximum banknote(O) =5

BanknoteTest [0.5]: Inserted amount(I) =0.5, Remaining amount(O) =5.1, Acceptable maximum banknote(O) =10

BanknoteTest [0.50]: Inserted amount(I) =0.50, Remaining amount(O) =10, Acceptable maximum banknote(O) =10

BanknoteTest [5, 0.1]: Inserted amount(I) =5, 0.1, Remaining amount(O) =10.1, Acceptable maximum banknote(O) =20

BanknoteTest [1]: Inserted amount(I) =1, Remaining amount(O) =20, Acceptable maximum banknote(O) =20

BanknoteTest [0.5, 0.2, 0.2]: Inserted amount(I) =0.5, 0.2, 0.2, Remaining amount(O) =20.1, Acceptable maximum banknote(O) =50

These are the necessary boundary value test cases.

Feature: Transaction OK

Inserting the remaining coins and/or banknotes for successful payment is very similar.

Categories and choices:

Inserted amount(I): 0.1; 5; 5, 0.1; 10; 10, 0.1; 20; 20, 0.1;
Remaining amount(O): 0(D)
Number of tickets printed(O): 1; 4; 5; 2; 10
Action(O): initial screen(D)

AC:

Print:
WHEN Inserted amount IS 0.1 | 5 | 5, 0.1| 10 | 10, 0.1 | 20 | 20, 0.1

THEN Number of tickets printed IS 1 | 5 | 4 | 5 | 2 | 10 | 10
Harmony generates the test cases below:

Print [0.1]:
Inserted amount(I) =0.1, Remaining amount(O) =0, Number of tickets printed(O) =1,
Action(O) =initial screen

Print [5]:
Inserted amount(I) =5, Remaining amount(O) =0, Number of tickets printed(O) =5,
Action(O) =initial screen

Print [5, 0.1]:
Inserted amount(I) =5, 0.1, Remaining amount(O) =0, Number of tickets printed(O) =4,
Action(O) =initial screen

Print [10]:
Inserted amount(I) =10, Remaining amount(O) =0, Number of tickets printed(O) =5,
Action(O) =initial screen

Print [10, 0.1]:
Inserted amount(I) =10, 0.1, Remaining amount(O) =0, Number of tickets printed(O) =2,
Action(O) =initial screen

Print [20]:
Inserted amount(I) =20, Remaining amount(O) =0, Number of tickets printed(O) =10,
Action(O) =initial screen

Print [20, 0.1]:
Inserted amount(I) =20, 0.1, Remaining amount(O) =0, Number of tickets
printed(O) =10, Action(O) =initial screen

Feature: Ticket selection

In this feature we connect the three parts of the TVM process: (1) ticket selection, (2) inserting less money than expected, (3) inserting the remaining money, (virtually) printing the ticket and going back to the welcome (initial) screen. Here we consider the ticket selection and then call the test cases from the other two features. Remember from Chapter 6 that we have three complex and three simple test paths to cover the all-transition-state criterion.

The ticket selection model has only one input category: TVM transition

TVM transition(I): increase St first; increase St; decrease St to 0; decrease St 9X; increase 24 first; increase 24; decrease 24 to 0; decrease 24 9X; increase short first; increase

short; decrease short to 0; decrease short 9X; increase St 9X; increase short 9X; increase 24 9X; increase short 4X; increase St 4X

Where, for example, *increase St 9X* means traversing t7 incStan in Figure 12.2 nine times. We have four outputs as we have the number of tickets for the three ticket types and one output for price:

Number of St tickets(O): 0; 1; 10; 5
Number of Short tickets (O): 0; 1; 10; 4; 5
Number of 24 tickets(O): 0; 1; 2; 10;
price(O):1.4; 2.1; 7.6; 5.6; 7; 10.5; 15.2; 21

The three complex paths described in Chapter 6, have been extended according to additional elements in the graph. We use the same abbreviations (**Init**, **St**, **Short**, **24, Payment** and **Success**) for states, and **insert** for insertMoney and **enough** for insertEnough Money for the transitions. We also use (10X) for repeating the transition 10 times.

Tpath1 = **Init** – incStan – **St** – incStan(10X) – **St** – decStan(11X) – **Init** – incStan – **St** – decStan – **Init** – incShort – **Short** – decShort – Init – inc24 – **24** – selectPay – **Payment** – insert – **Payment** – enough – **Success**

Tpath2 = **Init** – incShort – **Short** – incShort(10X) – **Short** – decShort(11X) – **Init** – incShort – **Short** – decShort – Init – inc24 – **24** – dec24 – Init – incStan – **St** – selectPay – **Payment** – insert – **Payment** – enough – **Success**

Tpath3 = **Init** – inc24 – **24** – inc24(10X) – **24** – dec24(11X) – **Init** – inc24 – **24** – dec24 – **Init** – incStan – **St** – decSt – Init – incShort – **Short** – selectPay – **Payment** – insert – **Payment** – enough – **Success**

You can see that pairs (insert/enough, Init/St/Short/24/Payment) are not covered. We execute these test cases together as one large test case, and in this way the test selection criterion is satisfied.

Note that we make sub-AC according to these test paths involving the underlined sub-path. You can see that we separate decreasing ticket number into three parts: (1) 9 times to reach 1, (2) decrease to 0, (3) try to decrease below 0. The case for ticket increase is similar. Here is the sub-acceptance criterion for the standard tickets:

First St Steps:
WHEN TVM transition GOES increase St first; increase St 9X; increase St; decrease St 9X; decrease St to 0; decrease St to 0; increase St; decrease St to 0
THEN Number of St tickets GOES 1; 10; 10; 1; 0; 0; 1; 0 AND Number of Short tickets IS 0 AND Number of 24 tickets IS 0
WHEN TVM transition GOES increase short first; decrease short to 0
THEN Number of Short tickets GOES 1; 0

Sub-acceptance criterion *First St Steps* is used for acceptance criterion *Test St and 10.1* below, where T5 is modeled involving the following steps:

- Increasing the number of 24-hour tickets 1 + 1 = 2 times.

- Checking the number and the price of the tickets (2, 15.2).

- Calling a test from the Buying process model, where €5 then 0.1 euro coin is inserted.

- Calling a test from the Transaction OK model (the third model, see below), where a €10 banknote then a 0.1 euro coin is inserted.

Here is the acceptance criterion:

Test St and 10.1:
WHEN First St Steps
WHEN TVM transition IS increase 24 first
WHEN TVM transition IS increase 24
THEN Number of 24 tickets IS 2
AND price IS 15.2
WHEN Buying process IS BanknoteTest [5, 0.1]
WHEN Transaction OK IS Print [10, 0.1]

Here we connect the three features by calling Buying process and Transaction OK in Ticket selection.

From this acceptance criterion Harmony generates a complex test case with almost 50 test steps.

To cover the six test cases based on STT and the seven test cases based on BVA we need eight test cases altogether. We cannot cover both test selection criteria with seven test cases.

Besides the three complex test cases representing Tpath1-first-try, Tpath2-first-try and Tpath3-first-try, we have five simpler ones. Here we use very short sub-AC such as:

First St:
WHEN TVM transition IS increase St first
THEN Number of St tickets IS 1 AND price IS 2.1

Here is the model of T7 (see Table 12.4):

Test 20.1:

GIVEN First St
WHEN TVM transition IS increase St 9X
THEN Number of St tickets IS 10 AND price IS 21
WHEN Buying process IS BanknoteTest [0.5, 0.2, 0.2]
WHEN Transaction OK IS Print [20, 0.1]

The generated test shows what happens:

Test 20.1:

First St {TVM transition(I) =increase St first }, TVM transition(I) = increase St 9X, Number of St tickets(O) =10, price(O) =21,

Buying process(F) =BanknoteTest [0.5, 0.2, 0.2] {Inserted amount(I) = 0.5, 0.2, 0.2, Remaining amount(O) =20.1, Acceptable maximum banknote(O) =50 },

Transaction OK(F) =Print [20, 0.1] {Inserted amount(I) = 20, 0.1, Remaining amount(O) =0, Number of tickets printed(O) =10 }

Finally, we connect the execution of the three complex test cases resulting in one even more complex test case:

Complex:
WHEN Test 24 and 5
WHEN Test St and 10.1
WHEN Test Short and 10

We can see that for simple features (when EP and BVA only can be applied) modelling is simple. This is also the case for pure STT test design. However, when multiple test design techniques are used in combination or there are several model layers, the modeller's task is more difficult. Fortunately, in most of the cases, we can separate the models related to the different test design techniques, and after that, we can connect them. In Appendix A of this book, you can study the whole model of this specification.

METHOD EVALUATION

Here we only evaluate the free tool Harmony and do not consider its test execution automation capability.

Applicability

The modelling method supports automated test design for testers and developers. It can be applied to projects where the specification can be divided into manageable parts. It can be used mainly for specifications, which can be tested by EP and BVA, STT and combinative testing. It can even be used for distributive and probabilistic systems.

Advantages and shortcomings of the tool

The main advantages are:

- Iterative modelling – categories, choices, AC and the generated test cases all serve as 'feedback' to the modeller to improve the model.

- Gherkin++ syntax makes the model and the generated test cases understandable for all the stakeholders. Therefore, everybody can validate the models.

- Due to simplicity, modelling can be done by a team led by the tester/modeller. In this way, model-based testing can be smoothly included in the Agile methodology.

- The modelling language is easy to learn and use.

- Models can be layered in a specific way. Usually, a model contains sub-models. Harmony models may contain only the necessary parts of a sub-model. For example, if we have a login feature with four test cases: success, wrong login, duplicate login and wrong password, we can use only two of them: success and wrong login.

- Harmony incorporates a unique test selection criterion, which makes the work of the modeller easier since they can concentrate only on the models.

- The modelling language is a real test model, where EP, BVA, STT and so on can be inherently used.

- Easy maintenance is the common advantage of model-based testing. By selecting the affected test cases based on model modification, maintenance becomes even easier and cheaper.

- Defect prevention is also a common advantage of MBT methods. Since the categories, choices and AC are created based on the specification, most problems are detected by the modeller.

- Models can be considered live specifications, since the generated tests and the code should match, otherwise, the test will fail. This understandable live specification can be used to implement the code with fewer bugs.

The shortcomings are:

- Harmony is a text-based method; however, lots of people like graphical models mainly because they are used to them, and in some cases, they are more understandable.

- Harmony is a web tool and currently doesn't support mobile and desktop applications.

- Harmony is not connected to test management tools, and its existing test management capabilities are weak.

THEORETICAL BACKGROUND

The starting point of Harmony is the **category-partition** method, for specifying and generating functional test cases (Ostrand and Balcer, 1988). Category-partitioning is a

> method for creating functional test suites which has been developed in which a test engineer analyzes the system specification, writes a series of formal test specifications, and then uses a generator tool to produce test descriptions from which test scripts are written.
>
> (Ostrand and Balcer, 1988, p. 676)

253

The first four steps of the method are similar to Harmony's modelling:

1. Decomposition of the system into functional units.
2. Creating the categories.
3. Partition the categories into choices.
4. Determine constraints among the choices.

The remaining steps are as follows:

5. Write and process the test specification. The category, choice and constraint information are written in a formal test specification. Then comes the test automation part, from which the test specification test frames are generated.
6. Evaluate the generator output. The tester checks the generated test frames and investigates whether any changes are necessary. If the specification has to be changed, Step 5 is repeated.
7. Transform into test scripts. When the test specification is ready, the tester converts the test frames into test cases.

One of the main differences between the category-partition and Harmony is that that the former generates test cases in combination, then the tester tries to reduce the number of test cases. The latter generates a linear number of test cases with respect to choices.

The other element of Harmony is the Gherkin language, which was originally used in Cucumber (Wynne and Hellesøy, 2012). Each line starts with a Gherkin keyword, which can be:

- Feature.
- Scenario – a concrete example that illustrates a business rule.
- Given, When, Then, And, But (Steps).
- Background – similar to PRECONDITION in Harmony.
- Scenario Outline – similar to Table in Harmony.
- Examples - A **Scenario Outline** section is always followed by **Example** section(s), which are a container for a table.

Now Gherkin is used in many testing tools, making test cases more understandable.

KEY TAKEAWAYS

- Use automated test design, which is much more fun, maintainable and understandable than traditional test design.
- Modelling starts with knowing the feature, then iterating the model until it is perfect or adequately represents the real system.

- The Harmony tool makes it possible to execute every test case only once.
- By applying a divide-and-conquer strategy, you can make complex test cases based on much simpler hierarchical models.

EXERCISES

E12.1 Consider the feature presented in E6.2. Create the extended Gherkin model for this feature by applying all-transition-state criterion.

E12.2 Consider E5.1 'Payment'. Create the extended Gherkin model of this specification.

13 MBT USING GRAPHS – GRAPHWALKER

WHY IS THIS CHAPTER WORTH READING?

In this chapter, you will learn how easy it is to start with a new MBT tool. GraphWalker is an open source MBT tool that can read models in the form of directed graphs and generate tests from them. We explain how to use GraphWalker for state transition testing, and how to write test code and execute random tests for our ticket vending machine example.

In the previous chapter, we introduced a text-based MBT tool. In this chapter, we provide an overview of GraphWalker (available at https://graphwalker.github.io/), an open source MBT tool for generating test sequences from (extended) finite-state machines.

The modelling language of GraphWalker is (E)FSM. EFSM's graph representations are created by another freeware tool, the yEd Graph Editor (available at https://www.yworks.com/products/yed). In the graph, the transitions contain the events, which call the application code.

The idea behind GraphWalker is to execute unpredictable test sequences. By applying random execution, GraphWalker creates an acceptable execution coverage of the SUT, by which faulty dependencies/interactions can be found with high probability. We do not consider non-random execution as we cannot satisfy our test selection criteria.

GraphWalker can manage the test executions. The user can select different test selection criteria by giving 'generators' and 'stop conditions'. The former generates different test sequences such as random, weighted random and so on. The stop conditions will terminate the execution. For example, 95 per cent edge coverage and random generation mean that the transitions are executed entirely at random and when 95 per cent of the edges have been covered the test process terminates.

Note that GraphWalker only drives how to traverse the model and terminates according to the stop criteria, but that's all. You need to use other tools to validate the outputs or interact with the SUT. To do this you can use jUnit, Selenium or Appium.

The process of applying GraphWalker consists of the following steps:

1. creating the graph model;
2. creating the adaptation code related to the graph that interacts with the SUT;
3. executing the test sequences.

The test code template is generated by the tool, which can be then extended by the tester/developer. The process is iterative; the model can be improved based on the execution paths. The first step can be done in a test-first way, but the others require the existence of the code to be tested.

One of the most important aims of this chapter is to show how to put a new testing tool in practice. The solution is step by step:

- First, we clone a sample example.
- We modify few things (usually one) in one step.
- During modification, we change the original graph model and the related code (e.g. GraphWalker generates basic tests without connecting the test code with TVM code).
- We extend the test code (e.g. to call methods of TVM).
- We improve the graph and the test code based on the test results.

MAKING GRAPHWALKER WORK

It is always reasonable to try an existing example first. Here we explain how to do this step by step, with all the necessary information needed to test our TVM. We use the Java programming language as test code.

1. Create a directory for the GraphWalker project: for example GW-Book. GraphWalker uses Maven, which is a software project management and comprehension tool. You can download it from here:

   https://maven.apache.org/download.cgi

   and install it according to:

   https://maven.apache.org/install.html

   As we use Java, make sure that Java Development Kit (JDK) is installed on your computer. Don't forget to set the environment variables correctly:

   variable name: M2_HOME

   variable value: C:\GW-Book\maven

   and

   variable name: JAVA_HOME

   value: C:\Program Files\Java\jdk1.8.0_152 – at the time of writing the book

Figure 13.1 Screen when executing Maven to start GraphWalker

```
[INFO] --------------------------------------------------
---
[INFO] Using following parameters for creating project from Archetype: graphwalk
er-maven-archetype:3.4.2
[INFO] --------------------------------------------------
---
[INFO] Parameter: groupId, Value: com.company
[INFO] Parameter: artifactId, Value: myProject
[INFO] Parameter: version, Value: 1.0-SNAPSHOT
[INFO] Parameter: package, Value: com.company
[INFO] Parameter: packageInPathFormat, Value: com/company
[INFO] Parameter: version, Value: 1.0-SNAPSHOT
[INFO] Parameter: package, Value: com.company
[INFO] Parameter: groupId, Value: com.company
[INFO] Parameter: artifactId, Value: myProject
[INFO] Project created from Archetype in dir: C:\GW-Book\myProject
[INFO] --------------------------------------------------
[INFO] BUILD SUCCESS
[INFO] --------------------------------------------------
[INFO] Total time: 24.734 s
[INFO] Finished at: 2017-11-08T19:53:01+01:00
[INFO] Final Memory: 14M/126M
[INFO] --------------------------------------------------

C:\GW-Book>
```

Figure 13.2 Directory structure of GraphWalker

(a)   (b)

2. If you are ready, you can run Maven from your GW-book directory:

```
mvn archetype:generate -B -DarchetypeGroupId=org.
    graphwalker -DarchetypeArtifactId =graphwalker-maven-
    archetype -DgroupId=com.company -DartifactId=myProject
```

The related screen is similar to Figure 13.1.

You have the directory structure shown in Figure 13.2.

3. Next, you can execute the tests by going to the myProject directory:

cd myProject

and run the tests:

mvn graphwalker:test

By executing Maven, the interface SmallTest has been generated (from the model SmallTest.graphml), named and placed into the folder:

GW-Book/myProject/target/generated-sources/graphwalker/com/company

The class **SomeSmallTest** implements the interface **SmallTest**. It contains the adaptation code and the test selection criterion, that is the generator and the stop criterion (see Figure 13.3).

If the build does not work with mvn graphwalker:test, some ideas for troubleshooting are as follows[1]:

- Try mvn clean (and optionally mvn graphwalker:generate-sources) before running mvn graphwalker:test.

- For Microsoft Windows, use only a user whose name does not contain spaces or accentuated letters.

- In Linux, change <version>1.0-SNAPSHOT</version> to <version>4.0.0-SNAPSHOT</version> in *pom.xml* file.

- Do not use a shared directory.

- Check the parameter of the generator in the Java code (but in the sample, delivered project it is right).

Figure 13.3 SmallTest.java in the directory structure

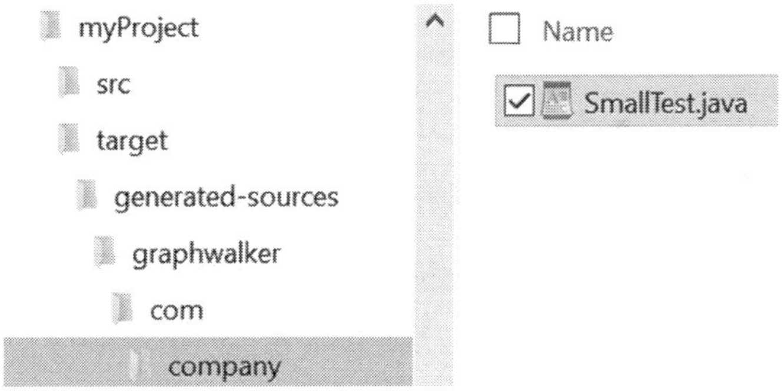

EXECUTING GRAPHWALKER FOR THE TVM MODEL

We have made a slightly different graph for the ticket selection of TVM described in Chapter 6 (see Figure 13.4).

You can see that we have inserted an edge back to the initial state, which makes it possible to generate long execution paths. We also differentiated the increase from zero and other than zero and decrease to zero and other than zero, as the related

---

1   Private communication with G. Á. Németh.

Figure 13.4 State transition graph of TVM made by yEd

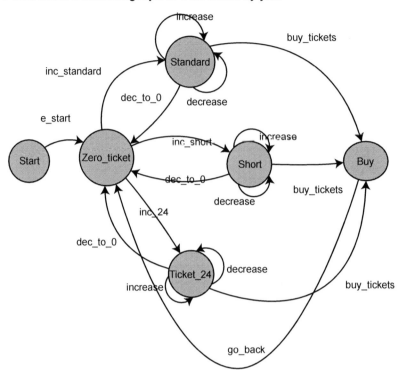

adaptation code is different. We have applied yEd, an easy to learn and use graph editor, and created TVMtest.graphml.

Our root node will be *Start*. This start node has no incoming edge and has one outgoing edge. The first real node corresponding to TVM is 'Zero_ticket'. There will be an extra edge from 'Buy' to 'Zero_ticket'. This is a real edge – we have not considered it intentionally in the former chapters as we neglect going back to the initial screen.

Executing the command

mvn graphwalker:test

results in the generation of TVMtest.java. Here all nodes – @Vertex() and the edges – @Edge()of our graph are generated:

```
@Model(file = "com/company/TVMtest.graphml")
public interface TVMtest {

@Edge()
void e_start();
```

```
@Vertex()
void Standard();

@Vertex()
void Ticket_24();

@Edge()
void dec_to_0();

@Edge()
void buy_tickets();
...
```

We can use this generated interface to modify the original SomeSmallTest.java:

```
@GraphWalker(value = "random(edge_coverage(100))", start =
    "e_start")
public class SomeSmallTest extends ExecutionContext
    implements TVMtest {

  @Override
  public void Standard() {
    System.out.println("Running: Standard");
  }

  @Override
  public void e_start() {
    System.out.println("Running: e_start");
  }

  @Override
  public void Zero_ticket() {
    System.out.println("Running: Zero_ticket");
  }
...
```

Note that our start node is **e_start**, and our model is **TVMtest**. Remember that our graph should be strongly connected. That's why we inserted an edge from 'Buy' to 'Zero_ticket'. Otherwise the execution would terminate without reaching any required coverage.

Now we can rerun the test cases, and it should work.

Finally, we modify the name of SomeSmallTest.java to TVM.java and modify the class name accordingly:

```
@GraphWalker(value = "random(edge_coverage(100))", start =
    "e_start")
public class TVM extends ExecutionContext implements TVMtest
    {
```

Let's summarise: we started with a working example, we validated its functioning and modified it step by step to transform it into our TVM example. The validation of each step makes it possible to detect any issues immediately. We successfully applied this method; it also works for other methods (such as test case minimisation (Zeller, 1999)).

TESTING OUR TVM WITH GRAPHWALKER

First, we determine the goal of testing. We would like to execute the TVM's ticket selection along many different execution paths to cover the all-transition-state criterion. We are interested in how many random executions are needed. We test the minimum/maximum amount of the selected tickets.

To make the appropriate adaptation code, we recall an important rule in test automation. This was originally introduced for agile testing (Black et al., 2017), however, it now seems to be generally accepted and is called the test automation pyramid (see Figure 13.5).

The concept of the test pyramid was introduced by Mike Cohn (2010). He considered three levels: unit, service/API and UI. There should be a lot of unit tests, comparatively fewer service/API tests, and even fewer UI tests. Unit tests are simple and short, and nowadays developers do them in a traditional or a TDD/BDD style.

A service is an implementation of business logic. Service-level testing is about testing the business logic of an application, ignoring the user interface. Sometimes we call this 'subcutaneous' testing. Service/API testing is much faster than UI testing. Another advantage of service/API testing is that business logic is much more stable than business logic and UI. The authors' opinion is that the importance of this level will grow quickly in the near future.

UI testing is the testing of the user interface and the connection of the UI with the service. UI testing is necessary; however, it is better to avoid it during testing the business logic as it is slower than API testing.

Figure 13.5 Test automation pyramid

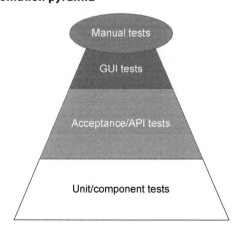

The original pyramid has been extended/modified in many ways by different authors. We believe the original concept is correct and we only include manual testing on the top of the pyramid (Crispin and Gregory, 2008).

When using GraphWalker for the TVM, we apply a service test as it is much simpler and faster. Let's improve our model according to our testing needs. Here our goal is to automatically execute lots of different execution paths to traverse the TVM code.

GraphWalker supports lots of random or specified walks along the graph such as:

- Random walk – randomly navigates through the model.
- Weighted random walk – extends random walk by weights. A weight is assigned to edges, and it represents the probability of an edge getting chosen.
- Quick random walk – tries to run the shortest path through a model.
- A* – generation of the shortest path to a specific vertex or edge.

The stop conditions can be

- Reaching a specified edge coverage percentage.
- Reaching a specified node coverage percentage.
- Total numbers of edge–node pairs.
- Total elapsed time and so on.

Considering our goal, we have selected the weighted random walk. Why? To cover all the necessary execution paths in accordance with our aim and traversing only a reasonable number of edge–node pairs, we have to 'cheat'. For example, we shall test whether the amount of tickets is less than or equal to 10. If the probability of traversing edges 'increase', 'decrease', 'dec_to_0' and 'buy_tickets' are the same, then we would generate very long test paths. To avoid this issue, we force 'increase' to execute with higher probability. GraphWalker has a command *weight = probability*, where *0.0 <= probability <= 1.0*. We select 0.8, meaning that 'increase' will be selected eight times from 10 on average.

Another issue is the coverage of edges, 'decrease' and 'dec_to_0'. If the amount of the tickets is larger than 1, then 'dec_to_0' cannot be traversed. Fortunately, GraphWalker can handle this issue as well, since it has 'guards' and 'actions'. A guard makes an edge traversable or not, for being walked. An action is JavaScript code that a tester wants to execute in the model. It is placed after a forward slash. The purpose of the action code is to assign values to the guards. Each statement must end with a semicolon. Hence, we can extend our model/graph by the following commands (where 'traverseDecTo0' is an attribute):

```
1.  /traverseDecTo0=true;
2.  [traverseDecTo0]
3.  [!traverseDecTo0]
```

The first will set this attribute to true. The second is a guard enabling 'dec_to_0' to be traversed only when 'traverseDecToO' is true. The third one enables 'decrease' to be traversed only when 'traverseDecToO' is false (see Figure 13.6).

Also, we use the method 'setAttribute()' to set 'traverseDecToO' to true or false for our TVM example in the following way:

```
a.   setAttribute("traverseDecTo0", true);
b.   setAttribute("traverseDecTo0", false);
```

Obviously, we use the first one in the methods related to 'inc_standard', 'inc_short', 'inc_24'. We also use the first one for the method related to 'decrease' under the condition of the ticket's amount being one. We use the second one for 'increase'. The code TVM. java can be found in Appendix B.

GraphWalker executes the software under test according to different test selection criteria, but the models do not involve output values. Therefore the output validation will be done in the adaptation code. This can be done for example, by applying JUnit.

Figure 13.6 Extended state transition graph for TVM

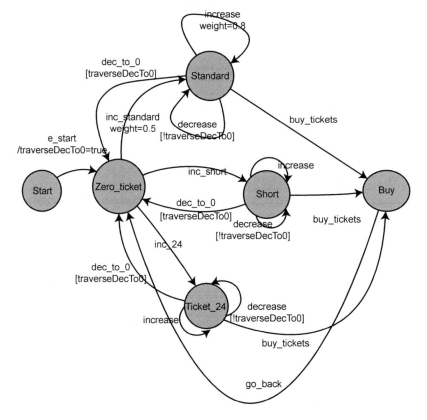

Making a test report is outside the scope of this book; however, the interested reader can use the Surefire Report Plugin (available at https://maven.apache.org/surefire/maven-surefire-report-plugin/). Our pom.xml file can be found in Appendix C containing the necessary JUnit part.

By applying JUnit, we test the correct number of tickets and the price of the tickets. In the code snippet below we validate two things: (1) while increasing the amount in the case of less than 10, then the number of tickets is increased by one (Assert.assertEquals), and (2) the amount of tickets does not exceed 10 (Assert.assertTrue).

```
public void increase(){
    int amountOld = model.getAmount(model.getTicket());
    model.addTicket(model.getTicket());
    int amount = model.getAmount(model.getTicket());
    if (amountOld <= 10)   //!!!
    Assert.assertEquals(1, amount - amountOld);
    Assert.assertTrue(amount <= 10);
...
```

Similar testing occurs for decreasing the amount. We also test the prices for the different types of tickets. The prices are in euro cents:

```
public void buy_tickets(){
    int amount = model.getAmount(model.getTicket());
    if (ticketType == "Standard ticket" && amount == 10)
    Assert.assertEquals(2100, price);
     if (ticketType == "Short distance ticket" && amount
  == 5)
    Assert.assertEquals(700, price);
     if (ticketType == "24 hour ticket" && amount == 2)
    Assert.assertEquals(1520, price);
}
```

As mentioned, GraphWalker generates test cases with stopping criteria, while other test automation tools/frameworks make the validation during the executions. Before we execute the tests the source of the TVM files has to be copied into the directory of TVM.java (see Figure 13.7).

Then, we can generate the tests by the command

mvn graphwalker:test >TVMtestResults.txt

and we can set the following stop criterion

```
@GraphWalker(value = "weighted_random(length(200))", start
    = "e_start")
```

which means covering 200 edge–node pairs. However, after executing some tests, an assert violation occurred:

```
16:53:33.538 [main] DEBUG org.graphwalker.core.machine.
    ExecutionContext - Execute: 'increase' in model:
    'TVMtest'
16:53:33.539 [main] ERROR org.graphwalker.core.machine.
    ExecutionContext - expected:<1> but was:<0>
16:53:33.539 [main] ERROR org.graphwalker.core.machine.
    SimpleMachine - java.lang.AssertionError: expected:<1>
    but was:<0>
16:53:33.539 [main] ERROR org.graphwalker.java.test.
    TestExecutor - java.lang.AssertionError: expected:<1>
    but was:<0>
[INFO] -------------------------------------------------
    --------------------
[ERROR] java.lang.AssertionError: expected:<1> but was:<0>
```

Very good, we have found a bug! Unfortunately, the bug is in the test code and not in the code to be tested. Let's consider the condition:

```
if (amountOld <= 10)  //!!!
    Assert.assertEquals(1, amount - amountOld);
```

When amount Old = 10, then amount will not be increased and amount − amountOld will be 0 instead of 1. Therefore, we have fixed this bug:

```
public void increase(){
    int amountOld = model.getAmount(model.getTicket());
    model.addTicket(model.getTicket());
    int amount = model.getAmount(model.getTicket());
    if (amountOld < 10)  //!!!
    Assert.assertEquals(1, amount - amountOld);
    Assert.assertTrue(amount <= 10);
    ...
```

and we have no assertion violation anymore.

The test results satisfied some of our expectations:

- When the number of standard tickets reached the maximum, it did not change when traversing 'increase'.

Figure 13.7 TVM source Java files

- The price of the tickets is correct for the different number of tickets.
- After decreasing the number of short distance tickets to zero, GraphWalker correctly traversed nodes and edges to simulate buying the 24-hour tickets.

However, there is no execution sequence: 'inc_X' – 'increase' – 'decrease' – 'dec_to_0' – 'inc_Y'. This is necessary considering the reliable all-transition-state criterion. To cover this missing execution sequence, we can change weight, or we can increase the length of the execution. We selected the second option. We increase the length to 500:

@GraphWalker(value = 'weighted_random(length(500))', start = 'e_start')

Executing GraphWalker, we found that such a sequence was missing from the previous execution paths:

- increase: 24-hour ticket: 1;
- increase: 24-hour ticket: 2;
- decrement: 24-hour ticket: 1;
- decrement to 0: 24-hour ticket: 0;
- increment short distance: 1.

The number at the end is the number of tickets to buy. In this way, we tested the missing execution sequence as well. Note that if we execute the tests again the execution will be different and the missing sequence may remain missing.

> We successfully tested a part of our TVM example with GraphWalker to satisfy our required test selection criterion. We validated some results. We haven't found any defects in the TVM, only in the test code.

METHOD EVALUATION

In the following section we briefly evaluate the GraphWalker open source tool.

Applicability

GraphWalker uses an extended finite-state machine model. The edges of the models contain method calls for the related parts of the application. GraphWalker (GW) can cover these edges in different ways such as random, weighted random and so on. In this way, we can test very long execution paths, that is, lots of influences among transitions and states/transitions. It is primarily applicable for state transition testing and especially for detecting program crashes. However, the adaptation code should be validated by other tools while GraphWalker executes the code.

On the other hand, it is difficult to apply for EP and BVA, as setting the appropriate input is difficult, though data-driven testing is possible by applying guards. For complex cases, when STT and EP and BVA shall be applied together, other MBT tools are more applicable.

Advantages and shortcomings of the tool

The advantages of the tool are:

- Open source and free.
- Support is excellent; documentation is appropriate.
- Random execution of the states and the transitions. This means:
  - Faults may be detected along paths that are not involved in the test selection criterion.
  - We can check the strength of a test selection criterion by executing very long tests randomly.
- The tool can be used together with other tools and frameworks such as Junit, Selenium and so on.
- Data can be exchanged between GraphWalker and the code. In this way, invalid execution sequences can be avoided; see our test code in Appendix B.

The shortcomings are:

- Test execution is random. Test cases are not repeatable. This is a problem in the case of retesting the code after fixing a bug or if we involve the tool in a continuous integration process. Note that although A* also exists it provides the shortest path only to a given vertex/edge.
- It is difficult to check whether all the necessary execution sequences are covered.
- The tool needs to be used together with other tools for functional validation.

KEY TAKEAWAYS

- When you use a new tool, start with the simplest existing example and change it step by step.
- Use the API test instead of UI test whenever possible.
- Use random testing to find exceptions and bugs along tricky execution paths.
- Use random testing to measure the quality of your designed tests.
- If a test fails, first check your test code. Bugs can be there as well.

EXERCISE

E13.1 Try GraphWalker as described in this chapter. Use the existing code of the ticket vending machine here: www.test-design.org. Make the state transition graph without using any weighting. Based on test selection criterion for STT, check the result and find the missing execution sequences.

14 TESTING THE TVM – SUMMARY AND METHOD COMPARISON

WHY IS THIS CHAPTER WORTH READING?

In this chapter we put together the TVM testing puzzles shown in the previous chapters. This is really interesting – please, believe us and read it!

The moment of truth has arrived. In this chapter we extend the test design for the TVM example, then, after executing all the tests, we investigate the results. We are curious to see if we can find any unknown bugs and those that our talented developer intentionally seeded into the code.

We compare the test design techniques based on the fault detection capabilities of the methods. The first obligatory step is the risk analysis. We use the result of our analysis from Chapter 3 (see Table 14.1).

We can only test the software part of the TVM, thus, risk item 2 is not considered. The remaining two highest risk items are 3 and 6. These risks are high but not critical, therefore we select STT with all-transition-state criterion and EP and BVA (with the test selection criterion used throughout the book). Before this, we consider the test cases for other methods written in our chapters.

TESTING TVM BY STT, EP AND BVA

The following steps can be used to extend the existing test design:

1. Design the test cases for the selected techniques separately.
2. Work out a plan of how to integrate the tests from the different techniques.
3. Select the larger set of test cases related to a test design technique, and map the test cases of the other technique to them (if possible).
4. Design additional integrated test cases for which the mapping is not possible.
5. Review and validate the result.

Table 14.1 Risk items for TVM

Risk item	Probability	Impact		
		On customer W = 0.7	On supplier W = 0.3	Aggregate risk
1. Inappropriate or missing information on the initial screen.	4	2	2	8
2. When issuing the tickets, the chosen and the printed number of tickets differs.	4	4	3	14.8
3. The ticket selection operation cannot be finished.	**4**	**3**	**3**	**12**
4. Inappropriate/missing transition to reduced mode.	2	4	3	7.4
5. The acceptable banknotes are improperly displayed.	4	2	2	8
6. Neither the timeout nor the reset selection feature is working.	**3**	**4**	**4**	**12**

Applying STT

First, we deal with the STT part. We created the state transition graph for some parts of the TVM in the state transition testing and Gherkin-based testing chapters. Here we extend the graph for the whole specification. For clarity, we exhibit a hierarchical description.

The first diagram contains the ticket selection process including the timeout and reset features (see Figure 14.1). Note that though reset/timeout can be executed from s2, s3 and s4, we inserted a common transition from the higher-level state s6. This is reasonable as we assume a unique implementation of both reset and timeout, based on CPH. Therefore, applying the test selection criterion we do not need to differentiate between states s2, s3 and s4. On the other hand, timeout or reset may not be called from states s2, s3 or s4. Therefore, we will test the application by executing reset/timeout from all these states. The second graph contains the entire statechart of the TVM including ticket selection in one state s6, the paying process on the normal and on the reduced mode, and the successful transition (showing the returned money), and then, going back to the initial welcome screen (see Figure 14.2).

Figure 14.1 Statechart for the ticket selection process

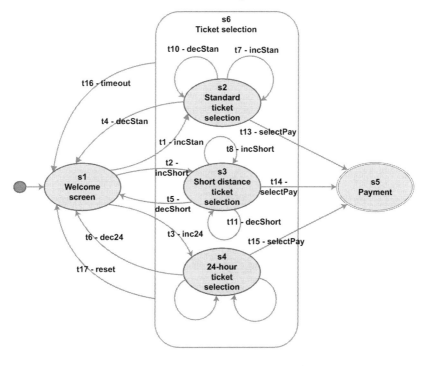

Figure 14.2 Statechart for the TVM

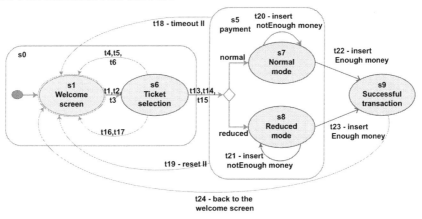

We can observe that the graph is symmetric for the ticket types to buy and for normal/reduced mode. We use the abbreviated versions of states as in Chapters 6 and 12, that is **St** for standard, **24** for 24-hour and **Short** for short-distance tickets). In addition, we use **Success** for Successful transaction, **Normal/Reduced** for the related modes and **Init** for

Initial state. With respect to the transition, we use incStan/decStan, incShort/decShort, inc24/dec24, pay, normal, reduced, enough, notEnough and back. We think that these abbreviations are obvious. In addition, (10X) means a transition occurs 10 consecutive times (however, reaching 10, further insertion is not possible for correct code). We also test for a negative amount of tickets by trying to decrease zero number of tickets. We have the following six test paths:

Tpath1 = **Init** – incStan – **St** – incStan(10X) – **St** – decStan – **St** – timeout – **Init** – incShort – **Short** – decShort(2X) – **Init** – inc24 – **24** – pay – **Normal** – enough – **Success** – back – **Init**

Tpath2 = **Init** – incShort – **Short** – incShort(10X) – **Short** – decShort – **Short** – reset – **Init** – inc24 – **24** – dec24(2X) – **Init** – incStan – **St** – pay – **Normal** – enough – **Success** – back – **Init**

Tpath3 = **Init** – inc24 – **24** – inc24(10X) – **24** – dec24 – **24** – timeout – **Init** – incStan – **St** – decStan(2X) – **Init** – incShort – **Short** – pay – **Normal** – enough – **Success** – back – **Init**

Tpath4 = **Init** – incStan – **St** – incStan(10X) – **St** – decStan – **St** – reset – **Init** – incShort – **Short** – decShort – **Init** – inc24 – **24** – pay – **Reduced** – enough – **Success** – back – **Init**

Tpath5 = **Init** – incShort – **Short** – incShort(10X) – **Short** – decShort – **Short** – timeout – **Init** – inc24 – **24** – dec24 – **Init** – incStan – **St** – pay – **Reduced** – enough – **Success** – back – **Init**

Tpath6 = **Init** – inc24 – **24** – inc24(10X) – **24** – dec24 – **24** – reset – **Init** – incStan – **St** – decStan – **Init** – incShort – **Short** – pay – **Reduced** – enough – **Success** – back – **Init**

You can see that we covered the transitions incStan, incShort, inc24, decStan, decShort, dec24, timeout and reset with all the states, and we also fulfilled the requirement to cover the transitions with a maximum possible time. For example, *timeout* precedes

- **Init**, **Short**, **Normal** and **Success** in Tpath1;
- **St** in Tpath3;
- **24**, **Reduced** in Tpath5.

We also have six simple paths where avoidable transactions are missing.

TPath7 = **Init** – incStan – **St** – pay – **Normal** – enough – **Success** – back – **Init**

TPath8 = **Init** – incShort – **Short** – pay – **Normal** – enough – **Success** – back – **Init**

TPath9 = **Init** – inc24 – **24**– pay – **Normal** – enough – **Success** – back – **Init**

TPath10 = **Init** – incStan – **St** – pay – **Reduced** – enough – **Success** – back – **Init**

TPath11 = **Init** – incShort – **Short** – pay – **Reduced** – enough – **Success** – back – **Init**

TPath12 = **Init** – inc24 – **24**– pay – **Reduced** – enough – **Success** – back – **Init**

Note that for all ticket prices the transition 'insert notEnough money' cannot be avoided.

So far we have not covered the transitions 'reset II', 'timeout II', 'pay', 'insert Enough/notEnough money' and 'back to the welcome screen'. However, you can see that the test cases terminate by going back to the welcome screen, that is the application does not exit after payment. This is the normal usage for such an application. In this way we can consider the execution of previous test cases. If you say that the test cases should be independent, you are right. However, we can cascade the test cases to form one large test.

In this way we cover most of the necessary pairs except timeout II, reset II and pairs (t21 notEnough/t23 Enough, s7). We cover timeout and reset at the ticket selection phase, and we can assume that it is enough to check whether the same feature is working at payment phase as well, that is after inserting any money into the machine. Therefore, we carry out one more test as follows.

Tpath13 = **Init** – incStan – **St** – pay – **Normal** – notEnough – **Normal** – reset II - **Init** – incShort – **Short** – pay – **Normal** – notEnough – **Normal** – timeout II – **Init** – inc24 – 24 – pay – **Reduced** – enough – **Success** – back – **Init**

Note that we should extend Tpath1–6 according to the test cases for EP and BVA. For example, when we test **T2,** in the next section, we modify Tpath3 so that the ticket price is 7 (5 x 1.4):

Tpath3 = **Init** – inc24 – **24** – inc24(10X) – **24** – dec24 – **24** – timeout – **Init** – incStan – **St** – decStan(2X) – **Init** – incShort – **Short** – incShort(4X) – **Short** – pay – **Normal** – notEnough(EUR2) – **Normal** – enough – **Success** – back – **Init**

We can consider each test case as a union of two parts: (1) STT and (2) EP and BVA.

Applying EP and BVA

We considered the test cases for EP and BVA for normal mode in Chapter 5. EP and BVA for reduced mode are simple. One equivalence partition is when the same maximal coin/banknote value is inserted. For example, when the remaining amount to be paid is in the range (20–49.9), we can insert banknote €20. Considering the boundary values: they are just 20 and 49.9.

We can see that the number of test cases exceeds the number of test cases for STT. Therefore, we map the STT test cases to these (see the far right column in Table 14.2). Note that one STT test can be used for several EP and BVA test cases.

RAP denotes the remaining amount to be paid. When the maximum value acceptable banknote is displayed, sometimes we try to insert a larger note than the maximum and then insert the maximum. This can be seen in the column 'Inserted amount'. We assume that the larger banknote cannot be inserted (we denote it by deletion, e.g. €10). Then, the right amount is inserted. Since we can insert several coins and banknotes one by one, we unite some test cases and mark them as 12/1, 12/2 and so on. In this case we insert 'C' (continue) into the column 'Inserted amount'.

Table 14.2 Test cases for the whole TVM

Test cases for normal mode							
Test	EP	Ticket price	Inserted amount before	RAP in EUR	Maximum acceptable banknote	Inserted amount	STTTest path
T1	1	2.1	2	0.1	€5	€5	Tpath7
T2	1	7 (5x1.4)	2	5	€5	~~€10~~, €5	Tpath3
T3	2	7.6	2, 0.5	5.1	€10	€10	Tpath9
T4	2	10.5 (5x2.1)	0.5	10	€10	~~€20~~, €10	Tpath2
T5	3	15.2 (2x7.6)	5, 0.1	10.1	€20	€20	Tpath1
T6	3	21	1	20	€20	~~€50~~, €20	Tpath7
T7	4	21	0.5, 0.2, 0.2	20.1	€50	€50	Tpath7
T8	1	1.4	2	-0.6	€5	-	Tpath8
Test cases for reduced mode							
Test	EP	Ticket price	Inserted amount before	RAP in EUR	Maximum acceptable banknote or coin	Inserted amount	STTTest path
T10/2	1	-	0.1	0.05	5c	~~0.1~~, 0.05	Tpath11
T11	2	2.1	2	0.1	10c	0.1	Tpath7
T10/1	2	1.4	1, 0.2, 0.05	0.15	10c	~~0.2~~, C	Tpath11
T12/8	3	-	-	0.2	20c	0.2	Tpath4
T12/7	3	-	0.5	0.4	20c	~~0.5~~, C	Tpath4
T13	4	2.1	1, 0.5, 0.1	0.5	50c	0.5	Tpath10
T12/6	4	-	1	0.9	50c	~~1~~, C	Tpath4
T14	5	1.4	0.2, 0.2	1	€1	2, 1	Tpath6
T12/5	5	-	2, 1	1.9	€1	~~2~~, C	Tpath4
T15	6	2.1	0.1	2	€2		Tpath10
T12/4	6	-	5	4.9	€2	~~5~~, C	Tpath4
T16	7	7.6	2, 0.5, 0.1	5	€5		Tpath12
T12/3	7	-	10	9.9	€5	~~10~~, C	Tpath4
T17	8	21	10, 1	10	€10		Tpath5

(Continued)

Table 14.2 (Continued)

Test cases for reduced mode							
Test	EP	Ticket price	Inserted amount before	RAP in EUR	Maximum acceptable banknote or coin	Inserted amount	STT Test path
T12/2	8		20, 10	19.9	€10	~~20~~, C	Tpath4
T18	9	21	1	20	€20	20	Tpath10
T12/1	9	76	20, 5, 1,0.1	49.9	€20	~~50~~, C	Tpath4
T19	10	76	20, 5, 1	50	€50	50	Tpath12
T20	10	76	1	75	€50	50, 20, 5	Tpath13

Now, based on Tpath1–11 and Table 14.2 we can design the test cases. For clarity, we use the following abbreviations and notations:

- '+st'/' -st' for increasing/decreasing standard tickets.
- '+sh'/'-sh' for increasing/decreasing short distance tickets.
- '+24'/'-24' for increasing/decreasing 24-hour tickets.
- (9) such as '-sh(9)' means increasing the number of short distance tickets nine times.
- 'RES' – reset.
- 'OUT' – timeout. Here we should have an output zero number of tickets, and it can happen after some seconds. If the timeout is different from that required, then we insert the actual time into 'Tested output'.
- st8/sh8/tw8 means eight standard/short distance/24-hour tickets (tw for twenty-four).
- For both input and output, a number such as 21 means the inserted/remaining price is EUR 21.
- A negative value means the amount to be returned.
- X means that the input is not possible, for example, if the maximum acceptable banknote is €5, then we cannot insert €10.
- OK means the transaction was successful. Remember that these outputs come from the implemented software as we cannot validate the real ticket printing.
- More inputs/outputs are selected by a comma, such as 12.
- M20 means the maximum banknote amount (20) that can be inserted.
- We omit pressing 'Pay' after setting the number of tickets – this is done for each test case, and the tester cannot omit it.
- We include pressing reduced mode 'ON' as this will be done for reduced mode only (R ON).

Test cases

After designing the test cases, we execute them. In the 'Tested output' row in Tables 14.3 and 14.4 we write either passed or failed with cause of failure or the faulty value. We omit transitions such as 'pay', as the input description is unambiguous without them. Even if an intermediate test step fails we try to execute the entire test case. Tests for normal mode are numbered T1–T8, tests for reduced mode are numbered T10–T20.

Table 14.3 Test cases for normal mode

T1

Input	+st	2	5	
Expected output	1st, 2.1	0.1, M5	-4.9, OK	
Tested output			5 not available	failed

T2

Input	+24	+24(10)	-24	OUT	+st	-st(2X)
Expected output	1tw	10tw	9tw	0	1st	0
Tested output				30 sec		

T2 cont.

Input	+sh	+sh(4)	2	10	5	
Expected output	1sh	5sh, 7	5, M5	X	0, OK	
Tested output	not possible					failed

T3

Input	+24	2, 0.5	10	
Expected output	1tw, 7.6	5.1, M10	-4.9, OK	
Tested output			passed	

(Continued)

Table 14.3 (Continued)

T4

Input	+sh(10)	+sh	-sh	RES	+24	-24(2X)
Expected output	10sh	10sh	9sh	0	1tw	0
Tested output						

T4 cont.

Input	+st	+st(4)	0.5	20	10
Expected output	1st	5st, 10.5, M20	10, M10	X	0, OK
Tested output	not possible				failed

T5

Input	+st	+st(10X)	-st	OUT	+sh	-sh(2X)
Expected output	1st	10st	9st	0	1sh	0
Tested output				30 sec		

T5 cont.

Input	+24	+24	5, 0.1	20
Expected output	1tw	2tw, 15.2, M20	10.1	-9.9, OK
Tested output	not possible			failed

T6

Input	+st	+st(9)	1	50	20
Expected output	1st	10st, 21	20, M20	X	0, OK
Tested output					passed

(Continued)

Table 14.3 (Continued)

T7

Input	+st	+st(9)	0.5, 0.2, 0.2	50	
Expected output	1st	10st, 21	20.1, M50	-29.9, OK	
Tested output				-19.9	failed

T8

Input	+sh	2	
Expected output	1sh, 1.4, M5	-0.6, OK	
Tested output		passed	

Table 14.4 Test cases for reduced mode

T10

Input	+sh	R ON	1, 0.2, 0.05	0.2	0.1	0.1	0.05
Expected output	1sh, 1.4, M1	ON	0.15, M0.1	X	0.05	X	0, OK
Tested output							passed

T11

Input	+st	R ON	2	0.1
Expected output	1st, 2.1, M2	ON	0.1, M0.1	0, OK
Tested output				passed

T12

Input	+st	+st(10)	-st	RES	+sh	-sh
Expected output	1st	10st	9st	0	1sh	0
Tested output						

(Continued)

Table 14.4 (Continued)

T12 cont.

Input	+24	+24(9)	R ON	20, 5, 1, 0.1	50	20, 10	20	10
Expected output	1tw	10tw, 76, M50	ON	49.9, M20	X	19.9, M10	X	9.9, M5
Tested output	not possible				enabled			

T12 cont.

Input	10	5	5	2, 1	2	1	1	0.5	0.5	0.2, 0.2
Expected output	X	4.9, M2	X	1.9, M1	X	0.9, M0.5	X	0.4, M0.2	X	0, OK
Tested output										failed

T13

Input	+st	R ON	1, 0.5, 0.1	0.5	
Expected output	1st, 2.1, M2	ON	0.5	0, OK	
Tested output		5 possible but clicking not possible			failed

T14

Input	+24	+24(10X)	-24	RES	+st	-st
Expected output	1tw	10tw	9tw	0	1st	0
Tested output						

(Continued)

Table 14.4 (Continued)

T14 cont.

Input	+sh	R ON	0.2, 0.2	1		
Expected output	1sh, 1.4, M1	ON	1	0, OK		
output	not possible					failed

T15

Input	+st	R ON	0.1	2	
Expected output	1st, 2.1, M2	ON	2	0, OK	
Tested output				passed	

T16

Input	+24	R ON	2, 0.5, 0.1	5	
Expected output	1tw, 7.6, M5	ON	5, M5	0, OK	
Tested output				passed	

T17

Input	+sh	+sh(10X)	-sh	OUT	+24	-24
Expected output	1sh	10sh	9sh	0	1tw	0
Tested output				30 sec		

T17 cont.

Input	+st	+st(9)	R ON	10, 1	10	
Expected output	1st	10st, 21, M20	ON	10, M10	0, OK	
Tested output	not possible					failed

(Continued)

Table 14.4 (Continued)

T18

Input	+st	+st(9)	R ON	1	20
Expected output	1st	10st, 21, M20	ON	20, M20	0, OK
Tested output					passed

T19

Input	+24	+24(9)	R ON	20, 5, 1	50	
Expected output	1tw	10tw, 21, M20	ON	50, M50	0, OK	
Tested output					10	failed

T20

Input	+st	0.1	RES	+sh	0.5	OUT	R ON
Expected output	1st, 2.1	2	0	1sh, 1.4	0.9	0	ON
Tested output						no timeout	

T20 cont.

Input	+24	2, 0.5, 0.1	5	
Expected output	1tw, 7.6	5, M5	0, OK	
Tested output		2, 0.5, 0.1	5	failed

The test cases were executed in less than one hour. However, the presented test design took more than two hours. Let's consider the code coverage. The total number of instructions is 1749, while the number of uncovered instructions is only 26. Therefore, the statement coverage is 98.5 per cent.

We did not consider the issue with regard to the reduced mode, that is, the returning money after reset/timeout/successful transaction. Our talented developer colleague inserted four bugs, and we found all of them, plus two bugs in the original code.

Defects found in TVM

1. An acceptable banknote has not been accepted in normal mode – one standard ticket for EUR 2.1, inserting €2 – €5 is then not acceptable.

2. No other type of ticket can be selected after selecting any ticket and decreasing the number to zero.

3. In both modes, when inserting €50 is possible, the remaining value is larger by EUR 10 and for normal mode the return value is less by EUR 10 – selecting 10 normal tickets, inserting €0.5, €0.2, €0.2, remaining 20.1, then inserting €50, the return value is smaller, that is, EUR 19.9 instead of 29.9.

4. In reduced mode, the software enables the insertion of a €50 banknote when the remaining amount is less than EUR 50 – selecting 10 lots of 24-hour tickets for EUR 76 and inserting €20, €5, €1, €0.1 the remaining amount is EUR 49.9, but the TVM accepts €50.

5. No timeout is working after inserting any money.

6. Timeout is 30 seconds instead of 20.

TESTING TVM BY USE CASE TESTING, EP AND BVA

The full test description can be found in Chapter 8. Here, we neglected the reduced mode, therefore only defects 1, 2, 3, 5 and 6 could be found. We designed four complex test cases, T1–T4. We tested the application, executing these four test cases and the result is the following:

- T1 and T2 failed because of defect 3.
- T3 failed because of defect 6.
- T4 failed because of defect 5.

Defect 2 has not been detected because use case testing did not involve tests selecting one ticket type, decreasing to zero and selecting another type. However, defect 1 should have been detected. A closer look at T1 revealed that the IN point (0.1) of EP1 in Table 14.2 accidently has not been tested.

COMBINATIVE TESTING

Applying combinative testing, specifically using diff-pair testing, we extended the boundary value test cases. We considered reset and timeout together based on our risk analysis (see Risk 6). As the risk may arise when inserting coins and banknotes, we considered only this part. Similarly to the test cases in Chapter 9, we insert one additional test case for each test case in Table 14.2, that is, the first new test case involves reset, the second involves timeout, and so on.

As we know, however, timeout is not working, therefore we always press reset. As we predicted, no more bugs have been found. This is because reset and timeout are totally separated from the payment process, thus they either work or they do not.

It is important that combinative testing extends the test cases for STT, EP and BVA, allowing us to use all these techniques together. The process is simple: when the test cases for STT and EP and BVA are ready, we insert additional test cases according to diff-pair testing.

TESTING TVM BY OTHER METHODS

We summarise in this section how the other methods can or cannot find the existing bugs in the TVM application.

Decision table testing

Here we considered the ticket selection process for defect 2 only. However, decision table testing is not adequate for this bug as the first seven test cases found no defects; the other nine test cases are non-executable. The first six test cases select 1 or 10 number of tickets for standard/short-distance/24-hour tickets, which is possible if the code is terminated for each test. The seventh test case validates that starting from no ticket selection, every type of ticket is selectable. The non-executable test cases require, for example, the selection of two ticket types in parallel, which is not possible for the implemented version.

Behaviour-driven test design

Here we have four test cases for demonstration; however, we did not claim to fully test any part of the TVM specification. Therefore, even if the four test cases have not detected any bugs, we cannot say anything about this method.

Gherkin-based MBT

The case here is similar to behaviour-driven testing. We can make any models involving STT, EP, BVA and so on, therefore a good model will find the same bugs as any combination of the test design techniques above.

GraphWalker

This tool will definitely find the STT-related bugs such as 2. However, neither EP and BVA errors are favourites of this tool, nor the bugs related to GUIs. It is more useful at finding bugs with unexpected bad influences.

COMPARISON

We know that our results are not statistically relevant. Yet, to the best of our knowledge, there are no comprehensive comparisons among the test design techniques, especially using more techniques together. Therefore, our results can be an important and valuable starting point, especially as the results and our predictions coincided. We think that the TVM is too simple to apply combinative or even combinatorial testing. Therefore we restrict it to a combination of non-combinatorial techniques. The comparison doesn't consider the maintenance phase, which may result in a different conclusion about cost effectiveness.

Table 14.5 summarises the test results.

Table 14.5 Comparison of the test design techniques

Test design techniques	Number of test cases	Bugs not found	Rank – reliability	Rank – cost-effectiveness	Comments
STT, EP and BVA	19/8	-	1	3	19 are the total number; eight test cases for the normal mode
Use case, EP and BVA	-/4	2	2	2	We consider all the necessary boundary values
ET	13/10	4, 5	3	1	

We cannot consider the other techniques as we have not enough test results for them. We can state that STT with EP and BVA is very reliable for the TVM application. However, the design time was considerable.

On the other hand, ET missed some faults; however, the total testing time of ET was only one hour. ET also caught bug 2, which is a bug ideal for state transition testing. However, ET is not good for the sophisticated bug 4 (it was a real bug and had not been seeded). Though ET seems to be very cost-effective, be very cautious. When you automate the tests or re-execute the test cases due to code modification, then ET is far from perfect. This case is similar to the 'capture and replay' tools. They were very popular about 20 years ago, but they turned out to be impractical just because of code maintenance.

Use case testing is not good for bugs related to states and transitions, however, the number of test cases was less. Decision table testing proved to be not appropriate for testing the TVM.

15 CONCLUSIONS AND RECOMMENDATIONS

Before we started our journey with this book, we believed our knowledge of test design was almost perfect. However, we realised through writing that there are unexplored territories in the jungle of test design. We made a huge effort to discover these territories, but we know that some remain unexplored.

Our goal with this book was to cover those parts of test design that can be used in practice. Contrary to other books, we believe we have used more complex, interesting and diverse examples. Our key contribution to the field is to show you how to use more test design techniques together, with the aid of realistic examples.

Test design is difficult. If you have read the whole book you already know that. We can offer you more help via our homepage, www.test-design.org, which contains all the examples, code and models from this book, along with further exercises.

Finally, some pieces of advice for you, to summarise:

On the test design itself:

- Software testing is a team responsibility. High-quality and efficient test cases can only be achieved when everyone involved in test design is aware of this.

- Never neglect risk analysis. Using risk analysis and some historical data, you can optimise both costs and quality. Although risk management is not a test design technique, it is not optional before test design. Without risk analysis, you will not be able to select appropriate test design techniques and either the quality of testing will be low or the costs will be too high, usually both.

- The cost of the project life cycle can be optimised by minimising the sum of the total testing and defect correction costs. This also results in adequate code quality. Hence, minimising this cost is one of the most important aspects of the test design.

- Defect prevention is unavoidable. As all the specifications are incomplete (as the famous philosopher Jacques Derrida called 'aporia'), we (testers) have to improve them. This results in significantly fewer bugs and more satisfied customers.

- It is not enough just to understand the specification on a basic level – you need to have an in-depth knowledge of it!

- Always develop test models separately. It is appealing to use the same models for both development and testing; however, this is a very dangerous approach, since the same starting point for both can result in the same faulty model.

In addition, testing requires the application of different test models, which support all the necessary test design techniques needed to test the implemented specification efficiently.

On test design techniques:

- In practice, you should use more test design techniques together. Plan it very carefully based on risk and complexity analysis. Favour linear methods over quadratic or higher degree ones, but let the decision depend on the criticality.

  - Carefully select the test design techniques for the specification.

  - Work out the test cases separately based on the related test design technique.

  - Harmonise the test cases by constituting more complex tests based on the original ones while paying attention to their independence.

  - Validate the test cases.

- Use automated test design if possible. But always think of its maintenance.

- In practice, according to the quality requirements (fault models) and risks, stop to refine the equivalence partitioning process where the fault detection capability falls below a certain level.

- Even if the single fault model is not prescribed, and the multiple fault model can be used for some reason, do not combine several invalid partition tests into one test case at the beginning of testing. If possible, test the invalid partitions separately.

- The test selection criterion of boundary value analysis requires testing an ON, an OFF and an IN/OUT point for each border so that the (ON, IN) points are on different sides of the boundary. Similarly, the (OFF, OUT) points should be the other side of the boundary. Note that the IN/OUT points can be the OFF/ON points of adjacent borders. When setting the ON–OFF pairs for a border, the variables (data) that are not related to that border have to be unchanged.

- Do not underestimate the importance of the random walk coverage. Many test design automation tools use this approach since for small–medium state transition graphs it works effectively. For simpler state diagrams the test cases can even be created manually.

- Regarding combinative and combinatorial test design, we suggest using:

  - On-the-fly test design for very low or low risks.

  - Non-combinatorial test design for low and medium risks.

  - Diff-pair test design in the case of medium or high risks. The number of test cases is linear, and therefore the test suite is manageable even when the previous methods are not sufficient. It is especially suitable for computational faults, but is also reliable for control-flow bugs.

  - N-wise testing in the case of high or very high risks.

  - Orthogonal/covering/sequence covering arrays for very large parameter spaces.

- Regarding exploratory testing:
  - The mixture of scripted and exploratory tests should be well-balanced.
  - Exploratory testing should be scheduled accordingly to the project progression.
  - Make exploratory testing measurable, so that testers' work and the method itself is comparable.

On output of test design:

- The output of the design process aggregates descriptions of prioritised test scenarios, test cases, appropriate test data and the controlled test environment.
- Be careful with implementation-dependent test cases. Your code probably has to be maintained long term, and technology changes rapidly.

APPENDIX A – TVM MODELS

Model for the buying process

//Ticket price(I): 1.1; 6; 10.1; 12; 20.1; 21; 25.1; 151
Inserted amount(I): 1; 1.0; 5, 0.1; 2; 2.0; 0.5; 0.5, 0.2, 0.2; 0.50
Remaining amount(O): 0.1; 5; 5.1; 10; 10.1; 20; 20.1; 75
Acceptable maximum banknote(O): 5; 10; 20; 50

BanknoteTest:
WHEN Inserted amount IS 2 | 2.0 | 0.5 | 0.50 | 5, 0.1 | 1 | 0.5, 0.2, 0.2
THEN Remaining amount IS 0.1 | 5 | 5.1 | 10 | 10.1 | 20 | 20.1 AND Acceptable maximum banknote IS 5 | 5 | 10 | 10 | 20 | 20 | 50

Model for the transaction OK

Inserted amount(I): 0.1; 5; 5, 0.1; 10; 10, 0.1; 20; 20, 0.1; 5
Remaining amount(O): 0(D)
Number of tickets printed(O): 1; 4; 5; 2; 10
Action(O): initial screen(D)

Print:
WHEN Inserted amount IS 0.1 | 5 | 5, 0.1 | 10 | 10, 0.1 | 20 | 20, 0.1
THEN Number of tickets printed IS 1 | 5 | 4 | 5 | 2 | 10 | 10

Model for ticket selection

TVM transition(I): increase St first; increase St; decrease St to 0; decrease St 9X; increase 24 first; increase 24; decrease 24 to 0; decrease 24 9X; increase short first; increase short; decrease short to 0; decrease short 9X; increase St 9X; increase short 9X; increase 24 9X; increase short 3X; increase short 4X; increase St 4X
Number of St tickets(O): 0; 1; 10; 5
Number of Short tickets (O): 0; 1; 10; 4; 5
Number of 24 tickets(O): 0; 1; 2; 10
Price(O):1.4; 2.1; 7.6; 5.6; 7; 10.5; 15.2; 21

First St Steps:
WHEN TVM transition GOES increase St first; increase St 9X; increase St; decrease St 9X; decrease St to 0; decrease St to 0; increase St; decrease St to 0
THEN Number of St tickets GOES 1; 10; 10; 1; 0; 0; 1; 0 AND Number of Short tickets IS 0 AND Number of 24 tickets IS 0

WHEN TVM transition GOES increase short first; decrease short to 0
THEN Number of Short tickets GOES 1; 0

First Short Steps:
WHEN TVM transition GOES increase short first; increase short 9X; increase short;
decrease short 9X; decrease short to 0; decrease short to 0; increase short; decrease
short to 0
THEN Number of Short tickets GOES 1; 10; 10; 1; 0; 0; 1; 0 AND Number of St tickets IS
0 AND Number of 24 tickets IS 0
WHEN TVM transition GOES increase 24 first; decrease 24 to 0;
THEN Number of 24 tickets GOES 1; 0

First 24 Steps:
WHEN TVM transition GOES increase 24 first; increase 24 9X; increase 24; decrease 24
9X; decrease 24 to 0; decrease 24 to 0; increase 24; decrease 24 to 0
THEN Number of 24 tickets GOES 1; 10; 10; 1; 0; 0; 1; 0 AND Number of Short tickets IS
0 AND Number of St tickets IS 0
WHEN TVM transition GOES increase St first; decrease St to 0
THEN Number of St tickets GOES 1; 0

First St:
WHEN TVM transition IS increase St first
THEN Number of St tickets IS 1 AND price IS 2.1

First Short:
WHEN TVM transition IS increase short first
THEN Number of Short tickets IS 1 AND price IS 1.4

First 24:
WHEN TVM transition IS increase 24 first
THEN Number of 24 tickets IS 1 AND price IS 7.6

Test 24 and 5:
WHEN First 24 Steps WHEN TVM transition IS increase short first
WHEN TVM transition IS increase short 4X
THEN Number of Short tickets IS 5 AND price IS 7
WHEN Buying process IS BanknoteTest [2.0]
WHEN Transaction OK IS Print [5]

Test St and 10.1:
WHEN First St Steps
WHEN TVM transition IS increase 24 first
WHEN TVM transition IS increase 24
THEN Number of 24 tickets IS 2
AND price IS 15.2
WHEN Buying process IS BanknoteTest [5, 0.1]
WHEN Transaction OK IS Print [10, 0.1]

Test Short and 10:
WHEN First Short Steps

WHEN TVM transition IS increase St
WHEN TVM transition IS increase St 4X
THEN Number of St tickets IS 5
AND price IS 10.5
WHEN Buying process IS BanknoteTest [0.50]
WHEN Transaction OK IS Print [10]

Test 24 and 5.1:
WHEN First Short
WHEN TVM transition IS increase short first
WHEN TVM transition IS increase short 3X
THEN Number of Short tickets IS 4 AND price IS 5.6
WHEN Buying process IS BanknoteTest [0.5]

Test 20:
GIVEN First St WHEN TVM transition IS increase St 9X
THEN Number of St tickets IS 10 AND price IS 21
WHEN Buying process IS BanknoteTest [1]

Test 20.1:
GIVEN First St WHEN TVM transition IS increase St 9X
THEN Number of St tickets IS 10 AND price IS 21
WHEN Buying process IS BanknoteTest [0.5, 0.2, 0.2]
WHEN Transaction OK IS Print [20, 0.1]

Test 0.1:
WHEN First St
WHEN Buying process IS BanknoteTest [2.0]
WHEN Transaction OK IS Print [0.1]

Complex:
WHEN Test 24 and 5
WHEN Test St and 10.1
WHEN Test Short and 10

Printed by Amazon POD

APPENDIX B – TEST CODE FOR DEMONSTRATING GRAPHWALKER

```java
package com.company;

    import org.graphwalker.core.machine.ExecutionContext;
    import org.graphwalker.java.annotation.GraphWalker;

import com.company.TVMtest;

import org.junit.Assert;

//@GraphWalker(value = "weighted_random(edge_coverage(101))",
    start = "e_start")
@GraphWalker(value = "weighted_random(length(500))", start =
    "e_start")

public class TVM extends ExecutionContext implements TVMtest {

    private TicketVendingMachine model;

  @Override
  public void Standard() {
    System.out.println("Running: Standard");
  }

  @Override
  public void Zero_ticket() {
    System.out.println("Running: Zero_ticket");
  }

  @Override
  public void Buy(){
      System.out.println("Running: Buy");
  }

  @Override
  public void Ticket_24(){
      System.out.println("Running: Ticket_24");
  }

  @Override
```

```java
    public void Short(){
        System.out.println("Running: Short");
    }

    @Override
    public void e_start() {
      System.out.println("Running: e_start");
      model = new TicketVendingMachine();
    }

    @Override
    public void dec_to_0(){
        model.removeTicket(model.getTicket());
        int amount = model.getAmount(model.getTicket());
        String ticketType = model.getTicket().getName();
        System.out.println("decrement to 0: "+ ticketType + ":   " +
      amount);
        Assert.assertEquals(0, amount);
    }

    @Override
    public void buy_tickets(){

        model.calculatePrice();
        int price = model.getPrice();
        System.out.println("buy_tickets for: " + price);
        String ticketType = model.getTicket().getName();
        int amount = model.getAmount(model.getTicket());
        if (ticketType == "Standard ticket" && amount == 10)
        Assert.assertEquals(2100, price);
        if (ticketType == "Short distance ticket" && amount == 5)
        Assert.assertEquals(700, price);
        if (ticketType == "24 hour ticket" && amount == 2)
        Assert.assertEquals(1520, price);
    }

    @Override
    public void inc_short(){
        model.addTicket(Ticket.SHORT_DISTANCE);
        int amount = model.getAmount(Ticket.SHORT_DISTANCE);
        System.out.println("increment short distance: "+ amount);
        Assert.assertEquals(1, amount);
        setAttribute("traverseDecTo0", true);
    }

    @Override
    public void inc_24(){
        model.addTicket(Ticket.DAILY);
        int amount = model.getAmount(Ticket.DAILY);
        System.out.println("increment 24h: "+ amount);
```

```java
        Assert.assertEquals(1, amount);
        setAttribute("traverseDecTo0", true);
    }

    @Override
    public void go_back(){
        System.out.println("Running: go_back");
        model.reset();
    }

    @Override
    public void increase(){
        int amountOld = model.getAmount(model.getTicket());
        model.addTicket(model.getTicket());
        int amount = model.getAmount(model.getTicket());
        if (amountOld < 10)   //!!! <=
        Assert.assertEquals(1, amount - amountOld);
        String ticketType = model.getTicket().getName();
        System.out.println("increase: "+ ticketType + ":   " + amount);
        Assert.assertTrue(amount <= 10);
        setAttribute("traverseDecTo0", false);
    }

    @Override
    public void decrease(){
        int amountOld = model.getAmount(model.getTicket());
        System.out.println("decrement: ");
        model.removeTicket(model.getTicket());
        int amount = model.getAmount(model.getTicket());
        if (amount > 0)
        Assert.assertEquals(1, amountOld - amount);
        String ticketType = model.getTicket().getName();
         System.out.println("decrement:  "+ ticketType + ":    " +
    amount);
        Assert.assertTrue(amount >= 0);
        if (amount < 2)
         setAttribute("traverseDecTo0", true);
    }

    @Override
    public void inc_standard(){
        model.addTicket(Ticket.STANDARD);
        int amount = model.getAmount(Ticket.STANDARD);
        System.out.println("increment standard: "+ amount);
        Assert.assertEquals(1, amount);
        setAttribute("traverseDecTo0", true);
    }

}
```

APPENDIX C – POM.XML FOR GRAPHWALKER

```xml
<?xml version="1.0" encoding="UTF-8"?>

<project    xmlns="http://maven.apache.org/POM/4.0.0"
    xmlns:xsi="http://www.w3.org/2001/XMLSchema-instance"
            xsi:schemaLocation="http://maven.apache.org/POM/4.0.0
    http://maven.apache.org/xsd/maven-4.0.0.xsd">

  <modelVersion>4.0.0</modelVersion>

  <groupId>com.company</groupId>
  <version>1.0-SNAPSHOT</version>
  <artifactId>myProject</artifactId>
  <name>GraphWalker Example</name>

  <properties>
    <graphwalker.version>4.0.0-SNAPSHOT</graphwalker.version>
        <project.build.sourceEncoding>UTF-8</project.build.
    sourceEncoding>
     <project.reporting.outputEncoding>UTF-8</project.reporting.
    outputEncoding>
  </properties>

  <dependencies>
    <dependency>
      <groupId>org.graphwalker</groupId>
      <artifactId>graphwalker-core</artifactId>
      <version>${graphwalker.version}</version>
    </dependency>
    <dependency>
      <groupId>org.graphwalker</groupId>
      <artifactId>graphwalker-io</artifactId>
      <version>${graphwalker.version}</version>
    </dependency>
    <dependency>
      <groupId>org.graphwalker</groupId>
      <artifactId>graphwalker-java</artifactId>
      <version>${graphwalker.version}</version>
    </dependency>
    <dependency>
```

```xml
    <groupId>org.graphwalker</groupId>
    <artifactId>graphwalker-maven-plugin</artifactId>
    <version>${graphwalker.version}</version>
  </dependency>
  <!-- https://mvnrepository.com/artifact/junit/junit -->
  <dependency>
    <groupId>junit</groupId>
    <artifactId>junit</artifactId>
    <version>4.12</version>
   <!-- <scope>test</scope> -->
  </dependency>
    </dependencies>

<build>
  <plugins>
    <plugin>
      <groupId>org.apache.maven.plugins</groupId>
      <artifactId>maven-compiler-plugin</artifactId>
      <version>3.1</version>
      <configuration>
        <source>1.8</source>
        <target>1.8</target>
      </configuration>
    </plugin>
    <plugin>
      <groupId>org.graphwalker</groupId>
      <artifactId>graphwalker-maven-plugin</artifactId>
      <version>${graphwalker.version}</version>
      <!-- Bind goals to the default lifecycle -->
      <executions>
        <execution>
          <id>generate-test-sources</id>
          <phase>generate-test-sources</phase>
          <goals>
            <goal>generate-test-sources</goal>
          </goals>
        </execution>
        <execution>
          <id>test</id>
          <phase>test</phase>
          <goals>
            <goal>test</goal>
          </goals>
        </execution>
      </executions>
    </plugin>
  </plugins>
</build>

<repositories>
  <repository>
```

295

```
        <releases>
            <enabled>false</enabled>
            <updatePolicy>always</updatePolicy>
            <checksumPolicy>warn</checksumPolicy>
        </releases>
        <snapshots>
            <enabled>true</enabled>
            <updatePolicy>never</updatePolicy>
            <checksumPolicy>fail</checksumPolicy>
        </snapshots>
        <id>sonatype-nexus-snapshots</id>
        <name>Sonatype Nexus Snapshots</name>
            <url>https://oss.sonatype.org/content/repositories/
    snapshots</url>
        <layout>default</layout>
    </repository>
  </repositories>
  <pluginRepositories>
    <pluginRepository>
        <id>sonatype-nexus-snapshots</id>
        <name>Sonatype Nexus Snapshots</name>
            <url>https://oss.sonatype.org/content/repositories/
    snapshots</url>
        <releases>
            <enabled>false</enabled>
        </releases>
        <snapshots>
            <enabled>true</enabled>
        </snapshots>
    </pluginRepository>
  </pluginRepositories>
</project>
```

APPENDIX D – SOLUTIONS TO THE EXERCISES

E5.1 Identify the EPs and one ON, OFF and IN/OUT point for each EP in the following specification.

Payment: for online shopping, the shipment fee is the following. If the final price is below EUR 50, then the shipment is not possible. If the price is below EUR 100, then the shipment fee is 10 per cent of the final price, in the case where the price is below EUR 500 the shipment fee is five per cent, and if the price reaches or exceeds EUR 500, the shipment is free. If the weight surpasses 10 kg, then EUR 1 is paid for each kilogram (where weight is rounded up to the next integer). Finally, if the shipment comes from abroad, the extra fee is doubled except for neighbouring countries, where the extra fee is only 1.5 times more. The price shift is EUR 0.1; the minimum non-zero weight shift is 0.1 kg. No negative or non-numeric cases should be considered.

Solution: In Table D.1 the ON1/OFF1/IN1 point is related to the lower border of an interval, while the ON2/OFF2/OUT2 point is related to the upper border of the same interval, for example for ≥50 – <100, ON1 relates to 50 and ON2 relates to 100. As during online shopping, the prices are given when an item is selected. We will consider neither negative nor non-numeric prices.

Table D.1 Equivalence partitions for solving Exercise 5.1

EP1 - price	0 – < 50	ON1: 0, ON2/IN1: 49.9, OFF2: 50, OUT2: 99.9
EP2 - price	≥ 50 – < 100	ON1: 50, OFF1: 49.9, ON2/IN1: 99.9, OFF2: 100, OUT2: 499.9
EP3 - price	≥ 100 – < 500	ON1: 100, OFF1: 99.9, ON2/IN1: 499.9, OFF2: 500, OUT2: 10,000
EP4 - price	≥ 500	ON: 500, OFF: 499.9, IN: 10,000
EP5 - weight	0 – ≤ 10	ON1/IN2: 0, ON2: 10, OFF2: 10.1
EP6 - weight	> 10	ON: 10.1, OFF: 10, OUT: 0
EP7 - shipment	Local	
EP8 - shipment	Non-local non-neighbour	
EP9 - shipment	Neighbour	

An alternative solution is shown in Table D.2.

Table D.2 Equivalence partitions for solving Exercise 5.1 – an alternative

Test design item no.: 5.10		Trace: Req. E5.1	
Based on: Input		Assumption: The smallest increment is 10 euro cents.	

Type	Description	ID	Belongs to
VB	Shipment normal price = 0 EUR	5.10-1	5.10-2 (ON)
VC	0 ≤ Shipment normal price < 50	5.10-2	
VB IB	Shipment normal price = 49.9 EUR	5.10-3	5.10-2 (ON, IN) 5.10-4 (OFF)
VC	50 ≤ Shipment normal price < 100	5.10-4	
VB IB	Shipment normal price = 50 EUR	5.10-5	5.10-4 (ON) 5.10-2 (OFF)
VC	100 ≤ Shipment normal price < 500	5.10-6	
VB IB	Shipment normal price = 99.9 EUR	5.10-7	5.10-4 (ON, IN) 5.10-6 (OFF) 5.10-2 (OUT)
VB IB	Shipment normal price = 100 EUR	5.10-8	5.10-6 (ON) 5.10-4 (OFF)
VB IB	Shipment normal price = 499.9 EUR	5.10-9	5.10-6 (ON, IN) 5.10-10 (OFF) 5.10-4 (OUT)
VC	500 ≤ Shipment normal price	5.10-10	
VB IB	Shipment normal price = 500 EUR	5.10-11	5.10-10 (ON) 5.10-6 (OFF)

Table D.2 (Continued)

Test design item no.: 5.11		Trace: Req. E5.1	
Based on: Input		**Assumption:** The weight is non-negative. The smallest increment is 0.1 kg.	

Type	Description	ID	Belongs to
VC	0 ≤ Shipment extra price for weight ≤ 10	5.11-1	
VB IB	Shipment extra price for weight = 0 EUR	5.11-2	5.11-1 (ON, IN) 5.11-3 (OUT)
VC	Shipment extra price for weight > 10	5.11-3	
VB IB	Shipment extra price for weight = 10 EUR	5.11-4	5.11-1 (ON) 5.11-3 (OFF)
VB IB	Shipment extra price for weight = 10.1 EUR	5.11-5	5.11-3 (ON) 5.11-1 (OFF)

Test design item no.: 5.12		Trace: Req. E5.1	
Based on: Input		**Assumption:** Neighbouring countries and other non-local, non-neighbouring countries are known	

Type	Description	ID	Belongs to
VC	Shipment extra price for local	5.12-1	
VC	Shipment extra price for neighbouring countries	5.12-2	
VC	Shipment extra price for non-local, non-neighbouring countries	5.12-3	

E5.2 Produce a test design for the specification above.

As the weight is rounded, it may occur that the weight is zero, yet the price is EUR 50 (consider a valuable stamp for example).

Table D.3 BVA for solving Exercise 5.2

Test	Price	Weight	Country	Shipment possible	Expected value for payment
T1	0	0	Local	N	0
T2	49.9	10	Local	N	49.9
T3	50	0	Local	Y	50 x 1.1 = 55
T4	99.9	10	Non-local, non-neighbour	Y	99.9 x (1 + 0.1 x 2) = 119.88
T5	100	10	Neighbour	Y	100 x (1 + 0.05 x 1.5) = 107.5
T6	499.9	10.1	Local	Y	499.9 x (1 + 0.05) + 11 = 535.9
T7	500	10	Local	Y	500
T8	10,000	10.1	Local	Y	10,011

E6.1 Construct test paths applying the all-transition–transition criterion for 'TVM ticket selection' (see Figure 6.7).

Let's consider the following six paths:

Tpath1= s1-t1-s2-t7-s2-t10-s2-t4-s1-t1-s2-t7-s2-t10-s2-t4-s1-t2-s3-t8-s3-t11-s3-t5-s1-t3-s4-t9-s4-t12-s4-t6-s1-t3-s4-t15-s5

Tpath2 = s1-t2-s3-t8-s3-t11-s3-t5-s1-t2-s3-t8-s3-t11-s3-t5-s1-t3-s4-t9-s4-t12-s4-t6-s1-t1-s2-t7-s2-t10-s2-t4-s1-t1-s2-t13-s5

Tpath3 = s1-t3-s4-t9-s4-t12-s4-t6-s1-t3-s4-t9-s4-t12-s4-t6-s1-t1-s2-t7-s2-t10-s2-t4-s1-t2-s3-t8-s3-t11-s3-t5-s1-t2-s3-t14-s5

Tpath4 = s1-t1-s2-t13-s5

Tpath5 = s1-t2-s3-t14-s5

Tpath6 = s1-t3-s4-t15-s5

Then

- (t1,T), (t4, T), (t7, T), (t10, T) satisfy for all T ∈ {t1, t2, t3, t4, t5, t6, t7, t8, t9, t10, t11, t12, t15} in Tpath1, T = t13 in Tpath2 and T = t14 in Tpath3.
- (t2, T), (t5, T), (t8, T), (t11, T) satisfy for all T ∈ {t1, t2, t3, t4, t5, t6, t7, t8, t9, t10, t11, t12, t13} in Tpath2, T = t15 in Tpath1 and T = t14 in Tpath3.
- (t3, T), (t6, T), (t9, T), (t12, T) satisfy for all T ∈ {t1, t2, t3, t4, t5, t6, t7, t8, t9, t10, t11, t12, t14} in Tpath3, T = t15 in Tpath1 and T = t13 in Tpath2.

On the other hand,

- (!t1, T), (!t4, T), (!t7, T), (!t10, T), (!t13, T) satisfy for all T ∈ {t2, t3, t5, t6, t8, t9, t11, t12} in Tpath2, T = t14 in Tpath5 and T = t15 in Tpath6 (there are no other possibilities).
- (!t2, T), (!t5, T), (!t8, T), (!t11, T), (!t14, T) satisfy for all T ∈ {t1, t3, t4, t6, t7, t9, t10, t12} in Tpath3, T = t13 in Tpath4 and T = t15 in Tpath6 (there are no other possibilities).
- (!t3, T), (!t6, T), (!t9, T), (!t12, T), (!t15, T) satisfy for all T ∈ {t1, t2 t4, t5, t7, t8, t10, t11} in Tpath1, T = t13 in Tpath4 and T = t14 in Tpath5 (there are no other possibilities).
- (!t4, t13), (!t7, t13), (!t10, t13) in Tpath4.
- (!t5, t14), (!t8, t14), (!t11, t14) in Tpath5.
- (!t6, t15), (!t9, t15), (!t12, t15) in Tpath6.

Hence, the all-transition–transition criterion is satisfied.

E6.2 Ordering water from an online shop. The types of water can be still or sparkling. We can buy bottles of one type only. If nothing is selected, then the quantity of either of them can be increased. After one has been selected, only one of the water types with a non-zero amount can be increased or decreased by one. The maximum number of bottles to be ordered is five. If the selected number of bottles is greater than 0, then the buying process can start. The output is the type and number of the selected bottles.

Model the buying process with a state transition graph and design tests for the following test selection criteria:

1. all-transition criterion;
2. all-2-transitions criterion;
3. all-transition-state criterion.

Precondition: the web page shows the initial screen where the buying process can start. The number of bottles is set to zero (NrB := 0) and the water type is empty (WaterType := '').

States:

- s1: initial state;
- s2: still water selection;
- s3: sparkling water selection;
- s4: payment.

Input:

- e1: increasing the number of still water bottles (inc-still);
- e2: increasing the number of sparkling water bottles (inc-spark);
- e3: decreasing the number of still water bottles (dec-still);
- e4: decreasing the number of sparkling water bottles (dec-spark);
- e5: selecting for payment (pay).

Output (actions)

- a1: increment the number of still water bottles (still+);
- a2: increment the number of sparkling water bottles (spark+);
- a3: decrement the number of still water bottles (still-);
- a4: decrement the number of sparkling bottles (spark-);
- a5: goes to the payment screen (payment) and passes the global data value NrB.

Transitions:

- t1: inc-still / still+;
- t2: dec-still / [NrB = 1] / still-;
- t3: inc-spark / spark+;
- t4: dec-spark / [NrT = 1] / spark-;
- t5: inc-still / [NrB < 5] / still+;
- t6: dec-still / [NrB > 1] / still-;
- t7: inc-spark / [NrB < 5] / spark+;
- t8: dec-spark / [NrB > 1] / spark-;
- t9: pay / <a5, WaterType := 'Still'>;
- t10: pay / <a5, WaterType := 'Sparkling'>.

Figure D.1 STT for solving Exercise 6.2

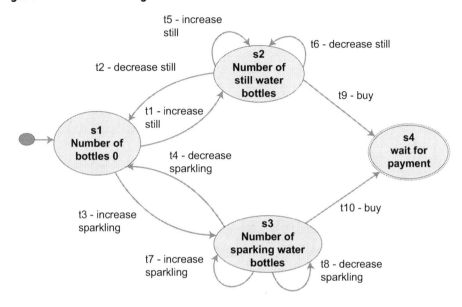

1. All-transition criterion:

   The following two tests paths are enough:

   Tpath1 = s1-t3-s3-t4-s1-t1-s2-t5-s2-t6-s2-t9-s4
   Tpath2 = s1-t1-s2-t2-s1-t3-s3-t7-s3-t8-s3-t10-s4

2. All-2-transitions criterion (for simplicity only the transitions are shown):

   Tpath1 = t3-t4-t1-t5-t5-t6-t6-t5-t9
   Tpath2 = t1-t5-t6-t2-t1-t5-t6-t9
   Tpath3 = t1-t2-t3-t4-t1-t9
   Tpath4 = t1-t2-t3-t7-t7-t8-t8-t7-t10
   Tpath5 = t3-t7-t8-t4-t3-t7-t8-t10
   Tpath6 = t3-t4-t1-t2-t3-t10

   These tests contain all the valid 2-transitions:

t1-t2, t1-t5, t1-t9, t2-t3, t2-t1, t5-t5, t5-t6, t5-t9, t6-t6, t6-t5, t6-t2, t6-t9,

t3-t4, t3-t7, t3-t10, t4-t1, t4-t3, t7-t7, t7-t8, t7-t10, t8-t4, t8-t7, t8-t10, t8-t8

Note that there are some invalid 2-transitions: t1-t6, t5-t2, t3-t8, t7-t4.

3. All-transition-state criterion

   The following four tests paths are enough:

   Tpath1 = s1-t1-s2-t2-s1-(t2-s1)-t2-s2-t5(5X)-s2-t6(4X)-s2-t2-s1-t3-s3-t4-s1-t3-s3-t10-s4

   Tpath2 = s1-t3-s3-t4-s1-(t4-s1)-t2-s3-t7(5X)-s3-t8(4X)-s3-t3-s1-t1-s2-t2-s1-t1-s2-t9-s4

   Tpath3 = s1-t1-s2-t9-s4

   Tpath4 = s1-t3-s3-t10-s4

   where (t2-s1) and (t3-s1) means the trial to decrease the number of water below 0.

   (t1,S), (t2,S), (t5,S), (t6,S), satisfy for all S $\in$ {s1,s2,s3,s4} in Tpath1, (t9,s4) in Tpath2.

   (t3,S), (t4,S), (t7,S), (t8,S), satisfy for all S $\in$ {s1,s2,s3,s4} in Tpath2, (t10,s4) in Tpath2.

   All the avoidable transitions (t2, t3, t4, t5, t6, t7, t8, t10) for s2, s4 excluded in Tpath3.

   All the avoidable transitions (t1, t2, t4, t5, t6, t7, t8, t9) for s3, s4 excluded in Tpath4.

   Tpath3 and Tpath4 are also appropriate for excluding all (ti, s1) pairs.

   Boundary value of the guard condition is reached: t5(5X)-s2-t6(4X)-s2-t2-s1 and -t7(5X)-s3-t8(4X)-s3-t3-s1

E7.1 Assignment

Consider the following specification.

A university course registration software assigns labs for the informatics faculty courses based on the number of registered students and the required software toolchains. There are three common toolchains used in teaching: GNU toolchain, Apache-Maven toolchain, and SharePoint Framework toolchain. There are four labs of different sizes (with a different number of computers) in the faculty.

1. If the number of registered students for a course is fewer than 10 and Apache-Maven is needed, then the course will be in lab A.

2. If the number of registered students for a course is between 10 and 30 and Apache-Maven toolchain is needed, then the course will be in lab B.

3. If the number of registered students for a course is fewer than 10 and GNU or SharePoint is needed, then the course will be in lab B.

4. If the number of registered students for a course is between 10 and 30 and GNU is needed, then the course will be in lab C.

5. If the number of registered students for a course is above 30, or between 10 and 30 with SharePoint requirement, then the course will be in lab D.

Model and design tests for the software.

We use the following notations:

- Category 1 (C1): The number of registered students is fewer than 10.

- Category 2 (C2): The number of registered students is between 10 and 30.

- Category 3 (C3): The number of registered students is above 30.

Table D.4 Decision table for solving Exercise 7.1

Conditions	R1	R2	R3	R4	R5	R6	R7
GNU?	Y	Y	N	N	N	N	-
Apache-Maven?	N	N	Y	Y	N	N	-
Sharepoint?	N	N	N	N	Y	Y	-
Number of registered students	C1	C2	C1	C2	C1	C2	C3
Actions							
Lab	B	C	A	B	B	D	D

Possible test suite:

TC1 = ([toolchain = GNU, student number = 9], [Lab = B])

TC2 = ([toolchain = GNU, student number = 10], [Lab = C])

TC3 = ([toolchain = Apache-Maven, student number = 9], [Lab = A])

TC4 = ([toolchain = Apache-Maven, student number = 30], [Lab = B])

TC5 = ([toolchain = Sharepoint, student number = 9], [Lab = B])

TC6 = ([toolchain = Sharepoint, student number 10], [Lab = D])

TC7 = ([student number = 31], [Lab = D])

E7.2 Police control rules.

A police department has specific rules that should apply in for on-road control. Measuring the speeds of all the passing cars, the police officer stops a car to check the driver's licence, vehicle registration, and the driver's alcohol level. If there are licence problems (it is non-existent or expired), a of EUR 350 penalty should be given, and the car is confiscated. In cases where the alcohol level is not zero, the penalty is EUR 300, the driver's licence is withdrawn, and the car is confiscated. If the vehicle is unregistered or the registration is expired, the penalty is EUR 200. If the driver has exceeded the speed limit by less than or equal to 10 per cent, the penalty is EUR 50. If the speed limit was exceeded by more than 10 per cent, but less than or equal to 20 per cent the penalty is EUR 100; above 20 per cent the penalty is EUR 200. Note that the penalties are added together. If the car is not confiscated, then the police officer returns all the documents and the driver can leave in the car.

Design tests for this specification based on the decision table technique.

We use the following notations:

- Category A: Speed limit exceeded by less than or equal to 10%.
- Category B: Speed limit exceeded by more than 10%, but less than or equal to 20%.
- Category C: Speed limit exceeded by more than 20%.
- Category N: Otherwise.

The 32 test cases can easily be created based on Table D.5, for example:

TC15 = ([Licence problems = N, Registration problems = N, non-zero alcohol level = Y, speed limit exceeded = 11], penalty = 400, car confiscated = Y, licence is withdrawn = Y])

Table D.5 Decision tables for solving Exercise 7.2

Conditions	R1	R2	R3	R4	R5	R6	R7	R8	R9	R10	R11	R12
Licence problems?	Y	Y	Y	Y	N	N	N	N	Y	Y	Y	Y
Registration problems?	Y	Y	Y	Y	Y	Y	Y	Y	N	N	N	N
Non-zero alcohol level?	Y	Y	Y	Y	Y	Y	Y	Y	Y	Y	Y	Y
Speed limit exceeded?	N	A	B	C	N	A	B	C	N	A	B	C
Actions												
Penalty (EUR)	850	900	950	1050	500	550	600	700	650	700	750	850
Car confiscated	Y	Y	Y	Y	Y	Y	Y	Y	Y	Y	Y	Y
Licence is withdrawn	Y	Y	Y	Y	Y	Y	Y	Y	Y	Y	Y	Y

Conditions	R13	R14	R15	R16	R17	R18	R19	R20	R21	R22	R23	R24
Licence problems?	N	N	N	N	Y	Y	Y	Y	N	N	N	N
Registration problems?	N	N	N	N	Y	Y	Y	Y	Y	Y	Y	Y
Non-zero alcohol level?	Y	Y	Y	Y	N	N	N	N	N	N	N	N
Speed limit exceeded?	N	A	B	C	N	A	B	C	N	A	B	C
Actions												
Penalty (EUR)	300	350	400	500	550	600	650	750	200	250	300	400
Car confiscated	Y	Y	Y	Y	Y	Y	Y	Y				
Licence is withdrawn	Y	Y	Y	Y								

Conditions:	R25	R26	R27	R28	R29	R30	R31	R32
Licence problems?	Y	Y	Y	Y	N	N	N	N
Registration problems?	N	N	N	N	N	N	N	N
Non-zero alcohol level?	N	N	N	N	N	N	N	N
Speed limit exceed?	N	A	B	C	N	A	B	C
Actions:								
Penalty (EUR)	350	400	450	550	0	50	100	200
Car confiscated	Y	Y	Y	Y				
Licence is withdrawn								

E8.1 Consider the specification of E7.2. Design tests by applying use case testing.

For simplicity we denote steps 1–4 as I and 9–10 as X. Covering an exception (5E or 7E) the process stops before the last step (10). The test cases are shown in Table D.6.

Table D.6 Use case for solving Exercise 8.1

Use case: *Vehicle stopped by police*			
Use case ID:	POL-UC-7.2		
Use case name:	Vehicle control	**Version no.**	1.0
Purpose:	The police check the licence and vehicle registration validity, the alcohol consumption of the driver and verify that the speed limit has been respected.		
Created by:	Attila Kovács	**Date:**	20-01-2019
Last update by:		**Date:**	
User/actor:	Police officer		
Stakeholder:		**Contact:**	
Trigger:	Police officer has pulled over the vehicle		
Frequency of use:	Often		
Safety:	Critical		
Other special reqs:			
Preconditions:	The police have the right to perform traffic stops		
Post-conditions:	The driver continues their journey or the car is confiscated		
Includes or extension points:			
Other notes (assumptions, issues):			

(Continued)

Table D.6 (Continued)

Basic flow

Step	Police actions	Vehicle driver actions
1	The police officer pulls over the vehicle	
2		The vehicle moves over to the hard shoulder and stops
3	The police officer asks for the licence and the registration documents	
4		The driver hands over the required documents
5	The police officer checks the licence and finds everything is OK	
6	The police officer checks the registration card and finds everything is OK	
7	The police officer checks whether the driver has been drinking alcohol and finds him clean	
8	The police officer checks the speed data of the vehicle, and everything is OK	
9	The police officer gives back the documents and wishes the driver a safe journey	
10		The driver goes on

(Continued)

Table D.6 (Continued)

Alternate flow

Step	Police actions	Vehicle driver actions
6A	The police officer checks the registration, which has expired, or the vehicle is unregistered. EUR 200 penalty is given.	
8A-1	The police officer checks the speed data, and the speed limit exceeded by less than 10% is noted. EUR 50 penalty is given.	
8A-2	The police officer checks the speed data, and the speed limit exceeded by more than 10%, but less than or equal to 20% is noted. EUR 100 penalty is given.	
8A-3	The police officer checks the speed data, and the speed limit exceeded by over 20% is noted. EUR 200 penalty is given.	

Exception flow

Step	
5E	The driver's licence has expired or is non-existent, then EUR 350 penalty is given and the vehicle is confiscated.
7E	The police officer checks the alcohol level of the driver, and it is not OK. EUR 300 penalty is given, the licence is withdrawn and the car is confiscated.

T1 = I-5-6-7-8- X   – happy path

T2 = I-5E-6-7-8

T3 = I-5E-6A-7-8

T4 = I-5E-6-7E-8

T5 = I-5E-6-7-8A-1

T6 = I-5E-6-7-8A-2

T7 = I-5E-6-7-8A-3

T8 = I-5-6A-7-8-X

T9 = I-5-6A-7E-8

T10 = I-5-6A-7-8A-1-X

T11 = I-5-6A-7-8A-2-X

T12 = I-5-6A-7-8A-3-X

T13 = I-5-6-7E-8

T14 = I-5-6-7E-8A-1

T15 = I-5-6-7E-8A-2

T16 = I-5-6-7E-8A-3

T17 = I-5E-6A-7E-8

T18 = I-5-6A-7E-8A-1

T19 = I-5-6A-7E-8A-2

T20 = I-5-6A-7E-8A-3

T21 = I-5E-6-7E-8A-1

T22 = I-5E-6-7E-8A-2

T23 = I-5E-6-7E-8A-3

T24 = I-5E-6A-7-8A-1

T25 = I-5E-6A-7-8A-1

T26 = I-5E-6A-7-8A-1

T27 = I-5-6-7-8A-1-X

T28 = I-5-6-7-8A-2-X

T29 = I-5-6-7-8A-3-X

T30 = I-5E-6A-7E-8A-1

T31 = I-5E-6A-7E-8A-2

T32 = I-5E-6A-7E-8A-3

The number of tests grows exponentially, because of the test selection criterion 'all path coverage'. We can select a simpler set in which some paths are tested together: (T1, T2, T8, T13, T27, T28, T29, T30, T31, T32). Now we have only 10 tests.

As the test cases are created based on the graph, obviously any graph-based test selection criteria can be chosen, and thus, control the number of test cases.

We can also apply defect prevention to improve the specification, which may modify the test cases.

E8.2 Consider the specification of E7.2. Design five important user stories based on it.

Scenario: My licence expired
    Given The police stopped my car
    When My licence has expired
    Then I shall pay EUR 350 penalty
    And My car is confiscated

Scenario: I drank some alcohol
    Given The police stopped my car
    When My alcohol level is not zero
    Then I shall pay EUR 300 penalty
    And My driver's licence is involved
    And My car is confiscated

Scenario: I exceed the speed limit by a little bit
    Given The police stopped my car
    When I exceeded the speed limit by less than 10%
    Then I shall pay EUR 50 penalty

Scenario: I exceed the speed limit by more than 10%
    Given The police stopped my car
    When I exceeded the speed limit by at least 10% and no more than 20%
    Then I shall pay EUR 100 penalty

Scenario: I exceed the speed limit by at least 20%
    Given The police stopped my car
    When I exceeded the speed limit by at least 20%
    Then I shall pay EUR 200 penalty

E9.1 Consider the specification of E5.1 (Payment). Design test cases by applying the diff-pair testing technique.

We start from the EP and BVA test cases and add those required for diff-pair testing. As the weight is rounded it may occur that a product with 'zero' weight can cost EUR 50 (consider a valuable stamp) (Table D.7).

E9.2 You want to test your favourite word processor. You are interested in the following attributes in combination:

- fonts: Arial, Calibri, Cambria, Comic, Courier, Times New Roman, Verdana (7 types);
- style: regular, italic, bold, bold italic (4 types);
- size: 8, 9, 10, 12, 14, 16, 18, 20, 24, 28 (10 types);
- effect: strikethrough, double strikethrough, superscript, subscript, small caps, all caps, hidden (7 types).

Construct test cases for pairwise testing.

Table D.7 Diff-pair tests for solving Exercise 9.1

Test	Price (EUR)	Weight (kg)	Country	Shipment possible	Expected value for payment (EUR)
T1	0	0	Local	N	0
T9	0	10	Non-local, non-neighbour	N	0
T2	49.9	10	Local	N	49.9
T10	49.9	10.1	Neighbour	N	49.9
T3	50	0	Local	Y	$50 \times 1.1 = 55$
T11	50	10.1	Non-local, non-neighbour	Y	$50 + 50 \times 0.1 \times 2 + 11 = 71$
T4	99.9	10	Non-local, non-neighbour	Y	$99.9 + 99.9 \times 0.1 \times 2 = 119.88$
T12	99.9	10.1	Neighbour	Y	$99.9 + 99.9 \times 0.1 \times 1.5 + 11 = 125.89$
T5	100	10	Neighbour	Y	$100 + 100 \times 0.05 \times 1.5 = 107.5$
T13	100	10.1	Non-local, non-neighbour	Y	$100 + 100 \times 0.05 \times 2 + 11 = 121$
T6	499.9	10.1	Local	Y	$499.9 \times 1.05 + 11 = 535.9$
T14	499.9	10	Neighbour	Y	$499.99 + 499.9 \times 0.05 \times 1.5 = 537.39$
T7	500	10	Local	Y	500
T15	500	10.1	Neighbour	Y	$500 + 11 = 511$
T8	10,000	10	Local	Y	10,000
T16	10,000	10.1	Non-local, non-neighbour	Y	10,011

Figure D.2 Parameter selection demonstration for Exercise 9.2

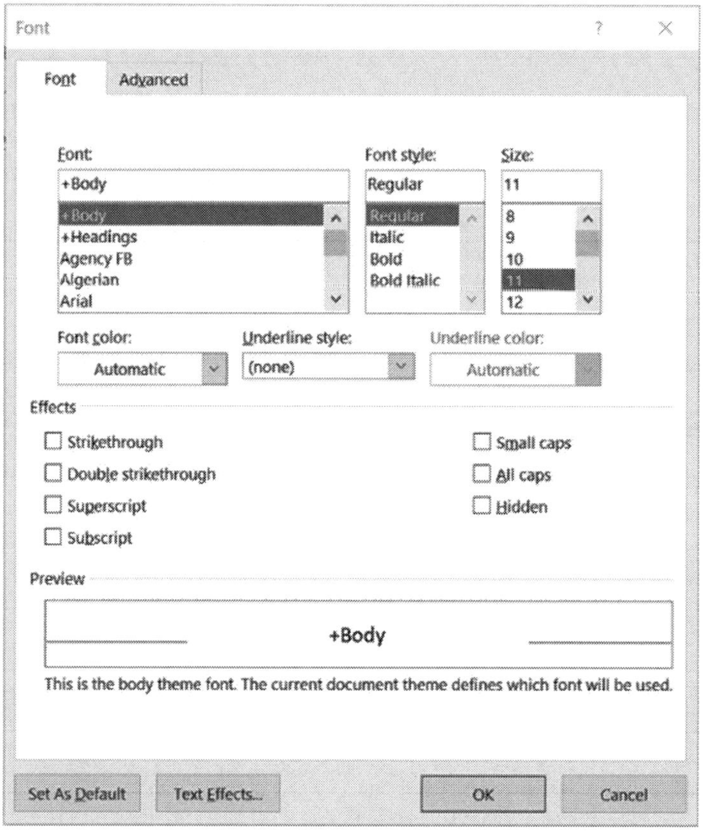

The test cases in Table D.8 cover the pairwise criteria.

Table D.8 Pairwise testing for Exercise 9.2

Test	Fonts	Style	Size	Effect
T1	Arial	Regular	8	Strikethrough
T2	Calibri	Italic	8	Double strikethrough
T3	Cambria	Bold	8	Superscript
T4	Comic	Bold Italic	8	Subscript
T5	Arial	Bold	9	Double strikethrough
T6	Calibri	Bold Italic	9	Strikethrough

(Continued)

Table D.8 (Continued)

Test	Fonts	Style	Size	Effect
T7	Cambria	Regular	9	Subscript
T8	Comic	Italic	9	Superscript
T9	Arial	Bold Italic	10	Superscript
T10	Calibri	Bold	10	Subscript
T11	Cambria	Italic	10	Strikethrough
T12	Comic	Regular	10	Double strikethrough
T13	Arial	Italic	12	Subscript
T14	Calibri	Regular	12	Superscript
T15	Cambria	Bold Italic	12	Double strikethrough
T16	Comic	Bold	12	Strikethrough
T17	Courier	Regular	14	Small caps
T18	Times New Roman	Italic	14	All caps
T19	Verdana	Bold	14	Hidden
T20	Arial	Bold Italic	14	Small caps
T21	Courier	Bold	16	All caps
T22	Times New Roman	Regular	16	Small caps
T23	Verdana	Italic	16	Strikethrough
T24	Arial	Bold Italic	16	Hidden
T25	Courier	Italic	18	Hidden
T26	Times New Roman	Bold	18	Strikethrough
T27	Verdana	Bold Italic	18	Small caps
T28	Arial	Regular	18	All caps
T29	Courier	Bold Italic	20	Strikethrough
T30	Times New Roman	Regular	20	Hidden
T31	Verdana	Regular	20	All caps
T32	Calibri	Italic	20	Small caps
T33	Cambria	Bold	20	Small caps
T34	Times New Roman	Bold Italic	24	Double strikethrough
T35	Calibri	Bold	24	All caps

(Continued)

315

Table D.8 (Continued)

Test	Fonts	Style	Size	Effect
T36	Cambria	Italic	24	All caps
T37	Comic	Regular	24	Small caps
T38	Calibri	Bold Italic	28	All caps
T39	Cambria	Regular	28	Hidden
T40	Comic	Italic	28	Strikethrough
T41	Courier	Bold	28	Double strikethrough
T42	Courier	~Regular	8	Superscript
T43	Times New Roman	~Italic	8	Subscript
T44	Verdana	~Regular	8	Double strikethrough
T45	Courier	~Bold Italic	9	Subscript
T46	Times New Roman	~Bold	9	Superscript
T47	Verdana	~Italic	9	Small caps
T48	Verdana	~Bold Italic	10	Superscript
T49	Calibri	~Regular	10	Hidden
T50	Comic	~Bold	10	All caps
T51	Courier	~Italic	10	Small caps
T52	Verdana	~Bold	12	Subscript
T53	Comic	~Bold Italic	12	Hidden
T54	Times New Roman	~Bold	12	Small caps
T55	Courier	~Regular	12	All caps
T56	Cambria	~Regular	14	Strikethrough
T57	Calibri	~Italic	14	Double strikethrough
T58	Comic	~Italic	14	Superscript
T59	Cambria	~Bold Italic	16	Subscript
T60	Calibri	~Regular	16	Superscript
T61	Comic	~Bold	16	Double strikethrough
T62	Calibri	~Regular	18	Subscript
T63	Cambria	~Italic	18	Double strikethrough
T64	Comic	~Bold Italic	18	Superscript
T65	Arial	~Italic	20	Double strikethrough
T66	Comic	~Bold	20	Subscript

(Continued)

Table D.8 (Continued)

Test	Fonts	Style	Size	Effect
T67	Arial	~Bold	24	Hidden
T68	Courier	~Bold Italic	24	Strikethrough
T69	Verdana	~Italic	24	Superscript
T70	Times New Roman	~Bold Italic	28	Superscript
T71	Arial	~Regular	28	Subscript
T72	Verdana	~Bold	28	Small caps
T73	~Arial	~Bold Italic	8	All caps
T74	~Calibri	~Bold	8	Hidden
T75	~Arial	~Italic	9	Hidden
T76	~Calibri	~Regular	9	All caps
T77	~Arial	~Bold	14	Subscript
T78	~Calibri	~Bold Italic	20	Superscript
T79	~Cambria	~Regular	24	Subscript
T80	~Cambria	~Bold Italic	8	Small caps
T81	Times New Roman	~Regular	10	~Strikethrough

E10 Let's extend our exploratory test cases with those related to the hardware of TVM including the testing of correct coins, banknotes and so on. Write the test cases in a similar way to how we have done it for the TVM example.

- Buy a maximum number of tickets of different types and check that all the tickets are printed.

- Insert different non-euro coins and validate that these coins are non-acceptable and will be given back.

- Select a maximum number of 24-hour tickets, and insert a €100 banknote to check that it is not acceptable.

- Insert some non-euro banknotes and validate that these banknotes are non-acceptable and will be given back.

- Take out coins and banknotes from the machine so that there is not sufficient to refund the customer during an applicable transaction. Validate that the machine changes to the reduced mode by performing that transaction.

- Buy some tickets to increase the supply of coins and banknotes in the machine. Validate that the machine changes back to normal mode.

- Unplug the machine during a transaction, when some money has already been inserted. Validate that the machine stored the amount and it can be refunded.

- Buy 10 tickets, and unplug the machine during the printing of the fifth ticket. Validate that the machine stored this failure and knew that only four tickets had been successfully printed.

E11 Consider the state transition graphs in Figures 11.2 and 11.3. Create test paths to satisfy the all-transition-state criterion by applying the reduced approach.

The simple test cases containing no avoidable transitions are the following:

Tp1 = s1-t1-s2-t4-s4-t8-s5

Tp2 = s1-t2-s3-t5-s4-t8-s5

Tp3 = s1-t3-_Sub_-t6-s4-t8-s5

We can see the symmetry for the states s2/s3/Sub, therefore we design test cases to cover pairs (t1/t4/t7, S), where S involves all the states:

Tp4 = s1-**t1**-s2-**t4**-s4-**t7**-s1-t1-s2-t4-s4-t8-s5

Tp5 = s1-**t1**-s2-**t4**-s4-**t7**-s1-t2-s3-t5-s4-t8-s5

Tp6 = s1-**t1**-s2-**t4**-s4-**t7**-s1-t3-_Sub_-t6-s4-t8-s5

For t2/t5 and t3/t6 we have the symmetric test paths below:

Tp7 = s1-t2-s3-t5-s4-t7-s1-t1-s2-t4-s4-t8-s5

Tp8 = s1-t2-s3-t5-s4-t7-s1-t2-s3-t5-s4-t8-s5

Tp9 = s1-t2-s3-t5-s4-t7-s1-t3-_Sub_-t6-s4-t8-s5

Tp10 = s1-t3-_Sub_-t6-s4-t7-s1-t1-s2-t4-s4-t8-s5

Tp11 = s1-t3-_Sub_-t6-s4-t7-s1-t2-s3-t5-s4-t8-s5

Tp12 = s1-t3-_Sub_-t6-s4-t7-s1-t3-_Sub_-t6-s4-t8-s5

We can see that _Sub_ is covered seven times. This means that we can cover all the transitions in it (no backward edge is in _Sub_). Therefore, the reduced approach results in 12 test cases.

E12.1 Consider the feature presented in E6.2. Create the extended Gherkin model for this feature by applying all-transition-state criterion.

The key part here is to create the categories and the choices. One possible solution is the following:

Categories

handle still(I): increase; decrease; increase 5X; decrease 4X; buy

handle sparkling(I): increase; decrease; increase 5X; decrease 4X; buy

possibilities(O): increase/decrease still; decrease still; increase both; increase/decrease sparkling; decrease sparkling; buy still; buy sparkling number of still(O): 0; 1; 5

number of sparkling(O): 0; 1; 5

The AC can be the following (we used sub-AC):

AC

happy still(ONLY):

> WHEN handle still IS increase
> WHEN handle still IS buy
> THEN possibilities IS buy still AND number of still IS 1

happy sparkling(ONLY):

> WHEN handle sparkling IS increase
> WHEN handle sparkling IS buy
> THEN possibilities IS buy sparkling AND number of sparkling IS 1

long still(ONLY):

> WHEN handle still GOES increase; decrease; increase; increase 5X; decrease 4X; decrease; decrease
> THEN possibilities GOES increase/decrease still; increase both; increase/decrease still; decrease still; increase/decrease still; increase both; increase both;
> AND number of still GOES 1; 0; 1; 5; 1; 0; 0

long sparkling(ONLY):

> WHEN handle sparkling GOES increase; decrease; increase; increase 5X; decrease 4X; decrease; decrease
> THEN possibilities GOES increase/decrease sparkling; increase both; increase/decrease sparkling; decrease sparkling; increase/decrease sparkling; increase both; increase both;
> AND number of sparkling GOES 1; 0; 1; 5; 1; 0; 0

long still and happy sparkling(ONLY):
WHEN long still WHEN happy sparkling

short still(ONLY):
WHEN happy still

long sparkling and happy still(ONLY):
WHEN long sparkling WHEN happy still

short sparkling(ONLY):
WHEN happy sparkling

E12.2 Consider E5.1 'Payment'. Create the extended Gherkin model of this specification.

Categories

Price(I): 0; 49.9; 50; 99.9; 100; 499.9; 500; 10,000

Weight(I): 0; 10; 10.1; 100

Shipment(I): local; abroad; neighbour

Shipment possible(O): yes; no

Payment(O): 0; 49.9; 55; 119.88; 107.5; 535.9; 500; 10,011

AC

Payment table:
WHEN Price IS 0 | 49.9 | 50 | 99.9 | 100 | 499.9 | 500 | 10,000
AND Weight IS 0 | 10 | 0 | 10 | 10 | 10.1 | 10 | 10.1
AND Shipment IS local | local | local | abroad | neighbour | local | local | local
THEN Shipment possible IS no | no | yes | yes | yes | yes | yes | yes
AND Payment IS 0 | 49.9 | 55 | 119.88 | 107.5 | 535.9 | 500 | 10,011

Test cases:

Payment table [0]:
Price(I) = 0, Weight(I) = 0, Shipment(I) = local, Shipment possible(O) = no, Payment(O) = 0

Payment table [49.9]:
Price(I) = 49.9, Weight(I) = 10, Shipment(I) = local, Shipment possible(O) = no,
Payment(O) = 49.9

Payment table [50]:
Price(I) = 50, Weight(I) = 0, Shipment(I) = local, Shipment possible(O) = yes,
Payment(O) = 55

Payment table [99.9]:
Price(I) = 99.9, Weight(I) = 10, Shipment(I) = abroad, Shipment possible(O) = yes,
Payment(O) = 119.88

Payment table [100]:
Price(I) = 100, Weight(I) = 10, Shipment(I) = neighbour, Shipment possible(O) = yes,
Payment(O) = 107.5

Payment table [499.9]:
Price(I) = 499.9, Weight(I) = 10.1, Shipment(I) = local, Shipment possible(O) = yes,
Payment(O) = 535.9

Payment table [500]:
Price(I) = 500, Weight(I) = 10, Shipment(I) = local, Shipment possible(O) = yes,
Payment(O) = 500

Payment table [10,000]:
Price(I) = 10,000, Weight(I) = 100, Shipment(I) = local, Shipment possible(O) = yes,
Payment(O) = 10,011

REFERENCES

Adzic, G. (2011) *Specification by Example: How Successful Teams Deliver the Right Software*. New York: Manning Publications.

Alexander, I.F. and Maiden, N. (2004) *Scenarios, Stories, Use Case: Through the Systems Development Life-Cycle*. Chichester: Wiley.

Arnicane, V. (2009) 'Complexity of equivalence class and boundary value testing methods'. *Scientific Papers*, University of Latvia. *Computer Science and Information Technologies*. 751. 80–101.

Bach, J. (2000) 'Session-based test management'. *Software Testing and Quality Engineering Magazine*, 32–37, available at: https://www.satisfice.com/download/session-based-test-management.

Beizer, B. (1990) *Software Testing Techniques*. New York: Van Nostrand Reinhold Co.

Bianchi, F.A., Margara, A. and Pezze, M. (2017) 'A survey of recent trends in testing concurrent software systems'. *IEEE on Trans Soft. Eng.*, 44 (8). 747–783.

Binder, R. (2000) *Testing Object-oriented Systems: Models, Patterns, and Tools*. Boston, MA: Addison-Wesley.

Black, R., Coleman, G., Walsh, M., Cornanguer, B., Forgács, I., Kakkonen, K. and Sabak, J. (2017) 'Agile testing methods, techniques, and tools'. In: Black, R. (ed.) *Agile Testing Foundations*. Swindon: BCS. Chapter 3.

Broy, M. et al. (eds) (2005) *Model-based Testing of Reactive Systems*, Part I. System Development, Berlin, Heidelberg: Springer.

Carroll, J.M. (ed.) (1995) *Scenario-based Design: Envisioning Work and Technology in System Development*. Hoboken, NJ: Wiley.

Chow, T.S. (1978) 'Testing software design modeled by finite-state machines'. *IEEE Transactions on Software Engineering.*, 4 (3). 178–187.

Cockburn, A. (2001) *Writing Effective Use Cases*. Boston, MA: Addison-Wesley.

Cohen, D.M. et al. (1997) 'The AETG system: An approach to testing based on combinatorial design'. *IEEE Transactions on. Software Engineering.*, 23 (7). 437–444.

Cohn, M. (2010) *Succeeding with Agile: Software Development Using Scrum*. Boston, MA: Addison-Wesley.

Crispin L. and Gregory, J. (2008) *Agile Testing: A Practical Guide for Testers and Agile Teams*. Boston, MA: Addison-Wesley.

Curtis, G. (1995) *Business Information Systems: Analysis, Design and Practice.* 2nd ed. Wokingham: Addison-Wesley.

Czerwonka, J. (2008) 'Pairwise testing in the real world: Practical extensions to test-case scenarios'. Microsoft Corporation, Software Testing Technical Articles, available at https://msdn.microsoft.com/en-us/library/cc150619.aspx

Dawson, M. et al. (2010) 'Integrating software assurance into the software development life cycle (SDLC)'. *JISTP,* 3 (6). 49–53.

DeMillo, R.A., Lipton, R.J. and Sayward F.G. (1978) 'Hints on test data selection: Help for the practicing programmer'. *Computer,* 11 (4). 34–41.

Elmendorf, W.R. (1973) 'Cause-effect graphs in functional testing'. IBM Technical report, Poughkeepsie, NY.

Fowler, M. (2004) *UML Distilled.* 3rd ed. Boston, MA: Addison-Wesley.

Garcia, A.M., Verhelle, M. and Vanthienen, J. (2000) 'An Overview of Decision Table Literature 1982-2000'. Presented at the Fifth International Conference on Artificial Intelligence and Emerging Technologies in Accounting, Huelva, Spain.

Goodenough, J. and Gerhart, S. (1975) 'Toward a theory of test data selection'. *IEEE Transactions on Software Engineering,* 1. 156–173.

Grady, R. and Caswell, D. (1987) *Software Metrics: Establishing a Company-wide Program.* Denver, CO: Prentice Hall.

GraphWalker, available at https://graphwalker.github.io/

Grochtmann, M. and Grimm, K. (1993) 'Classification trees for partition testing'. *Journal of STVR,* 3 (2). 63–82.

Gutjahr, W.J. (1995) 'Optimal test distributions for software failure cost estimation'. *IEEE Transactions on Software Engineering,* 21 (3). 219–228.

Hamlet, D. and Taylor, R. (1990) 'Partition testing does not inspire confidence'. *IEEE Transactions on Software Engineering,* 16 (12). 279–290.

Hamlet, R.G. (1977) 'Testing programs with the aid of a compiler'. *IEEE Transactions on Software Engineering,* 3 (4). 279–290.

Hao, D., Zhang, L. and Mei, H. (2016) 'Test-case prioritization: Achievements and challenges'. *Frontiers of Computer Science,* 10 (5). 769–777.

Harel, D. (1987) 'Statecharts: A visual formalism for complex systems'. *Science of Computer Programming,* 8. 231–274.

Harmony, available at https://trial.harmony.ac

Hopcroft, J. (1971) 'An n log n algorithm for minimizing states in a finite automaton: Theory of machines and computations'. Proceedings International Symposium Technion, Haifa. New York: Academic Press, 189–196.

Howden, W.E. (1976) 'Reliability of the path analysis testing strategy'. *IEEE Transactions on Software Engineering,* 2 (3). 208–215.

IEEE 1028 (2008) Available at https://standards.ieee.org/standard/1028-2008.html

IEEE 1044 (2009) Available at https://standards.ieee.org/findstds/standard/1044-2009. html

ISO 25010 (2011) Available at https://www.iso.org/standard/35733.html

ISO/IEC 20246 (2017) Software and Systems Engineering – Work Product Reviews, available at https://www.iso.org/standard/67407.html

ISO/IEC/IEEE 29119-3 (2013) Available at https://www.iso.org/standard/56737.html ISTQB (2018a) 'Glossary', available at https://glossary.istqb.org/search/

ISTQB (2018b) 'Certified Tester Foundation Level Syllabus', available at https://www. istqb.org/downloads/send/51-ctfl2018/208-ctfl-2018-syllabus.html

Itkonen, J. and Rautiainen, K. (2005) 'Exploratory testing: A multiple case study', *Proceedings of the 4th International Symposium on Empirical Software Engineering*, 84–93, available at https://wiki.aalto.fi/download/attachments/58922404/Itkonen_ Juha_ISESE2005.pdf

Jeffries, R. (2001) 'Essential XP: Card, Conversation, Confirmation', available at https:// ronjeffries.com/xprog/articles/expcardconversationconfirmation/

Jeng, B. and Forgács, I. (1999) 'An automatic approach of domain test data generation'. *Journal of Systems and Software*, 49 (1). 97–112.

Jeng, B. and Weyuker, E. (1994) 'A simplified domain-testing *strategy'. Journal ACM Transactions on Software Engineering and Methodology (TOSEM)*, 3 (3). 254–270.

Jia, Y. and Harman, M. (2011) 'An analysis and survey of the development of mutation testing'. *IEEE Transactions on Software Engineering*, 37 (5). 649–678.

Johnston, F.J.J. and Davis, J.C. (1970) *Decision tables in data processing: A report.* Manchester: National Computing Centre.

Jones C. and Bonsignour, O. (2011) *The Economics of Software Quality.* Boston, MA: Addison-Wesley.

Kaner, C. (2003) 'An introduction to scenario testing', available at http://kaner.com/pdfs/ ScenarioIntroVer4.pdf

Kaner, C. (2008) 'A tutorial in exploratory testing', available at https://www.kaner.com/ pdfs/QAIExploring.pdf

Kaner, C., Falk, J. and Nguyen, H.Q. (1987) *Testing Computer Software.* Boston, MA: Wiley

Kovács, A. and Szabados, K. (2018) 'Knowledge and mindset in software development - how developers, testers, technical writers and managers differ - a survey'. *Proceedings of the 11th Joint Conference on Mathematics and Computer Science*, CEUR. Vol. 2046. 161–184, available at http://ceur-ws.org/Vol-2046/.

Kramer, A. and Legeard, B. (2016) *Model-based Testing Essentials - Guide to the ISTQB Certified Model-Based Tester: Foundation Level.* Hoboken, NJ: Wiley.

Kramer, A., Legeard, B. and Binder R. (2017) 'Model-based testing user survey results', available at http://www.cftl.fr/wp-content/uploads/2017/02/2016-MBT-User-Survey-Results.pdf

Kuhn, D.R., Lei, Y. and Kacker, R. (2008) 'Practical combinatorial testing: Beyond pairwise'. *IT Professional*, 10 (3). 19–23.

Kuhn, D.R., Higdon, J.M., Lawrence, J.F., Kacker, R.N. and Lei, Y. (2012) 'Combinatorial methods for event sequence testing'. *Proceedings of the IEEE 5th International Conference on Software Testing, Verification and Validation (ICST)*, 601–609.

Kurani, A. (2018) 'TestOps in product engineering', available at https://www.sogeti.com/solutions/high-tech--global-engineering/products-and-engineering-services/testops/

Lee, D. and Yannakakis, M. (1996) 'Principles and methods of testing finite state machines - a survey'. *Proceedings of the IEEE*, 84 (8). 1090–1123.

Leffingwell, D. (2011) *Agile Software Requirements - Lean Requirements Practices for Teams, Programs, and the Enterprise*. Boston, MA: Addison Wesley.

Lei, Y. and Tai K.C. (1998) 'In-parameter-order: A test generation strategy for pairwise testing'. *High-Assurance Systems Engineering Symposium*, 254–261.

Maes, R. (1978) 'On the representation of program structures by decision tables: A critical assessment'. *The Computer Journal*, 21 (4). 290–295.

Mandl, R. (1985) 'Orthogonal latin squares: An application of experiment design to compiler testing'. *Comm. ACM* 28 (10). 1054–1058.

Martin, J. and McClure, C. (1985) *Diagramming Techniques for Analysts and Programmers*. Englewood Cliffs, NJ: Prentice Hall.

Mathur, P.A. (2008) *Foundations of Software Testing*. Denver, CO: Prentice Hall.

McDaniel, H. (1968) *An Introduction to Decision Logic Tables*. New York: John Wiley & Sons, Inc.

Micskei, Z. (2017) 'Model-based testing', available at http://mit.bme.hu/~micskeiz/pages/modelbased_testing.html

Myers, G.J. (1979) *The Art of Software Testing*. New York: Wiley.

Nagappan, N. et al. (2008) 'Realizing quality improvement through test driven development: Results and experiences of four industrial teams'. *Empir. Software Eng.*, 13 (3). 289–302.

Németh, G.Á. (2015) 'Incremental Test Generation Algorithms.' PhD dissertation, BME.

Nie, C. and Leung, H. (2011) 'A survey of combinatorial testing'. *Journal ACM Computing Surveys* (CSUR), 43 (2). Article 11.

OMG (2017) 'About the unified modeling language specification version 2.5.1', available at https://www.omg.org/spec/UML/About-UML/

Ostrand, T.J. and Balcer, M.J. (1988) 'The category-partition method for specifying and generating functional tests'. *Communications of the ACM*, 31 (6). 676–686.

Palmer, S.R. and Felsing, J.M. (2002) *A Practical Guide to Feature-Driven Development*. Denver, CO: Prentice Hall.

Pohl, K. and Rupp, C. (2016) *Requirements Engineering Fundamentals: A Study Guide for the Certified Professional for Requirements Engineering Exam-Foundation Level-IREB Compliant*. Santa Barbara, CA: Rocky Nook.

Pollack, S., Hicks, H. and Harrison, V. (1971) *Decision Tables: Theory and Practice*. New York: John Wiley & Sons, Inc.

Reid, S.C. (1997) 'An empirical analysis of equivalence partitioning, boundary value analysis and random testing'. *Proceedings of the Fourth International Software Metrics Symposium*. 64–73.

Roosendaal, E. (2018) 'On the 3x + 1 problem', available at www.ericr.nl/wondrous/

Sethi, I. and Chatterjee, B. (1980) 'Conversion of decision tables to efficient sequential testing procedures'. *Communications of the ACM*, 23 (5). 279–285.

Shwayder, K. (1971) 'Conversion of limited-entry decision tables to computer programs - A proposed modification to Pollack's algorithm'. *Communications of the ACM*, 14 (2). 69–73.

Shwayder, K. (1974) 'Extending the information theory approach to converting limited-entry decisions tables to computer programs'. *Communications of the ACM*, 17 (9). 532–537.

Sloane, N.J.A. (1993) 'Covering arrays and intersecting codes'. *Journal of Combinatorial Designs*, 1(1). 51–63.

Smillie, K. and Shave, M. (1975) 'Converting decision tables to computer programs'. *The Computer Journal*, 18 (2). 108–111.

Spillner, A., Linz, T. and Schaefer, H. (2014) *Software Testing Foundations: A Study Guide for the Certified Tester Exam*. 4th ed. Santa Barbara, CA: Rocky Nook.

Srivastava, P.R., Patel, P. and Hatrola, S. (2009) 'Cause effect graph to decision table generation'. *ACM SIGSOFT Software Eng. Notes*, 34 (2). 1–4.

Surefire, available at https://maven.apache.org/surefire/maven-surefire-report-plugin/

SWEBOK (2015) Software Engineering Body of Knowledge, available at http://swebokwiki.org/Chapter_4:_Software_Testing

Utting, M., Pretschner, A. and Legeard, B. (2012) 'A taxonomy of model-based testing'. *Software Test. Verif. Reliab.*, 22 (5). 297–312.

Wake, B. (2003) 'INVEST in good stories, and SMART tasks', available at https://xp123.com/articles/invest-in-good-stories-and-smart-tasks/

Weyuker, E. and Ostrand, T. (1980) 'Theories of program testing and the application of revealing subdomains'. *IEEE Transactions on Software Engineering*, 6 (3). 236–246.

White, L.J. and Cohen, E.I. (1980) 'A domain strategy for computer program testing'. *IEEE Transactions on Software Engineering*, 6 (3). 247–257.

Wiegers, K.E. and Beatty, J. (2013) *Software Requirements*. Redmond, WA: Microsoft Press.

Wynne, M. and Hellesøy, A. (2012) *The Cucumber Book. Behaviour-Driven Development for Testers and Developers*. Dallas, TX and Raleigh, NC: The Pragmatic Bookshelf.

yEd Graph Editor, available at https://www.yworks.com/products/yed

Zeller, A. (1999) 'Yesterday, my program worked. Today, it does not. Why?' *ACM SIGSOFT Software Engineering Notes*, 24 (6). 253–267.

INDEX

Printed by Amazon POD